CODE SWITCH

Hip-Hop, Hackers and Africa's Tech Revolutions

A Memoir

CONTACT:

JON GOSIER
Southbox Literary
Atlanta Financial Center
3343 Peachtree Rd NE Ste 145-1340
Atlanta, GA 30326

BY JON GOSIER

ISBN 978-1-7393143-0-9

ISBN Hardcover: 978-1-7393143-1-6

ISBN eBook: 978-1-7393143-2-3

Book design and layout by Misfit

First Edition: February 2023

Southbox Literary is a division of

Southbox Entertainment LLC

http://southboxent.com

Special thanks to:

EDITORS

Lindsay Alexander
(structure and pacing)
Alexis Gargliano
(characters and tone)
Kristin McTiernan
(line editing)
Peter Relic
(additional line editing)

ARTISTS

Sergio Ingravalle
Ed Fairburn

ADVISORS

Jud Laghi Agency
Tom Reilly and the TED
Fellows Team
Cyndi Stivers and the TED
Residency Team

LEGAL

Francelina M. Perdomo and
Gallet Dreyer & Berkey, LLP
Robert Labate, Kevin Gooch
and Holland & Knight

PUBLISHER

AJ Leon, Jessie White, Melissa
Leon and the team at Misfit

FRIENDS AND FAMILY

Margie Shorter (Mom)
Sarah Bramley
Maina Mwaura
Leila Chirayath Janah
Matthew Griffiths
Renee Millett

OTHERS

Hive Collab, Appfrica
and Apps4Africa
Tracy Sherrod, Amistad
and Harper Collins
Savannah College of Art
and Design
Tyler Perry and
Tyler Perry Studios
U.S. Department of State
The Navanti Group
The Guardian
The Knight Foundation
The New York Times
and Ron Nixon
Ken Banks and FrontlineSMS
Ben White and AfriLabs
Ushahidi and
SwiftRiver/Swiftly
Google, Facebook, and Twitter
The whistleblowers, leakers,
and digital activists working
to improve the world
and… Miite

TABLE OF CONTENTS

ACT #4 – CLEARANCE

ACT #5 – OPTIONS

Author's Note

Home is a string of digits.

Coordinates we call latitude and longitude are used to pinpoint every location on the planet, each location represented by a string of digits. Need more detail? Add more digits.

When I was growing up, I thought *home* was the house I grew up in. Familiar streets, lined by the sidewalk I used to walk to school. Nostalgic things I could sense. Sights, smells. The way my toes curled into a shag rug while I was shouted at for tracking dirt into the house.

As I got older, my idea of home changed. As I traveled the continents, to 50+ countries, that memory of home faded. *Home* was now just a data point that had been erased, replaced by new information written to disk. Home was wherever I found myself. Not my address—*my location*.

Through the decades the tools and technologies available to locate anything and anyone evolved dramatically:

Three years before I was born in 1981, the first Global Positioning Satellites went into orbit. Streaking through the sky, they carried within their payloads specialized equipment capable of pinpointing any location on Earth. The possibilities for mapping and navigation became limitless. From the heavens, they carefully scanned the planet, collecting as many of these data points as possible. Then, they beamed this *god's eye view* data back to us enabling the creation of the digital mapping software that would later power cellphones, smartwatches, and other devices.

When I was 10, I used my school's Tandy 1000 computer to look up my hometown in a digital Encyclopedia condensed to a 3.5-inch floppy disk. This was before people had access to the Internet, before most families even had a personal computer at home.

I marveled at the fact that my town was even listed and more surprised that the lat/lon coordinates were included in the article. I scribbled down those coordinates in a notepad. My street address had been committed to memory since the first grade, in case I ever needed to tell someone where I lived. To me it only made sense to commit the lat/lon string to memory as well—an even more accurate address, I decided.

When I was 20, I printed out maps from MapQuest with their accompanying turn-by-turn directions. I learned to correct my car's steering wheel with my knees while rustling through the printed pages in my hands, looking from the paper to the windows for landmarks and street signs.

When I was 30, I found myself in Uganda using an iPhone that could locate itself on a digital map by sending a 3G signal to cellphone towers relaying to satellites traveling through space at 17,000 miles per hour.

When I was 40, I virtually navigated the streets of a city in France. I was on vacation there, sitting in the bed of the luxury condo I'd leased. I woke up and wanted to know if there was a grocery store nearby to grab what I wanted to cook for breakfast. I could have gotten up and walked or asked around until I found one. Could have. Instead, I used a feature called street view to virtually tour the neighborhood. With street view I could look at different locations from afar—at signs, and even into the windows of stores, all from my smartphone. Once satisfied, I put on my clothes and left the condo. Then I clicked a button that read turn-by-turn directions aloud as I walked towards my destination.

"Bonjour! C'est une belle journée!" I said when I arrived to buy my milk and eggs.

"Au revoir, merci de m'avoir montré où était le lait." I said as I left

I didn't actually speak much French. A different app on my phone let me speak in English, then it repeated what I said aloud in French, translating in real time. It used a different type of turn-by-turn technology, strings of numbers that represent words. A map for languages. They navigated me to my next destination – a friendly conversation in French.

Technology increasingly intrudes into our lives, pinpointing our every location and action. The question of which ethical lines are at risk of being crossed has never been more apparent. This became most clear to me while working with individuals in situations where people's lives and safety depended on the answers. These location tools and others were used to help victims caught in catastrophic earthquakes, floods, and pandemics. They were sometimes used to hurt; in tragic bombings, injustice in police departments, and to attack fair elections.

The tools are indifferent to their use—it's all data.

These apps, which make life more navigable, now present us all with many tough choices. We can use tech to do many things, enabled by the *gods-eye-view* of satellites. What we *don't do* with them matters more as a result.

I wrote this book to share some of these experiences, to hopefully inspire other technologists to make better choices and better technology.

These tools have become an extension of our humanity; our collective ability to learn, fight, embrace, share, and sense the world. We use them to locate, communicate, and connect.

Everything has become a string of digits.

That string of digits is home.

Sincerely,
Jon Gosier

#Prologue

"An orange tree would rather die than produce lemons."
—Mokokoma Mokhonoana

Find comfort in the rooms you're in.

You're there, someone else isn't. You owe it to them.

We've all found ourselves the outsider at least once, needing to mold ourselves to integrate into the groups around us. If we don't, we get bullied as kids and ostracized as adults. This isn't just a defense mechanism to protect our egos. Sometimes we do it to bond with others. To show that our differences aren't a barrier to our common interests. We change our social cues because we may comfortably fit in with different groups who may not integrate with each other.

When you grow up between cultures and countries, you learn this early. It's the mask you don to gain acceptance as you navigate these groups. The new kid at school, black people in all-white environments, white people in all-black environments, Muslims with Christian co-workers, or the new person in town tasked with entertaining a group of people who've been friends since college.

In the early 2000s, I became a different type of outsider. I became a leader in a community of open-source hackers and GPS enthusiasts who transformed tech from a novelty into a critical tool for emergency response and, later, an everyday platform for ride-sharing and food delivery. We were data scientists and digital location experts, working at the frontier of emerging tech and policy. Later, I became an analyst in the global humanitarian sector of disaster responders, crisis mappers, digital activists, and U.S. intelligence agencies.

I was in well over my head.

Spearheading a network of technology hubs across Africa, I ended up joining a company that made humanitarian software that got us shortlisted for the Nobel Peace Prize. I watched as our open-source contributions to location technology made their way into other platforms, influencing the way Google and Facebook handled emergency scenarios and how companies like Uber and Waze handled logistics.

In 2005, tools for digital mapping were complicated and cumbersome. By 2010 they were crucial to the arrest of terrorists who carried out a horrible bombing. By 2020, they became an essentials tool in response to a global pandemic.

I was a self-taught computer programmer from the Baptist rural south who found myself contributing to community-driven software projects that became massive global movements. Ironically it was *hip-hop* that got me into computers in the first place. It, too, had become a global movement.

Along the way, I began investing in young African technologists who, like me, were outsiders. Outsiders in tech, outsiders in business, outsiders to most of the world. I didn't shy away from our otherness. I embraced it by investing in them, creating a network for digital tinkerers that now spans 30 countries and nearly 100 cities across Africa.

It wasn't supposed to be like this. When I was in my late teens, I just wanted to make movies and music. I worked my way in and out of the hardest-to-get-into rooms in the world, thriving in them all. I refused to stay outside. I worked my way in and adapted – *code switching*.

No one is more familiar with the necessity of adapting to overwhelming situations than first-generation immigrants trying to make their way in a new country. Like them, I would learn to get comfortable in whatever room I was in.

I became an African American man living and working in Uganda and remained a businessman traveling around the continent for years to follow. Growing up in the USA, especially in the rural South, I learned what it meant to be Black and American. It had never occurred to me what it meant to just be *American* until I moved to Africa.

"*Eh eh!* You are a clearly a Yankee," a Ugandan friend once teased in a deep-throated accent.

She was right. The cultural cues I knew, the music I'd listened to, the TV shows I watched growing up—American. The food I loved, my earliest memories, my friends—American. In Africa, though, I wasn't an African American. I wasn't African, and even to the extent that I am connected through distant ancestry, it was impossible to say my family was African. At least not African first. Before anything else, I had a blue passport. I was Black. I was American.

American Black.

As things become more chaotic and unpredictable, I find the linear path becomes the least safe. Instead, I learned to prepare for uncertainty, what the investors I now work with refer to as *optionality*. When I don't know the specifics of what needs to be done, I forget the specifics and focus on broader strokes.

As a child, my mother's career in government pulled us around the country and at times, pulled her away from me. We moved a lot, from Reston, Virginia to Dawson, Georgia to Fort Lauderdale, Florida to Lakeland, Florida to Ellenwood, Georgia—all before high school. My formative years were spent learning how to adjust while also learning to limit the bonds I formed with friends and classmates. I never knew when I'd be moving next. To be ripped away was painful if I got too attached to the people around me. That's how I got comfortable in the room by never getting attached to it in the first place.

Transitions became expected.

Farm to the city.

City to city.

Later in life, I moved from the United States to Africa. Then from Africa to Europe, and from Europe back to the U.S., I changed professions as well. Filmmaker to music producer, data scientist to humanitarian, to analyst sub-contracting for U.S. intelligence agencies, to venture capitalist, to film producer…to author.

I didn't plan my path; I exercised my *options* on the future.

I was sure to take careful advantage of new experiences as they came, acquiring as many skills and experiences as possible. The endgame wasn't always clear, but I could discern trends— which power circles I'd need to be in, the skills that would be in demand, which opportunities others might ignore. The only way I could thrive in so many different environments was to learn to get comfortable by adapting to new skills and languages (both figurative and literal). I learned to adapt to new countries and people to new cultures and norms. This optionality, the ability to fit in with any group in spite of uncertainty, has shaped my whole life. It's called *code switching*.

Everyone is born with a different hand of cards. We don't get to choose the circumstances we are dealt by life. Whether we are rich or poor. Whether we are Black, White, or Asian. Whether we are able-bodied or disabled. Whether our parents will be abusive or loving. Our personalities, our physical attributes – it's all part of the hand we're dealt. Some of it can be changed, most of it can't.

Code switching is knowing which hand to play in the moment.

It is one of the most important skills anyone can master if they are going to take the path less traveled. In business school, they teach you to read the room. Observe. Adapt. *Win friends! Influence people!* The thing business schools often ignore, though, is culture. Culture is the most important part of code switching because it's the part you can't fake. Your culture, the culture of the people around you, the culture of your country, your family, your friends. Culture is your chemistry. It's the part that's hard to quantify. It's DNA. Like DNA, it can emerge, mutate, and evolve, but you can never change its origins.

What allowed me to thrive living abroad wasn't throwing away my own culture; it was embracing new cultures alongside my own. I was comfortably the American Black living in Uganda who learned to appreciate *nyama choma, matoke,* and *cassava.* These were the staples of Ugandan cuisine that I learned to love. I became comfortable in Uganda, in Africa. I became comfortable outside of America—just a person in the world.

This became more apparent when I moved back to America. Living abroad for years, no matter who you are, will bring you back a changed person. I followed global news more intensely. I had more empathy for the suffering of people in other countries. I understood how nuanced issues around race were in the global context versus how *black and white* we viewed them in America.

I grew with the world beyond my country. Travel was the best education I could get. It was my crash course in code switching.

Act #1

Kernel

#CommandLines

"White lines, blowing through my mind."
**—Grandmaster Flash
and the Furious Five, White Lines**

The most important code that enables a computer to run is called the kernel. It's the core of the computer's operating system, the bridge between the low-level processes controlling the hardware of the machine and the applications and data processing that happens in the graphical user interface (also called the GUI). The user interface is just an illusion, a projection. Computers show us what we want to see. In fact, they show us what we demand.

Reality for the kernel is different. It knows the objective truth, that a computer is just electricity modulating at different frequencies, running through a litany of microprocessors. The real work that goes into computers starts here, with the people who lay the foundation that enables them to run — the manufacturers of the motherboards, the transistors, and other chips inside. Then comes the second wave, machine code, and assembly programmers who make those individual components talk to one another. Then comes the show. Through the components, the electricity becomes a series of on/off commands called binary code. It's through binary code that all things computing are possible. It's through the kernel that these machines, driven by manipulations of electricity, become human accessible.

The kernel is like awareness, consciousness, in humans. Without it, we are just wetware, a series of grey and pink fleshy microprocessors that add up to a biomatter machine finely tuned through millennia of evolution — but otherwise useless. We can all live without consciousness (in the same way that people who are brain dead are still alive). Alive in the biological sense, but not in a way that any human can fully understand or interact with. Consciousness is the kernel that runs our human code. Without it we can't perceive or interact with the graphical user interface we call reality. Everything we see, touch, hear, taste, smell and feel is because of it. So is every pain we suffer.

I felt most at home working in the command line. It was sort of like the computer was my patient and I was tapping its arm trying to find a vein so I could inject it with medicine that would change its condition. From the command line, you're able to manipulate the underlying processes, or the user interface itself.

You can change reality.

Everything becomes possible at the command line.

In movies where you see a black computer screen with rows and rows of white or green text, while someone bangs away furiously at the keyboard to 'tap into the mainframe', or they type some nonsense like 'restart the quantum drive'—that's the command line. It's through the command line that you learn to speak the way of computers (programming languages) and with proper grammar (syntax). If good programming is like proper grammar, *hacking* is like slang. You invoke your own rules; old phrases now take on new meaning. You make contractions and exceptions in the syntax. You make up new words and phrases. You ignore the proper order of things.

The system doesn't know how to handle this at first.

Initially, it might shut down or try to purge the intrusion of radical code trying to disrupt things. Radicals threaten everything. They present an existential crisis—change them or be changed by them. If left unchecked, eventually the system forgets its factory state and slowly but surely starts to recognize and accept slang as normal code. The system is corrupted. The slang becomes normalized. Slang is no longer slang. The syntax has been redefined. The radicals have changed the rules. This is how hacking works. It's not magic or rocket science; it's just redefining the rules.

Hacking was: phreaking, jamming, spoofing, phishing, scripting, and sniffing.

Hip-Hop was: remixing, scratching, sampling, spinning, bumping, and graffiti.

Both were radical forms of protest.

Both were activism.

Hacking was hip-hop.

I fell in love with computer hacking and making music. Hacking doesn't mean what most think it means. Yes, it can refer to using computers to attack and target other computers systems, exploiting them with malicious code. However, I prefer the meaning of the word as one might use it in music – *improvisation*. Hacking is figuring things out as you go along and adjusting course as things happen, just as many of us have to do.

It's freestyling.

* * *

In 2004, I was sitting in a car that probably cost as much money as the building it was parked next to. At the time, a Phantom Rolls-Royce retailed for somewhere between $300,000 and $450,000 dollars. In my short five years in the Atlanta music business, I'd learned one thing. Life was cheap but hip-hop beats were not. One super producer said as much to me as he was saving recording files to a computer. We were in a recording studio, a staple in Atlanta, called Patchwerk. I was interning as a recording engineer. My job was to follow behind the producers and recording artists who worked there and do anything for them they didn't know how to do on their own, or that they couldn't be bothered to do if they did. Things like setting up microphones, tuning guitars, and operating recording software for them on computers.

The producer had just sat down to create what would go on to become a big song on the radio that summer.

"This song is worth more than your whole life. Be careful," he said, flashing bright gold-teeth as he spoke.

He wasn't wrong. According to the USDA, a middle-class family will spend somewhere between $12,350 and $13,900 per year on child-rearing expenses, or just shy of $250,000 from birth through age 18. With college, you easily add another $100,000. The average person in the United States earns roughly $32,000 a year and gets in at most thirty working years before retirement, placing their total lifetime earning potential at $960,000. A star producer like this guy from New Orleans easily earned between $100,000 and $250,000 *per track*, paid by the record label either upfront or shortly after the beat was given to an artist to record. On top of that, producers often earned songwriting rights through publishing deals which could earn them a few hundred thousand dollars per year more if it was a hit, and tens of thousands if it wasn't.

This particular song was for another chart-topping artist, so the lifetime publishing revenue from this one song would easily be worth millions. One hit song, for one recording artist, would earn more than the average person over a lifetime.

I suppose the producer was right.

The way modern music producers work is through using computer software (called digital audio workstations) and beat machines to record music. The art of sitting down and either using software or the beat machines to place all the notes in the right place, by hand, to get the right sound is called *sequencing*. It's like rearranging the sentences and paragraphs in an essay you type in Microsoft Word, except for the music producer, the various parts of a song are sequenced in software like Pro Tools or Ableton.

I gravitated towards this area of music production because it was technical. Technology requires you to learn the rules of various systems—the rules of the software or machines someone else made. Digital sequencing was like programming computers, except you could *see* the code. This helped me see how computers understood the world, allowing me to better understand computers, and how to improvise with them later on.

Instead of having to remember complicated programming syntax and commands, these sequencing systems were visual and far more intuitive. I could tap beat patterns on soft drum pads instead of writing code. Or I could play chord sequences instead of writing Boolean statements that could generate the same tones. The digital workstation could be used to drag and drop notes around a digital canvas until I had visually painted the sounds I wanted. I didn't need to know how to play an instrument; I just needed to know how to put sounds together in a way that felt right. Somehow that felt more authentic to me than the folks who became virtuosi because they'd been playing the piano since five.

In a leaked 2015 deposition, prolific music producer Pharrell Williams was grilled by prosecutors in a dispute over the similarity of his song *Blurred Lines* to another song, the classic *Got to Give It Up* by Marvin Gaye released in 1977. The attorney tried to pin down whether a producer like Pharrell could read and write music. He was trying to make the point that if he couldn't read and write music like a classically trained pianist, that would prove Pharrell copied his client's song.

Every music producer in the world was probably screaming at their TV screens, thinking the same thing that I was. *Most music producers stopped reading music in the late 1980s!* This was because technology made reading and writing music virtually irrelevant to the music creation process itself. It was now possible to simply play notes. If they were off-key, computers could fix the notes for the singer. If something was impossible for a human to play, computers could create the melody easily. If you needed 808 bass tones that shook the room and had harmonics that people felt in their bones, computers could generate those frequencies. Modern producers had machine-assisted everything. They were cyborgs. Music is math. Computers helped non-mathematicians become virtuosos without having to be good at math or learning to read and write music. Through sequencing, synthesizers, beat machines, samplers, loop pedals, and digital audio workstations, it was possible to make any type of song, from hip-hop to electronic music, to rock or even classical, by clicking a few buttons.

There is a concept in tech called *the singularity* that describes the time when machine and human intelligence become indistinguishable from one another. It's become well-trodden ground in science-fiction in movies like *ExMachina*, *The Matrix*, and *Terminator*. For music producers, they had their own singularity twenty years ago when it became virtually impossible to tell the difference between human performances with instruments and the performances of synthesized instruments by machines.

There is a 1982 documentary that shows acclaimed producer Herbie Hancock demonstrating how music sampling works. In it, he used early digital audio workstations of the era – the Fairlight CMI and the Rhodes Chroma.

"We were sculpting," Quincy Jones says of the process. "Just like in a synthesizer, they're taking a pure electric signal and sculpting it into something of beauty."

He was talking about the original electronic synthesizers. These analog devices were bulky, made of wires and knobs that manipulated electricity through transistors. The knobs allowed the user to change the sound by manipulating electricity as it flowed through the machine. Every sound he heard emerge from these machines, no matter how jarring or how beautiful, was produced by dials. These analog filters and switches were manipulating electricity to create different tones and then organizing those tones into music sequences.

I was drawn to the increasing technical nature of music production. I like to understand how things work. Doing so was both fascinating and inspiring. Fascinating because of what they made possible, inspiring because of what they encouraged. I found music sequencing was intuitive for me. Later I experienced the same with programming, perhaps even more so.

This also shaped who my personal heroes were. For me, Quincy Jones, Herbie Hancock, Brian Transeau, Pharrell Williams, Chad Hugo, and Timbaland were as important as Steve Jobs, Bill Gates, Linus Torvalds, Larry Page, and Sergey Brin. They were all prolific in their respective industries but deeply technical, deeply thinking men, and it showed in their work. Tech and music. Computer geeks and beat geeks. Software engineers and sound engineers. Hackers and gangstas. Silicon Valley playboys and the hip-hop moguls. The context was different but the *swag* was the same. They were all radicals. They changed the rules.

Everyone has their own pace in life, our cadence for living, our unique personal rhythm for being. Sometimes we meet another person with whom we find resonance. We say things like *we just vibe*. "I *get* him", "he *gets* her", "we understand each other". "We finish each other's sentences." Your idea of the other person intertwines with theirs of you. His emotions trigger her impulses. Sometimes bodies intertwine only to find there's as much resonance physically as there is mentally. Their drums beat at the same rhythm.

When I was a DJ in college, I learned a technique called *beat matching*. Beat matching was where the DJ listens to two dueling records, each spinning on different turntables. (Yes, then DJs only had turntables and actual vinyl records to work with and not laptops.) The turntables each had their own switches to control the pitch and speed at which the two records rotated. In-between the turntables, there was a device called a mixer. The mixer allowed the DJ to control other things like volume. The most important feature of the mixer was a small sliding device called the fader. With the fader, the DJ controlled how much of each dual-laying record could be heard by everyone on the dance floor. In their headphones, only the DJ could hear both records playing at the same time. The goal was to listen to the drumbeat, the percussion of each playing record, and try to get them to align perfectly. If done well, it became hard to distinguish that there were two completely different records playing at all.

They synced, they *vibed*.

People on the dance floor usually were never aware of any of this. Only the DJ could hear what adjustments were being made to the music, that is, until he pulled the fader left or right to let the new record play through the speakers as it was in their headphones. The best DJs work the fader hard. This is called cutting – they use it to *cut* back and forth between two records. If properly beat-matched, cutting between two songs can make new rhythms altogether. The DJ can then cut in and out of dozens of songs so perfectly that at the end of their performance the people listening might wonder if one record was playing the whole night.

Sometimes there's a slip where the beats aren't perfectly matched. This is disastrous.

Suddenly, pounding bass drums begin to sound like galloping horses. The two records aren't in sync. They compete with each other and become *arrhythmic*. In DJ culture, this is referred to as a *train wreck*, where the DJ loses control of the two records and everyone can hear the mistake. Instead of resonance, they get dissonance. This is jarring and makes it impossible to dance. You are hearing two rhythms competing for your attention at the same time, and your brain doesn't know which to focus on.

When a train wreck happens, at some clubs, the audience will stop to stare at the DJ, or worse, boo them for ruining the night. This was the most terrifying part of DJing. I never wanted to flick the fader and let the rest of the world in on the secret that I had no idea what I was doing up there.

The goal of the DJ is to make the records match and then seamlessly transition from one song to the other. We try to keep the crowd moving without drawing too much attention. Scratching, mixing, spinning – sleight of hand. I remember these years in college spinning records every time I make a big life decision. No train wrecks…don't let your lack of confidence show…keep the records spinning…

Make the transitions seamless.

#TrapHouses

"I be on it all night, man I be on it all day,
Straight up, pimp. If you want me,
you can find me in the AYE!"

—Big Boi, Kryptonite

What chased me away from the music business was the business of music.

After interning at random studios around Atlanta, I landed a job at a prominent one, Doppler Studios. There, I worked my way up to a position as a staff engineer. On any given day at Doppler you might run into stars like Missy Elliot, Michael Jackson, Mos Def, Aretha Franklin, Pearl Jam, OutKast, Mariah Carey, or Stevie Wonder. Some, like Kanye West and Gwen Stefani, were there to record the decade's biggest singles. Music engineers like myself were responsible for making sure they didn't have to think about anything but being creative. We mastered the recording software, set up microphones, and tuned instruments.

There used to be a conductor at the front of the orchestra. They were responsible for shaping the sound of the players and extracting the best performances from them. With the arrival of tech, first analog then digital, the person at the front of the room became the music producer. The job of a recording engineer like myself was to do everything else the music producer needs other than actually make the music (though sometimes I did that too).

As someone working one-on-one with powerful pop stars and music producers, there was the unique opportunity to build a rapport with them. Sometimes you did trivial favors for them like parking their $350,000 car, or going to get food at 3 am so they could stay focused on their music. Other times it was more... interesting. Once a producer called me to engineer a session at his home studio. He wanted to record a bunch of songs but didn't want to pay the hundreds of dollars per hour it cost to record at Doppler. Instead, he would pay me directly for my time. It was a side hustle, and I was eager to earn the extra money. So I showed up, only to arrive at what was essentially a *trap house*.

For those unfamiliar, a trap house is a place where people came to buy or do drugs. From the outside, it was just an unassuming suburban house. Inside, random people lay passed out on sofas. Vials and used needles littered the carpet. Heavy clouds of marijuana hovered in the air, billowing from each room like fog over a city in the morning. A woman, moving as if in slow-motion, turned her head to see who had come through the door. Her head then dropped and bobbed like a needle on a vinyl record. She mumbled to herself, a conversation she was having in some distant universe. Pulsating lights cut through haze, pouring from a room down the hall. I assumed that's where the home's make-shift studio was. I walked towards it, careful to step over the bodies in the halls. Passed out from whatever high they were on.

I entered the room, mildly impressed. Whoever had set the studio up had outfitted it with all the right equipment: Auralex acoustic foam, a $5,000 microphone, a $25,000 state-of-the art mixing board. They used a closet to create a separate room for vocals, also with the proper acoustic treatments to deaden the noise for anyone outside the room. I walked in and started setting up software and saving files, carefully labeling zip disks so I could tell them apart later.

His studio was impressive, his entourage was not. There was an ever-present group of men and women who were just...around. I can't even tell you what they did. They were there to keep him company between recording takes, and probably for security if anything happened. That was the hardest part of being an audio engineer. You're the 'square' sitting at a computer in a room that has the vibe of a night club, where everyone else is having fun. Everyone but you. Your job is to stay focused and work without catching a contact high.

Even though it was your job to stay diligent, you also had to pass the group's vibe test or they'd fire you and hire someone who did. You might not have to do every little thing they did, but you needed to fit in. That meant code switching. I couldn't stand out too much even though I was there to work. A few weeks prior, I saw one engineer get fired because he told someone's manager to stop smoking blunts near him. It messed with his sinuses. He had mistakenly identified himself as the square in their circle.

"Man, get this Huxtable-ass, bitch-ass fool outta here!" they told him on his way out the door. They never paid him.

Being bad at code switching was not only bad for your career, it invited merciless harassment. It's more of an art than a science. There's no easy way to know how to behave when you're out of your element. At best, no one notices, and you fit in seamlessly. At worst, you get called out. Getting called out around guys like this could mean way worse things for you. Fights were common. Engineers got jumped, beat up for the audacity of demanding money they were owed. Others were shot at, caught in the cross-fire when a rival crew pulled up, trying to catch their enemies off-guard while recording. Anything could happen. Everyone was paranoid. Paranoid and high.

"Don't get caught lackin'," the rapper said to a friend, wincing as he took a drag from his blunt. "They outchea."

Translation: "Don't get caught without a weapon because you never know who might try to attack us today." For the uninformed.

The head of security for this guy was named Que; he kept a gun laying on one leg and a half-naked woman on the other. Robberies of recording studios, particularly home studios, were frequent. It wasn't just rap studios.

In 2009, a news article reported that the bassist of the rock band Pearl Jam, Jeff Ament, was violently attacked and robbed outside of a studio in Atlanta. The studio, Southern Tracks, was known for not hosting rap sessions at all. They mainly catered to the country, pop, rock, and alternative bands. Ironically, to avoid violence. Even studios like this weren't exempt. Any time you put fame, money, ego and drugs in the same room, you're bound to have problems.

I sat down to start the session. Kick drums rattled from powerful speakers, sending ripples through a Hennessey bottle on the floor. Each time the beat hit, soundwaves would move the air causing smoke to waft in and out of the speaker cone, as if dancing in rhythm. The heads of people in the room nodded along in unison. The rapper pulled out a Glock 9mm from his waist and literally tossed it on the table in front of me. It hit the desk and spun to a stop. It took every ounce of self-control not to flinch.

"Hol' dat fo me while I drop this verse!" the rapper said as he walked to the microphone. "Ayyyyeee," he began to rap. He either trusted me quite a bit or it was test. I could feel Que's eyes on the back of my head, daring me to make even the slightest wrong move.

I hated the unpredictability of these home recording sessions. I mostly kept to the professional environment of the studio where I would eventually move up the ranks, recording in million-dollar rooms with grand pianos and oak floors. Doppler has since closed, but in 2004, it was one of the most important music gigs in town. Music stars recorded albums while Hollywood films like "The Butler" and "Diary of a Mad Black Woman" did audio edits nearby. We recorded TV Shows like HBO's *True Detective* and Cartoon Network's *Space Ghost Coast to Coast*. As I gained more experience, I booked recording sessions of my own.

Even though I was surrounded by excess and success at a legendary level, I was rarely impressed. Chasing wealth in the music industry was a trap. For anyone who didn't make it, they had often spent their entire lives trying to make it. Chasing a dream that was unlikely to ever happen. When I was twenty, I told myself if I didn't have the career I'd imagined in music by twenty-five, I would quit altogether to do something else. I didn't want to get caught in the *trap*, a life spent chasing lottery numbers that would never land. A life of disappointment, passed out on the floor, high off a dream deferred.

Who cared about the glitzy world of famous musicians anyway? I had my own ambitions. I didn't want to ride on the coattails of others. If I was going to be great, I wanted to be great on my own. If I was going to fail, I'd do that on my own, too. Plus, I had a sobering view of celebrity from the inside. I saw these famous people at their best, but also their worst. I had to tend to them while they were having panic attacks, when they started fights, when they were screaming at our staff, or I had to guide them to a chair when they came stumbling in, barely able to put words together from all the drugs they'd consumed at a nightclub. I wasn't trying to join the entourage of people living vicariously through their fame. I was more comfortable as the outlier.

While young, nouveau-riche pop stars popped bottles at the club, I was more of a dive-bar guy. Most musicians like to record at night, so they could go to clubs after recording. This meant I often didn't leave work until well after 1 a.m. By then, most restaurants had closed. Instead, I went to grungy late-night bars, like the rugged bar for drifters called *Trackside* on the outskirts of Atlanta. It got its name for literally being on the wrong side of the tracks.

These kinds of bars, which seemed to be open all the time, were my escape. They were for vampires – nurses, off-duty cops, and music engineers like me who worked at night and slept all day. Places where people woke up with their faces stuck to the bar from dried alcohol, where the women tasted like cigarettes when you kissed them and made too much noise when they hooked up with men in the bathrooms. Where men didn't even bother fighting you when they got mad, they just bought you more shots and scoffed.

I was a studio rat and a music nerd. I wanted to know how producers came up with their sounds and melodies. Artists like Andre Benjamin of the group Outkast were endlessly engaging. He was one of those rappers who offered me work at his home studio, completely a different experience from the trap. He had a nice big home in the suburbs, gutted to turn every inch of space to record and make music. His home studio was outfitted with so much gear that it looked like the interior of a spaceship. Most artists ignored the engineer completely, but Andre sat like a student. He watched every move I made as I worked. He wanted to understand what every button did, what every click in the software was for. Why I selected one filter versus another. He had an endless curiosity about the methods, technologies, and the processes an engineer would use to make music. I did the same thing while he worked writing songs. We sat there absorbing knowledge together; students of each other's craft.

That isn't to say that all other musicians not named Andre Benjamin are assholes. Many were grounded and easy-going. Two R&B singers who I met shortly after they signed record deals, Keri Hilson and Ciara, were as eager to learn as they were to dance. Ken Block, of the band Sister Hazel, spent his down time teaching me guitar chords. Artists like these were obsessed with the secrets of music. They improvised. They figured it out as they went, adjusting course as things happened.

They were sound hackers.

#Boomer

"Peculiar things happen when you hit the speed of sound."
—Dave Hall

In a picture that sits on my desk, a black woman stands straight-backed, confident. She is poised, walking briskly to a destination unknown. Her aviator shades are pushed close to her nose. A thick, dark, puffy afro frames her face. Bell-bottom slacks lick at the wind. On the runway behind her, one of the inaugural flights of a jet capable of flying at twice the speed of sound is about to take place at Washington Dulles International Airport. The aircraft sits perfectly perched as engineers work diligently to prepare it for flight.

This turbojet-powered supersonic passenger airliner was called the Concorde. As it lifted from the runway, the roar of its Rolls-Royce Olympus engines shook the deck, bellowing thunder, torque pushing passengers backward into their seats. At the nose of the craft, air compressed, quadrupling the resistance against the plane. This meant the engines had to push harder than a normal plane, in order to break through the buildup of air. Eventually, the push of the engines accelerated the aircraft past the speed of sound. This resulted in a distinct burst of sound, called a *sonic boom*, which could sometimes be heard as far away as fifty miles.

* * *

The Concorde's first commercial flight took place on March 2, 1969, allowing passengers to cross the Atlantic, from New York to London, in under three and a half hours. For twenty-seven years, supersonic commercial air travel was not a fantasy. The last Concorde flight took place in 2003 after a fatal crash effectively bankrupted the company. The Concorde was a remarkable design for the time. Hell, it would be a remarkable feat of engineering today. Demand for air travel has never been higher. So where is the aircraft that will replace or surpass it?

The Concorde became a victim of retrograde innovation, or *retrovation*, where a technology breakthrough occurs but is abandoned for an objectively worse solution. Commercial aircraft used to fly faster than the speed of sound; now they don't. Sometimes things are better off the old way.

For example, switching from paper ballots to digital voting machines. Paper ballots worked decently for most of human history. Many solutions were developed to protect the elections that used them. When digital voting machines emerged, they almost immediately posed a new security risk due to the threat of computer hacking. Changing the method from paper to digital made it easier for attackers to compromise elections. They only had to click a few buttons to affect millions of votes whereas before it was considerably harder to affect votes at scale.

Another example: NASA went to the moon last with Apollo 17 in 1972. The agency hasn't produced a spacecraft capable of making a return trip to the moon since.

The Betamax video cassette was superior technology but lost the video format war to the poorer-quality VHS in the 1980s.

Petroleum still powers your car when electric and solar are more sustainable.

The Dvorak keyboard layout lost out to the Qwerty layout.

These are all retrovations.

My mother, the woman in the photo, was a plant pathologist for the U.S. Department of Agriculture. When I was a kid, she explained to me that pathologists were like disease detectives. They figured out where diseases came from, what crimes they committed, and what punishment they deserved. All this was to keep our crops healthy and safe from foreign-born diseases that could inadvertently (or intentionally) wipe out our crops here in the U.S., disrupting our food supply. It was a practice she dedicated thirty-five years of her life to, and she excelled in her position. She was a single mother striving to balance her career. When the government needed her to move, she moved. When the government needed her to work long hours, she worked long hours. For decades, she weathered obstinate threats of misogyny, objectification, and racism as a single mother in a male-dominated workforce.

She too was a code switcher. Later she became more radical, leading a class-action suit in the 70s in which women litigated for the right to wear pants to work instead of skirts.

She grew up in the reserved Georgia town of Dawson. Her early life was on a 90-acre farm on the outskirts of town. Our family owned the farm outright. Her parents, who worked the land for most of their lives as farmers, began renting it to other farmers in the area. They had acquired it by carefully saving their money, coming out of the era of sharecroppers and Jim Crow laws of the early 1900s. Everything in my family, everything she and her four siblings grew their own families from, emerged from that red earth and the hands that toiled on it.

The only time she changed jobs in that thirty-five years was early in her career, when she switched from being a school science teacher to join the U.S.D.A. Her generation had to choose careers young and rarely were there any wild shifts in the path. For people of my generation and younger, this is not the case at all. We are more like hackers and DJs; we have no choice but improvise. We have to make new rules as we go along.

"You should be a doctor or a lawyer," she would tell me.

She knew two things: these professions made money, and I liked to draw.

"...or an architect." she said. To her, these jobs meant financial stability and opportunity.

She knew a linear world, one where a single job could carry a person through their whole life—the world that defined her generation but no longer exists for ours.

I never saw the option of a linear path. Most people my age didn't, and it seems that younger generations won't either. We bounce from industry to industry, role to role, company to company. Many of us are entrepreneurs and freelancers, or if we do work for a company, we are independent contractors hire-at-will. We're told we're too impatient, that we can't stick to anything.

Actually, the world decided it doesn't want us to stick to anything for long.

What we call the *gig economy* or *share economy*, offers no benefits, healthcare, or life insurance. These jobs, where services are provided on-demand, make workers on both sides completely disposable. These jobs are like perpetual one-night stands. Friends with benefits. In this case, friends without benefits. You're invited to come over and do whatever needs to be done then leave immediately. A driver might work for Uber for six months, then Lyft the next six, or juggle both. Meanwhile, both Uber and Lyft claim to have no employees who are drivers. There's no minimum income guarantee. You just work. From what you earn for the company as you work, you get paid. This is all strangely familiar.

Work the lands, you don't need to own them. We'll pay you from what you produce for us!

It was familiar to me because I was raised by the offspring of sharecroppers. The concept of a career that existed for my parents, Black baby-boomers, doesn't exist anymore. That shouldn't be surprising. The concept of work that my mother's parents knew also no longer exists. They were wage farmers and sharecroppers, and their parents' parents were freed slaves. They had only the dirt but made it more.

The job market evolves with each generation, much like music, fashion, and culture. If someone is fifteen or sixteen right now, they probably can't begin to predict the job market that will exist when they're thirty. Adults who tell them the skills they should acquire, the courses to take, the people to network with, will more than likely be wrong. The prospects of the job market will have changed in fifteen years in ways that are hard to predict. In order to have more options down the road, young people will need to acquire as many skills as possible in emerging areas now. Experiment. Collaborate. Improvise. They'll have to build expertise in skill sets few others have to differentiate themselves and become less disposable.

They have to increase their optionality.

For my mom, there were few options. She stuck with the same job then retired into her pension and Social Security. Her job, working for others, became her life's work. Her career path was clear because the job market was different. Largely thanks to the Internet, we have fewer guarantees but far greater options. We have startups, gig work, micro-tasking, contracting, growth hacking, and temp working. We have everything but stability—a slew of innovations that resemble more of what my great-great grandparents experienced than what my mother did. We've gone backwards.

We've gone from Concorde-jobs to Wright Brother-jobs. What we have is a job market in retrograde. It's sub-sonic.

Given these circumstances, it's only natural that I was drawn to being an entrepreneur. Entrepreneurship was my way of freestyling through life. I've never had the type of job security my mom had. In fact, since college, over the past twenty years, while many of my friends went to work for Google or Facebook or Deloitte, I've never held a corporate gig. Instead, I mostly freelanced or started companies.

In the music and film industry, I was always an independent contractor hired for short periods of time. That contract could be renewed, or it could end abruptly at any moment. These companies didn't offer benefits either. The artists and studios I worked with could always just call someone else if I wasn't available. Or if no one was in town working on a music album or movie, I wouldn't get calls at all.

I was completely expendable. I had great opportunities in the entertainment business, working with some of the biggest stars in the world, but I didn't have any job security. I learned to keep multiple streams of income. I bought my own recording studio and rented it out to others. I had a side-hustle scoring independent movies. I set up home theaters for Fortune 500 executives, driving on-call to their gated homes in suburbia, far from the city. When you're that expendable and vulnerable, keeping multiple revenue streams is how to survive. You have keep your side hustles. You have to keep your options.

The entertainment industry was ruled by creatives and the people behind them. The singers, the songwriters, the managers, the lawyers, the directors, and producers. It's a business mostly driven by personal relationships or, because it's so competitive, the abuse of personal relationships. When I started my career, technical people like me were just sharecroppers on digital land.

In the early 2000s, the idea of the garage startup that grew to become a multi-billion-dollar company was still relatively new. Microsoft, Apple, Google, Amazon, and Yahoo were all companies that experienced unprecedented success and growth. The dot-com boom of the late 1990s had made legends of people who built massive companies from scratch. They made products that changed the way the world worked using technology. I grew bored with long nights with reckless millionaires in recording studios. The rise of software companies changed everything. I wanted to be a part of this other world, where people with my skills weren't at the bottom. A place where we were no longer expendable.

Where I was no longer the square in someone else's circle.

#Waypoints

"Mobiles squerking, mobiles chirping...
take the money and run!"
—Radiohead, Idioteque

Before YouTubers and vlogging became a thing and before Instagram made everyone under thirty an *influencer,* there were blogs. Bloggers were the original micro-celebrities of the late '90s and early 2000s. Prior to launching one of the more popular blogs in Africa, Appfrica.com, I had two of the least popular blogs in Atlanta, Georgia—StarkRavingBlack.com and HollaBackPack.com, where I shared my stories of growing up in Atlanta and my travels.

I first met Tyler Perry in 2004 when I was an intern at the studio where he was doing post-production on his first movie. A few years later in 2006, I received a voicemail from his staff. He was hiring and needed someone with a background in audio engineering. I was called back to accept the position where my job was – drumroll – to put the laugh tracks on his TV shows. Later, I got to place music in TV shows and movies, but that's where it started. *Laugh tracks.* At first, I was the only full-time person in the audio department until two other guys, more experienced sound engineers, joined me as our workload increased.

I was just a guy in the 'dungeon', a sound-proofed room that would get unbearably hot as the computing equipment and servers roared away. Still, Tyler would often visit. He wanted those laughs perfect. Given I was in the most uncomfortable room in the building, and no one seemed to understand what I did, I had a great deal of autonomy. So much autonomy that HR seemed to forget I worked there.

I had only been with Tyler and his company for a year when I got restless. I made myself a promise that if I wasn't where I wanted to be by twenty-five, I'd leave the Entertainment industry. It was time to decide if I was where I wanted to be. Working with this young, upcoming, film director, who was forging an unparalleled independent path through Hollywood, inspired me.

While I enjoyed being along for someone else's journey, it was time to forge my own path. It was a great job, and there were a lot of opportunities I'd be giving up, but I wanted to see what I could accomplish on my own. So, I turned in my resignation. I expected sadness and *fare-thee-wells*, a wet kiss on the cheek from an actress, or at least *a bon voyage*. I got nothing of the sort.

"We don't remember you," a person from the company told me years later when I invited Tyler to an awards ceremony. I shook my head as I typed, ego crushed. *They still don't remember me.*

I suppose I knew they didn't remember me because I was a part of Tyler's staff when it too resembled a chaotic startup. I had been lost in the shuffle. Buried under a pile of sitcom laughs.

I was one of the early hires, maybe in the first batch of twenty or thirty. Within three months, the company exploded to a head-count of more than one hundred. They also didn't remember to take me off payroll after I turned in my resignation. For the better part of six months, I was living on another continent while everyone, including HR, forgot about me.

It was a sign from the universe to go do something memorable.

I took off to Europe. I didn't have an agenda, I just wanted to get out of the trap. I backpacked across Europe, from West to East and then back. Twenty countries. Britain, Ireland, Norway, Sweden, Denmark, Finland, Estonia, Poland, Spain, Portugal, France, Belgium, The Netherlands, Germany, Switzerland, Austria, Slovakia, Hungary, Slovenia, Croatia – in that order, before taking the train from Zagreb to Frankfurt and then to London on my way home.

On the trip, I traveled with a device called a Garmin. The Garmin is a single-purpose hand-held electronic device that uses satellites for real-time mapping and geo-location. It was one of the first global positioning systems (GPS) available to consumers and hobbyists. In the days before everyone had Google maps on their smartphones, this was how it was done.

I wanted to create a digital map of my trip, something that wasn't easy then. Getting the location data into a computer required a patchwork of cables and software databases that I had to learn to program. First, you extracted the data from the device then ran software that made sense of it all. To make digital maps, you had to translate latitude and longitudinal coordinates into code and overlay them onto mapping software that you also had to download and learn to program. Often this took a lot of trial and error, and if you were wrong, all the data displayed in the wrong places. It took a decade for marking your location on a map to become as simple as pressing the *add location* button on Instagram. Working with these Garmin devices was how I first learned to work with data.

There were no photos or vivid colors, just dull greys and greens. You could locate yourself on the screen by pressing a button or you could use a dial to move around the map's canvas. Up, down, left or right – those were your only options if you wanted to see what lay ahead. The Garmin unit spoke to satellites like smartphones do now and felt a lot more accurate. It only had one thing to do, track your location. Smartphones now have ten thousand other priorities to focus on at the expense of accuracy. If you've ever hit the *current location* icon and ordered an Uber or Lyft, you know what I'm talking about.

As I traveled, I became an expert at dropping *waypoints*—digital signals that marked location. I used them to mark places that were important to me. Waypoints were so accurate that they could guide you back to a hole in the ground you dug a decade ago (assuming no one had changed the landscape). It was for this reason that it became popular to plant hidden treasure and play scavenger hunt games with other Garmin users. These were called *geocaching games* and took place all over the world, sometimes leading to hidden prizes.

If one were to trace my plots from 2006 using these digital waypoints, the only treasure they'd find are pubs, landmarks, museums, hostels, and the occasional residence of a couch surfing host.

Some people take photos in front of a building to preserve their memories.

I dropped waypoints.

* * *

"It's not so bad. At least the weather is good," I said into my phone.

My cash had run out. I found out while trying to book a hostel. My card was declined. I asked the receptionist to run it again. *Declined.*

"Lo siento," the woman at the desk said. I wouldn't be staying at the hostel that night. I had an expensive Canon camera that I offered to trade for a few nights' stay. She looked up unimpressed and pointed to a sign. *Cash only.*

It was October 1st, 2006, and other than a travel wallet full of random coins collected across Europe, I was out of money. What I did have left, I was saving for emergencies. A warm meal and soft bed weren't what I considered an emergency. I could get by without either. Without any real money left, I decided it was simply cheaper to remain homeless – at least then I could afford to eat when I needed to.

I improvised.

At night I slept on the streets of Madrid, Spain in an open courtyard in front of the Royal Palace of Madrid at Calle de Bailén. It wasn't the most comfortable place but it helped stretch the little money I had left. Unless it rained, the 80-degree weather in Spain made it perfect for sleeping outside. I used my backpack as a pillow and my blue hoodie for a blanket

In the square, I felt safer than other areas around town. Orange tinted streetlights came on at night giving a soft glow to the whole area. Also, from my corner in the square, I could see 270 degrees around me. With my back against the wall and a view of all sides, I could see any passersby who might represent a threat. I slept no more than two or three hours at a time. If I heard voices approaching, I got up and walked away, exiting the square and roaming until it felt safe to come back. You never knew if it was just some random passersby, a cop, or someone looking for trouble. Better safe than sorry. At times, I felt alone and beaten by the world. Other times, I felt like I was the star of a movie and this was the lowest point in the lead character's life.

I really, really hoped it was the lowest point in the lead character's life.

During the daytime, I'd go to coffee shops to use the Internet. A friend's dad once referred to being homeless in a city as "urban camping." You might not have much, but if you were resourceful, you could find ways of letting the city's infrastructure take care of you. I made sure that the little cash I did have was enough to pay for a coffee or pastry to keep the proprietors from harassing me if I sat on my laptop too long without buying anything. I had money to fall back on in my accounts back home but it required a call back to the States so my mother could initiate a wire transfer. This was a call I dreaded. I didn't want her to worry. I was also prideful and didn't want to give her the opportunity to say *I told you going to Europe without a plan, or a job was a bad idea!* I waited almost a week, surviving on instant noodles and continental breakfast buffets before I sucked it up and made the call home. I used a payphone.

Well, I used a payphone—but I didn't pay for it.

The fraternity of hackers is powerful. Relationships were formed, virtually, in chatrooms and web forums for months, sometimes years, before they manifested in the real world. This allowed bonds to form between, say, a black hip-hop producer from Atlanta and a bunch of computer geeks in Spain. Walking down the street, we might not even have glanced at each other but online we found we had a lot in common. We didn't let our differences get in the way. It was another type of code switching, the best kind. Computer screens and chatrooms obfuscated the prejudices of real-world first impressions. The virtual world, what they now called the metaverse, masked you from what people thought you *might* be. Instead, we got to know each other first online, *then* we met in person.

With a lot of time to spare and nowhere to go as a broke backpacker, I frequented websites like Slashdot, 4Chan and Phrack. org, stumbling my way into web forums run by the Spanish hacker community. Many of the sites are no longer around but, one, *hackstory.es* is still active and preserving the history of hacking culture in Spain.

Their manifesto reads:

Porque no queremos que los viejos días de Internet se desvanezcan en bits muertos.

Porque estamos orgullos de los hackers.

Porque queremos su memoria viva.

Y en marcha.

It was a fractured community, but members were still active and knowledgeable in 2006. These early hackers were known as

Phreakers and they pre-dated what we now know of computer hackers by at least a decade. Phreakers emerged as early as the 1950s, using their knowledge of analog electronics and audio frequencies to hack telecommunications systems. From then, into the early aughts, they were active, compromising telephone networks, racking up huge bills and off-loading them to individuals or corporations, testing vulnerabilities of digital phone systems to see what was possible, what rules could be rewritten.

That's right. Before hackers, there were phreakers. The phreaking community was about improvisation and experimentation with phones before computers were pervasive. Growing up, I discovered these communities online, mostly related to an underground magazine called 2600. The people in those communities were eager to share knowledge, give advice, and share ideas. In these magazines, I read stories about popular hackers of the time. People like John "Captain Crunch" Denver, Loyd Blankenship, Kevin "Dark Dante" Poulsen, RedBoxChilliPepper, Lord Digital, and the now-legendary Kevin Mitnick. Though he wouldn't become famous for hacking, another of the most famous from that era was Apple Computer Co-Founder Steve Wozniak.

In the early-Internet era, these people forged the path for hackers and created the businesses that would change the world. The software and hardware exploits that originally made them legends, though, was from phreaking. Phreaking was a way of hacking pay phones when they still used analog switches.

To be successful, the person seeking to *phreak* the phone played tones into its microphone through the mouthpiece. Tones played at exactly 2600 hertz triggered devices in the phone responsible for keeping the phone locked until the user paid. This is why the famous computer magazine was called 2600. Tones played at that frequency allowed the phreaker to trick the phone services into thinking they had paid when they, in fact, had not. Other times the tone might serve as a passcode, giving the phreaks author-ity to access underlying systems of the phone service provider. For instance, they might secretly piggyback off corporate phone networks, freely making long-distance calls that appeared to be coming from a business whose owners had no idea. This type of hack was called *line emulation*.

Any device that could record audio could play these tones but *phreak boxes* were the original tools of choice. Each box was named after its color. There were black, beige, clear, red, gold, green, magenta, and orange boxes. *Black boxes* were devices that, when attached to an analog phone line (a method dubbed as the *click-it method*), allowed all inbound calls to be received for free. The *beige box* allowed users to hotwire phone lines with clips that looked like a tiny version of the ones you might use to jumpstart a car. By clipping the analog cables, the user could intercept incoming and outgoing calls to essentially eavesdrop on them. *Clear boxes* were used to avoid paying phone toll fees. *Gold boxes* allowed the user to use one phone line to hijack another – basically making calls that were secretly billed to someone else. *Green boxes* were used to fool payphones in situations where the call receiver had to input coins to stay on the line (think of someone dialing from jail or overseas but not having to pay). *Magenta boxes* were used to spoof incoming call signals. *Orange boxes* were for spoofing caller ID information through a technique called frequency-shift keying.

The last was the elusive holy grail of phreak boxes, known as *the Vermilion*. The vermilion box was a mythical device that com-bined the features of all these other phreak boxes into one. The vermilion box could do many things at once where the others were each single-purpose. In other words, it could code switch.

The Spanish phreaking community had been decimated by an event in January 2000 called *Operación Millennium*. Complaints from several corporations including Microsoft, Toshiba, and Novartis triggered an investigation that prompted Spanish authorities to arrest fifty-five people from across the country in a sting operation, charging them with fraud. The unit that investigated the crimes, which spanned more than 200 phone calls, was called the Telematics Crimes Group of the Civil Guard. The main group hit in the round-up was a group of phreakers called *COM 30*. The crackdown hit members of the group as well as civilians who had used information about how to hack from COM 30's online chat rooms. Even though many of the individuals were eventually acquitted, the Operación Millennium raid had successfully spooked the Spanish hacking community.

"It wasn't the same after that," my friend from Spain told me.

In 2006, although U.S. telecom operators had already gone through a mass transition from analog phone networks to more secure digital ones, in Western Europe, the transition was still underway. Eastern Europe was even further behind. That left the door open for two urban hikers to get crafty.

"I need to call home but I don't want to spend the money," I typed, thinking about what would be an expensive long-distance call. My new Spanish friend took pity. We'd only met in person a few times and because I spoke limited Spanish and he spoke limited English, we could mainly only speak to each other via web chat.

Instead, we sat side by side in Internet cafés in our *Bonjour* internet chatrooms, copying and pasting what each other wrote into a translation service called *Babel Fish*. Even though we were from different backgrounds and spoke different languages, in the chatroom we were connected.

We found our rhythm, our vibe.

"It's okay. Let me show you a trick," he typed. He motioned to a Telefonica payphone outside .

At the pay phone, he looked over his shoulder to make sure no one was watching. He proceeded to use line emulation to hack the phone to get me a free call.

Even if I could share what he taught me, it's all irrelevant now. Since 2006, the underlying telecommunications systems in Spain and around the world have changed half-a-dozen times. What worked then won't work now. Nonetheless, at the time my concerns about being able to afford a call home disappeared. I was able to contact my mom and get my wire transfer initiated.

Before I left, I made sure to pin our location to another waypoint.

* * *

Watching the landscape while traveling by rail from Western Europe to Eastern Europe is like watching blood as it drains from a body. Colors faded as infrastructure became sparser, older. Highways gave way to stone roads and worn buildings. Polished skyscrapers were replaced by castles and other relics of history that look like they hadn't been visited in decades. The journey took me from Salzburg, Austria to Bratislava, Slovakia to Budapest, Hungary to Zagreb, Croatia to Celje, Slovenia, where I was to get off and transfer to a different train, which would take me to a smaller town called Rogaška Slatina. There, I was told, I'd find my hotel. Crossing the border between these five countries in the Schengen Area of Eastern Europe was meant to be painless.

If that was their goal, they failed.

As the street poles and hills whizzed past the train window, I took pictures and left notes in a paper journal that I carried.

When I dropped new waypoints on my device, I wrote down the coordinates and left corresponding notes about the things I saw or did in that place. That way, I thought, if I ever wanted to retrace my steps, I could.

Wouldn't this be a lot easier if I could do all this via computer? Or better yet, my phone?

The other challenge was that this part of the world was still largely unmapped by products like MapQuest and the then-new Google Maps. Even where the areas were mapped, the Garmin had to be updated manually by connecting it to a computer to upload location data. When I didn't have Internet access, which was frequently, updating the maps wasn't possible at all. This meant at times even the Garmin couldn't help me figure out where I was. I'd look for myself on a road or intersection and just find I was staring at a blank space on the map.

So, I improvised.

I used a different device to help: a digital camera. This was before smartphones had the high-quality cameras they do now. Instead, I used my higher-quality digital camera to take pictures of paper maps I got from tourist shops. That way, I could use the digital viewfinder to zoom in and trace the roads around the image as if I was moving a satellite looking down on my location. With its massive amounts of storage, I could digitize dozens of paper maps in my camera, effectively creating my own digital maps. This was 2006, less than a year before Steve Jobs would take the stage at Macworld on June 9th, 2007 to introduce a device that would soon make all these hacks redundant – the iPhone.

The whole trip would have been so much easier with a goddamn iPhone!

I rifled through instructions I'd written in my journal to find my hotel. Some of the pages became crumpled and sweaty from being tucked in my pocket for so long. From what I could still see, they read:

Train between Budapest and Celje

Cross-border at Hodoš, border crossing (Prekburje Region)

Celje

Train from Celje towards Rok ob Sotli

Get off at Rogaška Slatina

The train ride was overnight and would take eight hours. As we pulled away from the train station in Budapest I followed along with my gadgets and makeshift digital maps. I turned to the window and watched a foreign world pass by. I was just one person among ten million strangers separated by language and culture. My skin defined me differently here. There was no legacy of slavery, Jim Crow, or civil rights. It was a different type of *otherness*. Sure, to many, I was a curiosity, a visual anomaly with black skin. But in a sea of immigrants, refugees, and tourists, the one thing that united us was our mutual anonymity.

We had come from everywhere and were headed anywhere. Strange passersby who could only look at each other and wonder. I thought of the millions of faces I must have crossed in my trip so far, and I couldn't quite remember a single one. I dozed off trying.

* * *

A loud *CLANK* startled me awake.

The door to the cabin swung open and banged against the train's steel frame. There was a draft as snowy air rushed in from outside. A dark figure was now shining an intense beam of light in my face. I blinked and rubbed my eyes.

When did I fall asleep? I squinted to make out what was happening. Shielding my eyes, I tapped around to make sure my backpacks were still there. They were. My worst fear was being robbed – losing my passport, computer, and other electronics would have been devastating.

Silhouettes of unknown men flanked me, military-grade semi-automatic rifles hanging low by their sides.

"Putovnica."

"What?"

"*Putovnica!* ......Passporte," the shadowy figure repeated in English after realizing I didn't speak the local language.

"Oh…yeah." I reached into my bag, raising my hand to shield my face from the beam of his flashlight.

Moments like this happen while traveling. Moments you should have planned for but didn't. Otherwise-benign things that snap you to attention and put you on alert. Like being awoken by border crossing guards at the nexus of Croatia and Slovenia. Suddenly, I no longer felt anonymous and only slightly uncomfortable. The light loomed over me. I code switched again, from relaxed tourist falling asleep on a train to cautious American Black far from home. Don't make any trouble, I told myself.

The man shifted the flashlight to the passport, then back to me. He was silent and stern, like he'd seen too much in his lifetime. He flipped through the pages looking for my visa stamp from visiting Croatia. Satisfied, he flipped back to the first page and raised it to eye level to compare my face to that in the book.

"Hvala," he handed the booklet back and moved up the aisle to the next person.

"Putovnica," he said again, moving up the aisle.

* * *

I got used to being looked at.

Quixotic looks. Casual looks before the bashful glance away. Intimidated looks. Black people, people of color generally, were rare in this part of the world. The locals couldn't help themselves. They were curious. It was awkward but otherwise harmless. I had been on the road for months, occasionally making friends but mostly alone. Loneliness was refreshing. It gave me time to think. Time to appreciate the fact that, briefly, I had no worries, reacting only to the moment I was in. I became hyper-aware of my own internal monologue. I became more introspective and more self-aware.

The standoffish stares weren't the only reaction I got in Eastern Europe. There was also a great deal of fascination from some individuals who wanted to lean into my otherness. At nightclubs, the looks were not so shy. Shyness gave way to flirtation and lust. I was told it was because of my *African body*.

In Estonia, I visited a club called *Prive*. I sat down at the bar and dumped my bags on the floor. I let out a deep sigh and stretched. I was exhausted from travel but energized by constant discovery.

Nearby, a stocky man of about two-hundred and fifty pounds was pounding vodka shots. He was surrounded by blonde women who drank and laughed with him. He shook hands with security and joked with the bartenders. He was Russian. Not what most would consider handsome, but '*strong*' as they say. He looked like a backyard wrestler – square jawline, protruding belly, hands that seemed like they could crush a baseball. He wasn't so much muscular as he was *immovable* and *dense*. His interactions with the staff made it clear that he had a reputation. People respected him or feared him. It didn't take long before he noticed me at the bar.

"Hey, *Hip-Hop*!" It sounded like he was was saying *heep-hope.*

I continued sipping my vodka soda, assuming he couldn't possibly have the audacity to talk to me that way. I continued chatting with the bartender.

"Hey Hip-Hop!" He pointed. *"You! African!"*

Great. I turned: "I'm American."

"Oh! American Negro! I like Negro music. I buy you shot!"

I guess he took my pause and dumbfounded look as an open invitation. He and his harem of girls made their way over. At the time, I was growing short dreads called twists, perfect for traveling because it meant I didn't require a haircut. I was doing what I could with a straight razor to keep my beard trimmed.

Experience had taught me to sometimes code switch out of caution, to diffuse a situation. In this case, I didn't know if the guy trying to get my attention was a friend or a threat. He was massive enough that the answer to that question would change the situation a great deal.

"You're Russian?" I asked, trying to distinguish his accent from that of the Estonian men I'd met.

"Ja! My name is Miite, from Yaroslavl. You visit Yaroslavl?"

"Nah, I'm headed to Moscow."

"Ničevó sebé!" he exclaimed. Something along the lines of *Wow!* "What you drinking? We must celebrate!"

"Vodka soda."

"Vodka good. Vodka soda for *devochka*! Tell me, Hip-Hop. Do they have Absinthe in United States?"

Restraint. Restraint is a big part of code switching.

Despite my initial annoyance, after a few rounds of drinks, I found myself enjoying the company of Miite. He told me that when I got to Moscow, he'd take great care of me: "You must come. See my country! See our women! They love you, Hip-Hop!"

I laughed.

"But Estonia ist better... they have expression here in Estonia. When country formed, it was only filled with beautiful women who had fled war in Soviet Union. Blondes and brunettes, as far as eye could see. All lovely!"

"When the borders were being drawn, Russians realize there was no men here in Estonia. Before drawing border was finished, all the ugliest men in Russia from St. Petersburg to Krasnoyarsk rushed over and closed border behind them! Now, only the only potato that grow in Estonia is the men!"

He roared with laughter that shook the room, slamming his fists on the table. The glasses jumped as if they, too, were startled. The group of women flanking him giggled.

I awoke the next morning entangled in the limbs of these women from Miite's entourage. My head was throbbing and my throat parched. I walked over to the sink to pour myself a glass of water. As I drank, I realized Miite wasn't there. At some point during the night, I'd lost him, and I couldn't even recall to who or what. The whole evening after the Absinthe shots was a blur. I vaguely remembered more shots and many more jokes that I only barely understood.

I hazily remember a street scuffle, the girls asking to touch the twists in my hair, and lots of Russian marijuana. We stayed overnight at an apartment I'd been renting that overlooked Tallinn Town Hall Square. There had already been many weeks of my friends back home following my exploits around the world through my blogs. Thankfully those years weren't immortalized on video and social media apps like they are for this generation. The next night, after nursing a brutal hangover, I wrote about my night out in Tallinn with Miite. I wrote about the shots of absinthe and my exploration of the city's nightlife.

A comment was posted to the blog in response almost immediately.

"Watch your back in the Baltics, nigga," the anonymous person wrote.

My anonymity and comfort were shattered.

Historically, the region was known for incidents where immigrants had been targeted and persecuted. In the early aughts in Russia, there was a string of racially motivated violence against immigrants and foreign exchange students. On February 9th, 2004, a gang of teenage skinheads armed with chains, metal rods and knives, attacked the unassuming family of Yusuf Sultanov as they walked through the streets of St. Petersburg. The family were natives of Tajikistan (sandwiched between China, Uzbekistan, and Afghanistan). Police speculated that the fact that they were immigrants was the reason for the attack. Yusuf was pummeled by the assailants and helplessly watched as they stabbed his eleven-year-old nephew in the neck. His nine-year-old daughter, Khursheda, was killed. When his attackers were brought to trial, the murder charges were thrown out. The judge instead declared it a case of "hooliganism." Boys will be boys. Murders? Just good old-fashioned hooliganism.

On April 7th, 2006, Senegalese student Lamzar Samba and a group of friends were leaving a club when someone fired a shot from behind. The bullet tore through Lamzar's neck and left him dying in the streets as his friends fled for safety. After his death, a neo-Nazi website applauded the murder, writing that "the clean-up of the city continues." Russian authorities wrote off these acts as the work of extreme nationalists, but the inaction to properly investigate and prosecute and such acts of violence spoke volumes. There were many more cases of ethnic aggression and warnings found in the news of the time.

I later spoke to a friend, a French-African DJ, who told me about his apprehension of taking gigs at clubs in Moscow. He had seen the reports of a fire at a University in Moscow, the People's Friendship University of Russia, that was suspected arson. All the exits to the building had been blocked, forcing many students to jump to their deaths from the fifth floor. All forty students killed were immigrants from other countries. Days later, four Jamaicans and a Colombian student were viciously attacked by skinheads on the same campus.

"I never left my hotel room. Not to party, not to get food, not even to see the city. The promoter who booked me had me escorted to the club and back, and then to the airport. He protected his investment, " my DJ friend explained. "Moscow is different, though." He encouraged me to go there. "There's a lot more tourism so it's cool, but in St. Pete and anywhere else, just be careful."

I had planned for my first trip to Russia to be to St. Petersburg the following day. I was already close by in Estonia and the train ride was cheap. Most of my trips in Europe were planned on impulse, looking at maps to see what was near (and what was cheapest to get to). When I failed to obtain a travel visa in time for Russia, I didn't give it a second thought. Between all the warnings, that impulse had now passed. Instead, I'd decided to stay a bit longer in Tallinn. Plus, I was still haunted by the comment...

Watch your back.

While most people were harmless, there are always troublemakers. In Estonia, I was warned the gangs there were mostly Russian youth, disgruntled, and ready to make trouble with anyone. Especially foreigners. They were dangerous and unpredictable.

One morning around 2 a.m., I was walking back from a club to my apartment. A car passing with four teenagers inside jeered towards me abruptly, slowing to a crawl. I quickened my pace, trying not to look back at them. I listened for sounds of a car door opening or the scuffle of footsteps. I heard nothing, just the low hum of the car engine. It was an old Peugeot.

I thought to myself... *this is it. I'm going to be shot in Estonia, no one will find my body for a week.*

The car rolled a few more feet behind me and stopped. I reached into my pocket and clutched the Swiss Army knife I carried with me. It was all I had.

My breaths got deeper and quicker. It was cold out, so my every exhale danced wildly, like my nerves in that moment. I tried to conceal my fear by breathing more shallowly. I didn't want to give any signal, no matter how small, that I was scared. Doing so would certainly be an invitation for them to get out of the car.

Instead, I kept walking as if they weren't there. I waited, head straight, tracing my peripheral vision for any sudden movements. As I put distance between myself and the car, it began to creep forwards again. The engine snarled and groaned like a dog on a leash. The car crept along beside me for a few more feet, then – BANG!

I couldn't look.

The tires squealed in place before the vehicle swerved off into the night.

"Lahkuda meie riigist!" one of the passengers was hanging out the window waving his middle finger up. The banging was him slapping the side of the car with his palm.

I kept walking briskly as if I hadn't noticed a thing. Restraint.

In my pocket, my hand loosened and let the knife sink back into the pit of my pocket.

I hurried on my way.

No waypoint necessary. I wouldn't be visiting this place again.

Act #2

Vermilion

#Mutungo

"It Began in Africa."
—Jim Ingram

As the plane hovered in darkness just prior to touching ground, I glanced out the window. Pitch black.

The only lights were dim pinholes of lights in the distance littering a dark landscape and a hazy maroon horizon. These lights made the visibility only marginally better. I was used to streetlights being bright and white in America, illuminating roads for long distances. Here, though, the lights were bright at the source but didn't carry long distances. Torrential red clouds swallowed the view of the landscape as we approached the runway. The plane's engines kicked Ugandan red earth into the air. It was what I imagine landing on Mars might feel like.

The plane touched the runway and stumbled to a stop. Applause erupted. It was the first time I heard people on plane clap for a safe landing. This itself was jarring – I hadn't been worried on the flight at all. *Should I have been?*

I later learned this is common on international flights, especially African flights. For a long time, African countries were the dumping ground for the world's retired planes, particularly second-hand Russian planes. After these planes had been decommissioned in Russia and other countries, Africa's airlines would buy them at a reduced cost, refurbish them, and put them back in the air. From a financial perspective, this is absolutely practical. With the refurbishments, the planes still ended up being close to a third of the cost of a brand-new plane. Still, it's a little unsettling to think that planes that would be considered at or near end-of-life in other parts of the world were getting another fifteen to twenty years of life here on the continent.

Entebbe was the former capital of Uganda and rested on the peninsula of Lake Victoria. It was the home of Uganda's only international airport. Between Entebbe and Kampala, there is an hour and a half drive. The road is full of potholes and wayward pedestrians who don't seem intimidated by vehicles at all. Cattle roamed the streets as well, also stubborn in the face of imminent death by truck or car.

As we left Entebbe, the silhouettes of people faded in and out of pockets of light cast by overarching street poles. Velveteen bodies reflected that light or absorbed it, pulsating highlights of red, purple and brown. The stench of cow manure and open sewage from the streets was eye-watering. Blankets of crimson dust loomed over everything. It coated my nose and the inside of my glasses. It covered the walls of buildings, the cuffs of pants, and the wheel wells of cars. It colored the banks of Lake Victoria and the fields of outdoor parks. It colored the air and my mucus when I sneezed. I coughed to clear my throat.

This was Africa.

It was a place I had heard about my entire life but realized I knew nothing about. My experiences with Africa up to that point were limited to commercials about poverty or people recovering from mysterious wars that no one could ever explain to me. Some people spoke of Africa as if it had all the answers, but no one could articulate any of the questions. No one, on any continent, seemed to be able to tell me anything about Africa other than it was beautiful or to be careful. It was distinct from all the continents. Old and new, mysterious but well-known, infinitely poor and infinitely rich, all at once. It was an oddity that garnered the same looks of curiosity and lust from around the world that I got in Estonia.

Africa was an outlier.

As we drove, I watched the profiles of strangers walking long distances in darkness. Their elongated silhouettes were stretched by harsh light cast by low-voltage bulbs on tilted poles. They crossed in front of cars, unflinching as motorbikes whizzed around them. Some sat with friends and family around a fire where they grilled meat, laughed and shouted. Occasionally one or two stared into the vehicle, heads turning to watch us. What was my story I imagined them wondering?

My head turned to follow and wonder about them, too.

* * *

As you may now be able to tell, this isn't the *moving to Africa* story that most people envision. I wouldn't imagine most people think of moving to Africa for any reason at all.

When they do, if they do, it's likely an image drawn from pre-colonial nostalgia or the outrage of activists. For most people, Africa exists in a pervasive binary state of poverty or war. That's all they know from the news and documentaries. Others simply don't know Africa at all, or they romanticize it with safaris and charity photo-ops with the continent's colorful, humble people.

The year after my trip through Europe, briefly back in America, I bonded with a woman who had as much love for travel as I did. Her name was Sarah. She did humanitarian work across Asia and Africa and hopped from country to country like I did—only she got paid to do it. She worked in developmental aid, helping poor countries on their path to property and progress. Her work meant visiting orphanages and farms or rebuilding the plumbing systems of remote villages. She was impressed I had done as much traveling as I had. We were familiar and exotic to each other all at once. She was driven by a desire to change the developmental course of nations; I was driven by curiosity and restlessness. It wasn't long before we fell for each other.

Soon we were living together and had settled into the routines that couples do. We'd found our rhythm, our resonance. For a while, that seemed like that was going to be the end of our story.

For a while…

"Yes," I told her.

For some couples, the big question is: *Will you marry me?*

For us it was: *Will you move to another continent and live with me there for three years?*

"I'll come with you."

She had received a job offer to work for a non-profit organization that did work improving access to water for the poor in developing countries, the bulk of it in Africa. It meant living abroad for the better part of three years in Uganda. She wanted to know if I'd join her. I weighed my options. After returning to America from my trip across Europe, I briefly returned to my work in entertainment. It felt even less fulfilling than before.

The rigid definitions of race, class, and culture in America now made me feel claustrophobic. It was like visiting your old high school after being away at college Freshman year. When you go back, the things that once seemed to loom over you in their importance now felt tiny and irrelevant. The students running the halls used to look like thirty-year-olds; now they resembled toddlers.

I longed for that feeling of being an anonymous mind among millions of people again, collectively coming from everywhere and each headed anywhere. An opportunity had been extended to reshuffle my hand again – this time, with a woman I loved.

When I tell people now about moving abroad for several years, they respond with questions like, "Weren't you afraid to leave everything behind? I could never just move to a country I've never visited."

My response is, "How could I be afraid of something I hadn't yet experienced? That's just being afraid of change, any change."

I look at it this way – if everything changes at once, there are only three possible outcomes. Things change for the better. They change for the worse. Or they don't change at all. That makes a 66.67% chance everything's going to be alright. Those are pretty good odds. Is it worth the 33.33% risk that it won't work out? To me, it almost always is, especially as it relates to seeing more of the world. A two in three chance to try something new, to increase your opportunity for serendipity, to explore the unknown.

Three months later, I moved with Sarah to Uganda.

For many reasons, this didn't make sense to my friends and family. It was the mid-2000s, and I was in my twenties earning six-figures working with the powerful people in TV and film. I had bought a small recording studio. I was being hired to produce records for burgeoning stars. None of it excited me as much as my time on trains in Eastern Europe. I was willing to give it all up to find that sense of serendipity again. I found it in her.

Beyond being my lover, she was someone I looked up to. She exemplified a sense of purpose and commitment to serving others. She was tall and gentle with long auburn hair. She was the type of kind and empathetic person who made it her life's purpose to make the world a better place. I left my freelancing behind and ended my side-hustles. I sold everything in my studio to save for our move. She put her midtown Atlanta apartment up for rent which gave us a consistent revenue stream while abroad. We needed every penny we could save for Uganda.

The late comedienne Gilda Radner wrote in her memoir *It's Always Something*: "Some stories don't have a clear beginning, middle, and end. Life is about having to change, taking the moment and making the best of it without knowing what's going to happen next. Delicious ambiguity." When Sarah asked me about the move, I knew a moment had arrived that could change everything. There it was, our own delicious ambiguity.

Kampala, Uganda in 2008 was neither as war-torn nor as poor as it had once been. It is often referred to as 'the Pearl of Africa' and likened to Europe's Norway for its rolling hills, green valleys, and serenity. Travel an hour outside of Kampala, and the biome completely changes multiple times. from rocky and mountainous, to tropical and wet, to humid and swamp-like, and in some places to completely arid. Even in the big city of Kampala, the atmosphere was peaceful and quiet.

Plus, the organization Sarah worked for covered our first-year housing and moving expenses. They gave her a stipend and helped us get established by covering furnishing costs. They helped us rent a home in a nice neighborhood with a concrete security wall that encircled the grounds.

Prior to leaving the U.S., she and I researched Uganda's history – the terrifying hijacking of a plane bound for Israel in the 1980s, the expulsions of its merchant Indian class in the late '70s, its contemporary political scandals, and corruption. We wanted to be as informed as we could possibly be. The relocation expenses were covered and could include shipping our belongings via freight, meaning by ship, which can easily cost tens of thousands of dollars. We declined. We didn't even have enough stuff for that to make sense.

I had already liquidated my recording studio and sold everything else I owned for my trip to Europe. The most valuable possessions I had left were dusty vinyl records I was given by my mom or that I collected during my time as a DJ, plus thousands of comic books from childhood. Some art. Clothes. That was pretty much it. Instead, we used most of the relocation budget to tie-up loose ends like paying off the last of our bills in America.

In comparison to the living standard of most of the citizens in a country like Uganda, life as an expat is unreasonably nice. Not quite as nice as it is for ambassadors or diplomats, who sometimes live as lavishly as the President of the country himself, but pretty close. We had a live-in guard, called an *askari* in the local tongue, Luganda. His name was Godfrey. Our full-time maid was named Charmise.

When we asked them to do things for us, they would respond, "Yes, ssebo," or "No, nnyabo." In Luganda, *ssebo* was sir and *nnyabo* was madam. This was the custom here. Our landlord was a prominent member of Ugandan high society himself — the chairman of Makerere University Business School. The street we lived on was named after him.

Expats living as we did, with corporate budgets and U.S. salaries, were among the country's wealthiest by default. We had privileges that locals struggled their whole lives to obtain. As such, expats were accused of abusing their status as guests of the country, accused of abusing our authority as foreigners. The relationship between local and expatriates was tenuous at best.

Most of these feelings were reserved for white expats. I was never quite sure what they made of me, the American Black who had moved to Africa. Most people in Uganda assumed I was African, like them. But many knew I wasn't. They could tell I was foreign by my gait. The way I carried myself. Even without speaking, a few were very good at identifying and calling out my *otherness*. It was hard for some Ugandans to reconcile that I was both black and American but that I had no familial connections to Africa, at least not for several generations. Of course, some knew quite a bit about American history and knew about the removal of black populations in America from their African ancestors. Others asked if I was from *the ghetto*. I explained that I wasn't. I wasn't poor, wasn't rich, wasn't the child of African immigrants to America, and wasn't there to visit African relatives. I was just – there.

I found myself having to code switch for them as well. I didn't want to come off as condescending, aloof, or arrogant.

The next question was often, "Why are you here? Why do you come here?"

Good question.

"For a girl," I would often say trying to keep it simple.

"Is she African?"

"No."

The questions continued. I didn't have a good answer for that one. Still just – there.

I couldn't really explain why I came, but I knew exactly why I stayed. It was for an Africa that was different than everything I'd imagined growing up. I couldn't even say it was new; it was just new to me.

While researching the country and what life would be like in Uganda, I discovered the work of a man by the name of Andrew Mwenda. Andrew was the editor and writer behind Uganda's most popular political newspaper, *The Independent*. A YouTube video featuring Andrew had come up in my search about Kampala. In the talk, he spoke about standing up to a corrupt administration in Uganda and the numerous times he'd been arrested for doing so. Andrew's call was ultimately for more equitable philanthropy, where the people in poorer countries were treated as equals in decision-making. Where African countries, and African citizens, relied upon each other instead of foreign aid or even local governments. It was *neo-pan-Africanism*. Arguing that Africa's people need to take a more active role in Africa's growth and progress. Otherwise, the Neo-Pan-Africanists would say, we couldn't complain when the content's resources were exploited by others.

Many successful first-, second-, and third-generation Africans returned to invest and start companies, bringing their Western education, skills, money, and connections with them. A decade later, in Ghana, an official *Year of Return* was established to welcome well-to-do Africans and Black Americans back to the continent. It was a rallying cry to the diaspora across the world, an evolution of the philosophy of people like Andrew Mwenda and economist George Ayittey. A philosophy that arose in response to many years of misspent philanthropy, the shadow of colonialism, and poor governance by a handful of African leaders out of control. Neo-Pan-Africanism was a call for social responsibility by Africans. Asking, in short, *What are we Africans going to do for ourselves?* In his writing, Mwenda argued Africans were the solutions to their own problems.

I wrestled with whether I was *African* enough. Sure, I lived there but that didn't feel sufficiently authentic. Africa was clearly in my oily skin and coarse hair. Did I have to code switch to become African or to remain African?

A group of Ugandan friends coined the phrase *reaspora* to reference this homecoming of self-sufficient Africans. We were the *returning diaspora*. We were members of the African diaspora who had returned to use our skills to improve the continent. It wasn't about kicking expats out of their homes or taking back land from whites as had been done in Zimbabwe. It also wasn't necessarily about forgiveness for the worst parts of history. Equally, it wasn't about persecuting people for the sins of their ancestors. This reaspora movement was more introspective. It was a movement focused inward, on improvising for each other's benefit. There was no room for racial or colonial bitterness.

This was a movement focused on building a better future, not settling the debts of the past.

* * *

The first morning after arriving in Kampala, Uganda's capital and most populous city, I was eager to get out of bed and explore. We didn't move to our house on Mutungo Hill right away. For the first few weeks, we lived in a well-known Chinese-owned hotel called Fang Fang. The hotel was something Sarah's company had arranged. By living there first, it reduced the pressure to buy furniture and style a home right away.

Fang Fang was quaint, a reserved mix of Chinese minimalism and Ugandan pragmatism. The restaurant was excellent with floral gardens typical of the region adorning an open-air courtyard where the children of guests played with live rabbits in grass so well-manicured it looked like carpet. Ironically, rabbit was also on the restaurant menu.

The flavors at the restaurant were delicious and new. At least one distinct good thing that has come from the mixing of Chinese and African cultures is ChinAfrican food, the Chinese cuisine that arose from migrants trying to make their traditional family dishes with the ingredients available to them in Africa. The mix of traditional Chinese aesthetic on the interior, coupled with East African styling, was intriguing. I had read a bit about Asia's scramble for Africa but here I was, standing in a Chinese family-owned hotel that had been in East Africa for nearly a generation. Was this a Chinese take on the African experience? Or was this Africa's take on the Chinese experience?

Other Chinese people, some might say the vast majority in Uganda, remained isolated and had limited desire to consort with locals. I suppose in their minds, they were there to harvest cheap resources and to form strategic geopolitical relationships, not make friends. By trading with Africa for minerals, timber, oil, etc., China could avoid competing with America and Russia for resources in the Middle East. It was strategic.

Likewise, many African leaders didn't care about any potential downsides of trade with China. They saw it as a transactional means-to-an-end. Their countries were starving for infrastructure and industrial mass production. They may have understood China didn't care for Africa's culture and people, but it *was* spending generously to gain resources. This was a relationship unlike the Western powers who had taken the continent's resources by force and colonoization. China, on the other hand, was investing. African governments didn't care about Chinese motives, only that this was a much better deal than the ones history had provided.

Still, proximity breeds familiarity and familiarity fosters kinship. Despite wariness of each other, the Ugandan hot pot of Chinese and African cultures was brewing here at Fang Fang.

The Asian move into Africa has been part of the continent's history for hundreds of years. In the 1970s, during Idi Amin's reign in Uganda, there was a forced expulsion of all Asians living in the country including Indians, Chinese, and Saudi Arabians. By the thousands, they had to either return to their own countries or seek asylum in places like Canada, the United Kingdom, Kenya, or Germany. Amin felt they were creating too many businesses and that the danger of them dominating control of the economy was too great. He looked to Kenya, where it appeared to be happening as well.

Idi Amin's thesis was at least partially correct. The foreigners did run much of the business in his country. Unfortunately, he grossly misjudged how much he needed them. How much their experience and expertise mattered to the sustainability of it all.

After the Southeast Asians were extradited, Uganda's economy imploded.

Entrepreneurship can't exactly be taught, at least not quickly. It's even harder when all the people with skills that could be taught are gone, chased away by a short-sighted, xenophobic mandate. Even where it can be taught, there has to be room for those learning to try and, if necessary, fail. The economy of a country does not have much margin for error.

What Amin failed to see is that experience and ambition are what create successful entrepreneurs. Lack of business experience meant his plan was doomed from conception. Likewise, simply giving someone a business because they were born on a certain soil has no bearing on their skills, aspirations, or interests. Ironically, many of the Asians forced out were natives of Uganda, born or relocated when it was still a British colony. Amin didn't expel colonizers; he expelled his own countrymen and women. These Southeast Asians had originally arrived as unwilling passengers of the British — as slaves. Yet, they were targeted because of Amin's racist and irrational fear of losing control of his economy to hard-working immigrants.

On the other hand, it could be argued that the Asians who left didn't make it easy for anyone to take their place. They were bankers and business owners who were forced to give up their livelihood and companies in a place they had made home, bitterly. It would be plausible that some would deliberately sabotage a transition.

Whatever the reason, businesses began to falter under their new Ugandan owners. It was an event that reports said would set the economy back twenty years. Ironically, things didn't begin to turn around until Uganda's current leader Museveni took power in the '90s – twenty years later. After taking power, Musevini encouraged the people and families who had been expelled to return to the continent, without restriction. The family that owned Fang Fang was one of the few to return after the great Asian expulsion. Even though they weren't Southeast Asian, they were still expelled. They loved the country so much they returned, even after being betrayed. Home was home.

The restaurant at Fang Fang acted as the perfect entry point for expats. Unusual, intriguing, inspiring.

I woke up in this new environment – a city that would be our home for the next three years. The morning after we arrived, Sarah and I walked the winding streets of Kampala. We had the same curiosity as when we digitally explored the city streets using Google Street View, an application that lets users virtually navigate real-world locations from a digital device. At the time, the app returned a blank canvas where many of Kampala's streets were supposed to be. This was long before Google's camera-equipped cars had made it to the city to capture and map the streets of this part of the world. Years later, mapping the streets of East Africa for Google became a project my company, Appfrica, would contribute to directly. I arrived at a blank canvas and did my part to help paint the rest of the picture.

* * *

While exploring the city, Sarah and I found ourselves in the densest, most chaotic part – *the taxi park*. In the taxi park, for almost half a mile, all you could see in any direction were hundreds of vehicles. Buses called *matatus*, taxis called *share cars*, and motorcycle taxis called *boda bodas*. These vehicles littered the landscape as if they were once in a box of toys that had fallen over and spilled everywhere.

Somehow, these matatus could weave in and out of each other's way on the roads without incident. No matter how crowded or close, it was like there were hidden lanes of order, visible only to the drivers. They shouted out the window at each other if that order was violated. The taxi park was a jungle for vehicles. Taxis lay in wait for prey like tigers.

I walked through the madness of it all, eyes wide. Our guidebook warned us muggings were common. Expats were the most common victims. The park was a cacophony of sights and smells that assaulted the senses. Open sewage and rotting food, loud and schizophrenic with rushing cars and scurrying people. When not in their cars, taxi drivers bumped between passers-by, pushing past them as if they weren't there at all. Unaccompanied children wandered around, begging for food. They stopped to stare in awe at Sarah. The tall white girl with hair the color of cinnamon.

The muzungu.

"Muzungu! Muzungu!" they shouted as they ran up to her.

The word meant *foreigner*, mostly reserved for Caucasians. Apparently, there was no distinct word for me – a foreign black in Africa. The American Black. It was even harder for them to fathom that we were a couple.

"How is your wife?" people would ask. For the entirety of our time there they ignored the fact that we weren't married.

For two weeks, we traversed the city like this, familiarizing ourselves with the city's personality and features. We went into the overcrowded markets where we bought souvenirs for friends and family. After exhausting all the ChinAfrican food on the menu at Fang Fang, we ventured out to find new places to eat.

I found the traditional food of the country to be bland and tasteless. Lumps of grey matoke (boiled banana turned into a mashed potato-like mush) covered in purple G-nut sauce (made from purple peanuts called G-nuts) and boiled meats (chicken, beef, or goat). Nothing was seasoned. The only flavor was survival. These were recipes passed on through years of famine, drought, and civil war, made for people who needed nutrients and energy, not indulgence. Nyama choma (grilled meat), on the other hand, was the opposite. Lamb, beef, and succulent pork, slow-grilled or roasted on kabobs and seasoned with salt and pepper sauce. Delicious.

I later learned that nyama choma had its roots in Kenya where the food was a thousand times better. Kenya was home to one of the busiest ports in Africa, Mombassa, which would have made it critical in the early days of shipping to and from the continent. These foreign ships opened Kenya to the spice trade, and its Rosetta Stone of flavors and the people introduced the country to their cultural influences. Uganda, on the other hand, is land-locked. It is closer to Africa's interior and surrounded by harsh mountains, the torrential Nile, and dense jungles. I assumed that pre-colonial spice traders only made their way so far inland.

Either way, the cuisine of the countries changed to reflect the visitors.

After living in Fang Fang for weeks, we finally moved to our home in Mutungo. Looking out from the home's gardens, you could see for miles into the valley below. In the mornings, the sounds of construction echoed across the canvas of Kampala and into its stone walls. These were echoes of what I'd been chasing – the unknown but necessary.

The house was near the top of a hill overlooking the city. At the very top were houses that belonged to distinguished Ugandans like our landlord, diplomats, and expatriates like us. As we walked, the fortified walls, barbed wire, and armed security of the more expensive houses gave way to much smaller homes, ones that didn't have the protection of concrete walls or razor wire. Towards the bottom of the hill was a shantytown community with homes made of scrap wood, discarded aluminum, and in some cases, cloth. Some were literally no more than tents – the four feet of land someone had been able to claim for their family. In the early days of Uganda, before the courts documented land rights, if you settled somewhere no one else claimed, it became your land. It was a free-for-all – what you claimed was yours. As one might imagine, many land disputes arose in a time when record-keeping was non-existent.

The pace of life was slower here. No one was in a hurry. Unless they had jobs in the city, people were content to watch life as it happened around them. They weren't stressed. They were as calm and relaxed as the country itself. Some waved, others watched, unsure of who we were or where we had come from.

At the bottom of the hill, we hailed a share-car to take us to the city center.

"Can you come now?" we'd ask, respectfully trying to match the intonations and inflections of the Ugandan accent. It was the type of switching I had to do when speaking to people who have a hard time understanding me. I wondered if it was condescending. Otherwise, our own accents became a barrier to communication. Even though English was the common language in Uganda, without mimicking their accent, we often weren't understood.

"Now now," meant immediately, not when they felt like it. The distinction had to be made otherwise you'd wait for a ride forever.

To get around the city, there were *matatus*, compact vans that could fit between eight and fifteen passengers. They were usually decorated with decals representing the owner's favorite music, movies, or football teams. Before smartphones existed, we would text message drivers who came to pick us up as needed. (Years later, companies like Uber and Lyft would reference how the inspiration for their billion-dollar apps came from their experiences like this across India and Africa.) We had to compile our own lists of driver's phone numbers, a pool of them we learned to trust. Then we'd use our mobile phones to call whichever was available, on-demand, the old-fashioned way.

Text a driver, get a car.

#TalesFromDispatch

"In a banana republic, one might slip on a banana peel but things do work now and then for the people, albeit inefficiently and unreliably."

—George Ayittey

"They call it waragi. Bathtub gin," he said holding up the mysterious bottle of clear liquor.

"What is *bathtub gin*?" I asked.

"It's crude gin, made from bananas. What I've heard is people here used to let it ferment in bathtubs during colonial-imposed prohibition and the following wars when it wasn't possible to get liquor or to own distilleries." He crossed his legs and passed the shot he'd poured me.

"Made from bananas. In a bathtub?"

"Yes, sir. Warigi," he laughed at my exasperation. *"East African Moonshine.* Hell, you're from Georgia. You should know all about moonshine."

He flung his head back and drank, wincing as he swallowed.

I did the same, drinking after him. "Oh…that's…not good." My chest burned as I coughed heavily.

Everyone in the circle laughed.

It was dusk at a cocktail party in the suburban hills of Nakasero neighborhood of Kampala. It was a posh neighborhood mainly for diplomats and foreign aid workers, government workers, and the occasional local Ugandan celebrity. The rows of diplomat homes were manicured and ornate, like a 1940s film set. The roads seemed to unravel and twist their way up and through the hills, snaking past houses that got more extravagant as they climbed. The lawns were grand and immaculate. Towering Borassus palm trees encircled the property just outside the wall, their line broken by the waist-high shrubs neatly trimmed to form a path alongside a walkway that led right up to the front door. The house had eight rooms and three bathrooms split across three floors. It was white and concrete with orange slatted tiles adorning the roof. During the day, ceiling-high windows let in lots of light and air. A terrace wrapped nearly completely around the house on the second floor. The perimeter was lined with a brick security wall that had spirals of barbed wire at the top.

Nakasero had become in many ways the hub of Kampala as the city's population stretched from one million people during the evenings to nearly two million in the day. Day laborers and their children would drive in from other parts of the country for work and school in the mornings, then make the long journey back in the evenings. The lower slopes of the hill accommodated local business. This was the lifeblood of the city — the taxi parks, a large open market, banks, and countless restaurants.

Gatherings like the party we were attending weren't uncommon here – where journalists, expats, diplomats, and foreign aid workers got together to drink and share stories about life and work. We met frequently to joke and commiserate about local things that never changed, like how bad traffic had become in the city or how much we missed the changing of seasons. Though we had nothing to complain about with Kampala's year-round 80-degree weather.

These rooms required intense code switching. At any moment you might be talking to a Ugandan official, an Israeli diplomat, war correspondents or people from Interpol. Casual conversation usually didn't cut it. I learned to know a little about everything that was happening around the world and across Africa. That way I could at least not look uninformed in conversation with people from various disciplines. I absorbed as much as I could when others spoke, they became my unwitting tutors about global events, African politics, and local gossip.

"So, you are American?" The woman was Israeli, here in Uganda working for her country's embassy. Her wavy black hair draped over her shoulders and seemed to be on the verge of falling into her face until, with a wave of her hand, she'd pull it behind her ears. "It is rare to meet Black Americans in this region. No?"

I nodded. "Rarer than it should be." I took a sip of the wine a cocktail waitress was walking around with pouring for guests. "I like it so far."

"Don't we all!"

"I suppose," I said, smiling. We continued to make small talk before she politely excused herself to go say hello to another friend in the room.

The party was a suit and tie affair – glamorous by any measure. Despite that, even at the most exclusive events in Africa, there were guests who seemed to just…show up. They arrived wearing whatever they were wearing when they got the invitation. Often these were journalists and war reporters who couldn't be bothered with trivial things like putting on stuffy suits. That wasted precious time that could be spent on adrenaline-fueled coverage of village bombings, political coup d'états, and the migration of refugees. They would arrive wearing their field clothes, fatigues, and cargo vests with camera rolls or bullets (or both) tucked away in vest pockets.

These galas would have impressed anywhere in the world. Expensive wines from vintage collections, freshly butchered meats, and fresh seafood flown in from the coast of neighboring Kenya. Politicians and journalists shimmied like Hollywood actors and actresses. Occasionally actual Hollywood actors and actresses were present, there to visit orphanages or shoot their newest film. Meanwhile, barely half a mile away was Kisenyi, one of the largest slums in the country.

"We are so disconnected from the streets around us," said a slim British man wearing a suit. He was much older than I was and wore those years on his face.

I chuckled, "I was thinking that, actually. We're in here drinking like this is Caligula in one of the poorest countries on the planet."

"Welcome to Africa! Not that bad for the likes of you and me, ay?" The man smiled and sipped from the scotch glass in his hand.

I stuck out my arm to introduce myself. "I just moved here a few months ago."

"Welcome, son. I'm going on eight years. Stephen, retiree, and journalist. What about you?"

"Wow, eight years! You're an OG."

"OG?"

"Original Gangster...never mind. American slang. I'm here....to be honest still trying to figure that out. I'm building a software company now. I used to work in the music industry back home."

As we spoke the sounds of the party rose – laughter, high-heels clacking on tiled floors, glasses clinking together, a bed of soft music underneath it all. My new normal.

"Ah, a techie. We need more like you here...and less of these bobble-heads who don't do anything but talk at each other all day and push paper around. Eh...who am I to talk I'm a journalist!"

"Retired journalist," I reminded him.

"Correct. I left my old role at U.N. Dispatch years ago. Since then, I've found a second calling freelancing as a journalist for the Associated Press. It's hard for them to find people willing to live here in Kampala. Job security for me, I suppose." He looked around the room. "'Bet this isn't how you pictured Africa before you got here. Is it?"

"I guess I didn't know what to expect, but this is nice. Odd juxta-position, though. On the way here we drove past Nakasero mar-ket. This feels more like Buckingham Palace."

Nakasero Market was the oldest outdoor market in Uganda. It was a popular tourist destination for buying local crafts and foods. It was divided into two areas, an open space that seemed to be a writhing pit of traders and barterers and a covered por-tion which was less crowded with people shopping for clothing and other goods.

"Well put, but this is the Africa more people should know. There's plenty of wealth here and plenty of opportunities to distribute that wealth. There's little will to change things…at least not from those with the actual power to do so. So, it goes on and on."

The thought resonated deeply. A Ugandan woman with a serv-ing tray walked by carrying a plate of something that looked and smelled delicious. She was wearing a red vest and white shirt, with a black skirt. "You could be anywhere in the world right now but you choose to stay. What's keeping you?" I asked him.

Stephen sighed. "Despite the faults, there are endless possibilities here. Plus, someone has to keep the elite on their toes." He mo-tioned towards the folks in the room. He began to explain how he knew people in the room.

"That guy over there is C.I.A. You can tell because he never does any work yet is somehow at every important event in the city. He claims to run some NGO, and no, not all NGOs are fronts for the alphabet boys, but as far as I can tell it's also not uncommon for real organizations to be cover for CIA operations – less conspic-uous that way.

"That woman is our host's wife. Her husband is the head of an Embassy. While he travels the world playing James Bond all day, she stays here and plays Mrs. Robinson with the Ugandan pool boys." He bounced his eyebrows suggestively and laughed.

"You don't say."

"That's not gossip, lad. Circles here are small and word travels fast. If people are talking about it, it probably happened. But what do I know."

Over the following weeks, I would find my way back to this world of expatriates regularly. The hardest part of being an expat was wanting to socialize with locals where I stood out, knowing the only social group I really 'belonged' to was amongst these eccentric foreigners. I hung out with non-expats at Ugandan bars and nightclubs on occasion, but I was never going to be able to blend in. Every new person I met was a challenge. As an expat I had to find a way to relate to the poor, the rich, the powerful, and the meek on a daily basis. Every day was an opportunity to code switch.

A group of Stephen's friends formed around us. They chatted with the familiarity and urgency of old friends catching up after some time apart. They shared stories of expats sent to places like Goma in Congo where the staff of an NGO lived in compounds much like the one we were presently in. They often didn't step foot outside of the walls for months because it was so dangerous to step out. The Congo had been ravaged for years by civil war and political unrest. Liquor and food were flown in by helicopter every month. At the same time, workers would remove any waste from the compound the estate guards hadn't already burned in a pit in the backyard.

"You can't imagine what it's like to have to stare at the same walls, the same views, the same cabinets, the same twelve people, day in and out for months", one of them said. He was drinking wine at an alarming rate. "It's enough to drive one mad. Thank heavens for co-ed compounds!"

One guest spoke of fleets of motorcycle drivers who lined up opposite each other to play *motor ball* in an open field as local kids watched, cheering them on. Motor ball was like soccer except the players on each team were on motorbikes. They weaved in and out of each other, kicking the ball as best they could without the bike falling over. Usually, each bike had two people. One person sat upfront steering, while the other held on tightly in the rear using their free legs to kick the ball. If it sounds like a sport created by drunk British hooligans, it's because it was. Copious amounts of the local brand *Club Beer* were often involved.

But mostly there were more stories about sex.

Sex with Presidents. Sex with diplomats. Sex with wives. With daughters, with husbands, fathers, celebrities – you get the point. There was one rumor that a young woman who had joined the United Nations as an outspoken feminist and champion against human trafficking had previously starred in hardcore porn movies. When the room chastised him for going too far, the man refused to back down.

"Do I need to show you the scene?" he said drunkenly, swaying with his phone. "I will press play! I will do it!"

"Are you crazy! This is someone's home! Put that away!" a woman scolded.

"Sounds like a non-stop frat party out here," I said, shaking my head.

"An idle mind is the devil's playground," Stephen sighed. "What else are you gonna do when you're locked in a bunker in Kinshasa for months?"

They spoke of incestuous relationships where colleagues and their partners would break up and get together with other colleagues until everyone in the office had slept with everyone else.

Then there were the truly questionable incidents. What some might consider an abuse of power. Highly-paid expats having sex with the groundsmen and maids who worked for them. This caused much debate about the ethics of workplace power imbalances and the appropriateness of such relationships. Whenever that happened, it would usually last for a few weeks before someone would get concerned about appearances and the aid worker would be sent off to a different compound to work for a different group of ex-pats where the same things would inevitably happen again.

Another guest overheard the conversation and interjected with their own gossip. Apparently, United Nations private planes were occasionally flown to Europe or Asia under the auspices of an international emergency. In reality, a high-ranking official wanted to take his family shopping in the South of France for the weekend and used the UN plane to do it. To watchdogs back in the U.S., this would be considered misuse of public money. To the expatriates here in Uganda, it was business as usual. Rarely would any of these people be caught or reprimanded. In Africa, people got away with whatever they could. If caught, they simply transferred to a different part of Africa and did it again.

It was a strange world of extreme excess amongst dire disparity. Power and debauchery superimposed on the poor. Local people fought for their basic dignities while others fought for discretionary expense accounts. When you're a foreign aid worker or missionary, there's no one to really hold you accountable. The people who come here are *doing good.* They are people on foreign assignment: the journalists covering hardships of the poor, people digging wells for villages, and building orphanages for abandoned children. They are also still people. They make mistakes and sometimes cause a lot of harm. A 2018 report accused U.N. staff of over 60,000 cases of sexual assault in poor countries all over the world. The reports and rumors about charities have persisted over the years.

"Did you hear about that guy Sam?" a British woman whispered.

"Who lets a pedo' into an orphanage? It's shameful to think about what he may have done to those children. He was here for a whole year!" another woman exclaimed.

"It's fucked up is what it is," Stephen said. "Abusing people who have so little to begin with."

"Using tax dollars, as a public servant no less," a woman said.

I sighed. I suppose I shouldn't have been surprised. Where there are people with unchecked power, scandal usually isn't far behind. I learned to expect the absurd.

"Well, you know the saying," Stephen began, "You either die the hero or live long enough to see yourself become the vil—."

The drunken man interrupted: "Or you live long enough to see yourself on camera!"

He pressed play on the video.

#LandOfDialUp

> *"The real question is not where do ideas*
> *come from, but where do they go."*
> **—Paul Beatty**

"You're going to come someday?" The investor smiled as he signed the last document.

"I'd love to. I've never been. Is it safe?"

"Is it safe!? In Beirut!? Tell me, is this *Kampala* safe?" he scoffed.

I smiled. "Touché."

November 4th, 2009. I leaned back and reviewed the terms one last time. Raising money from venture capitalists takes a lot of work. You've got to have product-market fit, a low burn rate, a disruptive product, a pitch deck, etc. But first, you need to know what all those terms mean before signing a lopsided contract. All things I've learned since, but at the time, they were still new and intimidating. Another way to get an investor to commit is to sell them on a vision. If they believe the entrepreneur's vision is possible, they're more likely to take the risk. Before that vision is reality, they have to trust that it's attainable and the person in front of them is the right one to make it happen. When you're a startup and first-time entrepreneur, you don't yet have past successes to point to, so you point to your vision. Vision is what connected me with this investor.

I was an active blogger, writing about doing business in Africa. My blog about African tech attracted a number of readers curious about what was happening across the continent. As one of those readers, he came to appreciate the stories of my work in Africa.

I frequently wrote about Africa's ecosystem of innovators, entrepreneurs, and builders. While covering them, I learned that what was needed was a place to pool resources and bring down the costs of doing business in Uganda. They wanted shared Internet, shared electricity, shared office space, and if they all needed the same things, why pay separately? The investor was from Lebanon, a place that had its own resource constraints. He read my ambitious plans to start technology hubs in Africa. He could empathize with the problems of technologists in a still-developing country because he came from one. He understood the opportunity and shared my vision.

The man was slender and sharp-looking and wore the type of designer clothes that might get you kidnapped in this part of the world. He moved like he didn't care. I assumed Beirut had prepared him for the worst.

"I've got 36 hours before my flight departs, so let's not waste time," he told me, looking down at his Rolex.

After signing the term sheet, he walked me right into a bank where we opened a joint account at Standard Chartered. He deposited $15,000, which at the time felt like half a million. It wasn't a lot, but it was a start. "If your team delivers, I'll put in another $50,000 in three months. Who knows, if it's going well in a year, I'm capable of bringing in a few million," he continued.

In Beirut, he ran an e-commerce software company and was investing with money drawn from the balance sheet of his business. Essentially, pulling profits to buy equity in other businesses. This was something I would emulate myself. Reading my blog, it occurred to him that there may be an opportunity to grow his own software company by expanding into Africa the same way other tech companies had been growing with partners in Southeast Asia or Eastern Europe. These were countries where labor was cheap and the cost of doing business was low. In addition to seed capital, he agreed to send a certain amount of business our way. He became both our first investor and our first customer.

Appfrica was the software consultancy that I operated from my house on Mutungo Hill, land that was previously owned by Uganda's first President Edward Mutesa II. Tech companies around the world were outsourcing to India which inspired an idea to do the same. *Why not have them outsource to Africa?* When we weren't building software for corporate customers around the world, I envisioned Appfrica as a *house of ideas*. The staff received company laptops and equipment. They spent four days out of our five-day work week working on client projects. The last day was time they could use to tackle whatever projects they wanted.

This was a concept I borrowed from Google's early days. In their 2004 IPO letter, founders Larry Page and Sergey Brin highlighted the twenty-percent concept:

> *"We encourage our employees, in addition to their regular proj ects, to spend twenty-percent of their time working on what they think will most benefit Google. This empowers them to be more creative and innovative. Many of our significant advances have happened in this manner."*

They had.

Several major Google innovations came from the twenty-percent time experiment. Products like Google News, Gmail, and AdSense eventually became the basis of the company's $ 150-billion-a-year revenue model. For my team at Appfrica, things ran a little differently. For us, the twenty-percent time was for pitching. Staff presented ideas that I would invest in if I saw the merit. I'd go as far as doing the legal work for them, creating legal entities on their behalf. They would be the owners and CEOs of these ventures. I put up the capital needed to get their companies started, as the investor from Beirut had done for me.

Typically, I invested anywhere between $10,000 and $25,000 on top of their salaries. In 2009, in Uganda, this kind of money went a long way. They were the ones who had grown up in Uganda and across Africa. They would come up with ideas and solutions I would even be aware were needed. I doubled down on them and their ideas. In turn, they invested their time and energy into Appfrica. They were Barbara Birungi, Moses Mugisha, Victor Miclovich, Emmanuel Oluka, Apac Manac, Ahmed Maawy, Matthew Griffiths, Bahiyah Yasmeen-Robinson, Dennis Senyonjo, Muwanga, Frankie Raiderson, Michael Rutalo, Oliver Haas, Richard Jeong, Theresa Carpenter, Victor Oguli, Jerry Opolot, Joshua Goldstein, Brian Ndyaguma, Glen Mehn, Brandon Sheats, Felix Kitaka.

This was the staff who made Appfrica a success.

I found that my technical skills put me in a position to act as the bridge between cultures. Multinational corporations in Africa didn't trust the local workforce to have the computer science skill that were required. They didn't think their education was good enough or that the people were reliable enough. Likewise, the local software developers, consultants, and analysts often didn't know how to get meetings with these foreign companies. They didn't have the right connections. I didn't have that problem. As an expat, I ran in the same circles as many of these executives. I could go back and forth. I turned code switching into my business.

"Why aren't you hiring any local staff?" I asked one executive. "Surely it would be cheaper than flying consultants in from Europe and America. Local wages are like a tenth of what you must be paying."

He answered, "We're not sure they can deliver the quality we need." I could tell he was uncomfortable at the prospect of working with locals. This was odd.

"Why come thousands of miles to other countries just to cling to the familiar?" I asked. "There are hundreds of qualified people here. Makerere University is one of the most famed universities in Africa. You don't think there aren't at least a few qualified locals you can hire here in-country?"

He thought about it, "I suppose so. But we don't know how to find them."

"Are you really looking?" I asked. No answer. I continued, "Tell you what. Hire my company. I'll go out of my way to find the right talent for you."

That became my pitch to win business. My customers didn't have to become experts in hiring African talent. Appfrica could do that for them. They hired us, so they didn't have to worry about training, vetting, or managing local software developers.

Appfrica had a team of brilliant software engineers. Corporates could subcontract work to our company, or we would temp out our staff to work with them on their projects indefinitely. It was like a mini management consulting firm like Deloitte or McKinsey & Company. *"The Startup in the Land of Dial-Up"* was how one New York Times headline wrote about us. The phrase referred to the days of 56 kbit/s dial-up Internet in the U.S. The article was on how Appfrica challenged the western bias that Africans couldn't hold their own when it came to technical work.

One of our first partners was a company called Samasource. Samasource was founded by an Indian-American woman from San Francisco named Leila Chirayath Janah. Samasource's major innovation was leveraging a methodology called *micro-tasking* to provide work to people in developing countries. Micro-tasking allowed corporations to break large tasks (like editing a stack of documents) into much smaller tasks (like editing one sentence in a paragraph) to thousands of workers around the world. By aggregating the work of many contributors, each working on small parts of the larger task, edits to the whole stack finished in record time. Faster than any single worker could do alone. Leila championed the idea of giving work to people in developing countries instead of just philanthropy. Work, she argued, was more dignified and created jobs that boosted the economy. It also gave people skills. It expanded their options.

She already had a staff in Uganda and when she learned of Appfrica, she was excited to work with us. Companies in Silicon Valley hired Samasource because of the number of contractors it could supply them in its workforce. By partnering with companies like Appfrica, she could add our staff to her pool of talent as needed, expanding temporarily without having to hire new staff long term. Leila was one of the most fearless and incredible people I'd met in humanitarian circles. She too frequented cocktail parties and lavish events organized by philanthropists and wealthy investors like the one in Nakasero. She was quick to call out the hypocrisy and indifference on display. It endeared her to investors cynical about philanthropy which, in turn, helped her become successful at raising capital. She didn't need to code switch for the room. She made the rooms switch for her.

It was Leila who convinced me that we could get a young, newly minted Mark Zuckerberg to support a coding event in Uganda. A year prior, Microsoft had purchased 1.6% stake in Facebook for $240 million, giving the company a valuation of more than 15 billion dollars. Mark, as the holder of more than 50% of Facebook's shares, was now worth over $7 billion. He was around 24 years old. Facebook was talked about at the time, but it wasn't quite the behemoth it is now. It was still very much a startup, albeit a well-funded one.

I didn't expect this precocious billionaire to care at all about potential customers in Uganda. Surprisingly, through a series of emails, Leila managed to convince Mark's company to host an event for software developers in Kampala. This would mean flying Facebook staff to Uganda and paying for a venue that could hold hundreds of people. It was one of the first times one of the world's leading software companies held such an event in Africa. The event would not focus on executives or salespeople, but on developers and their ideas.

We were living in the land of dial-up in an era of wi-fi.

To its credit, Facebook didn't shy away from the challenges of getting things done in the African market. The company wanted to support their users wherever they were around the world. The event was a huge success. After it was over, Leila and I took turns responding to inquiries from the international press who wanted to cover our collaboration.

What was Facebook doing in Uganda?

The day-long event was part of a series called *Facebook Garages*. In the early days of Facebook, these Garages were semi-organized events where software developers could learn about Facebook software directly from the company's engineers. Facebook didn't want to be in the business of making a thousand products; they saw themselves as creating the platform from which other products could blossom. To do that successfully, they needed to encourage software developers around the world to come up with new ideas built on Facebook. It was also an excellent way for the company to discover new talent and potential hires.

Around the world, developers made games like Angry Birds and Words With Friends, games that leveraged Facebook so users could play with each other. Others made software that automated posting photos or videos to Facebook, so users didn't have to log in every day manually. The purpose of the events in Africa, Facebook told us, was to encourage software innovations that made sense for a market unfamiliar to them. Hundreds of aspiring Ugandan software developers turned out to share their ideas. The event consisted of workshops and brainstorming sessions that happened in parallel. Groups of developers huddled in smaller teams, working quickly to code prototypes of their various ideas. It was a rare opportunity to code with more experienced engineers eager to share their knowledge.

Leila was the mastermind behind the experience. She shared her philosophy of leveraging business for altruism and development. I didn't know it at the time, but many of the people who become

Appfrica's first employees were in the room that day. A handful were among the hundreds of other developers who showed up to get the opportunity to demonstrate their skills. Luckily, it wouldn't be the last time we'd cross paths. As Leila and I led the workshops, a young man approached me.

"This is a great event. I can't believe Facebook is here in Uganda," he said, smiling as he introduced himself. "My name is Moses."

"I can't believe it either. Thanks for all your help today," I told him. He had been impressive during the workshops, pushing his peers to work harder while sharing great ideas and knowledge.

"Thanks. This is big for Kampala. I know all about Facebook, but can you tell me—what does Appfrica do?"

* * *

I was fortunate to have hired Barbara Buringi. Barbara wasn't afraid to tell me what I needed to do. "You need to buy computers for our staff," she told me, referring to Appfrica's other new hires. "They can't afford them on their own, and if you give them the money to buy them, they will use it for other priorities."

"Makes sense," I responded.

"And we should cater lunch. If they leave for lunch, you won't see them again till the next day. Traffic is too bad to come back and forth midday."

"I didn't think about that."

"You should also get mobile hotspot subscriptions for each of them. The power goes out often. When it does, the internet router will go off, too. They will get bored sitting around and leave the office, and likely won't return until the next day. Which means we'll lose time doing work. If they have the hotspots, when the main internet goes down, they will stay connected and can still get a few hours of work done."

"I didn't think about that either."

"That's why you hired me," she smiled.

Barbara was one of the first people I'd hired for the company. I had conducted a string of interviews from my home in Kitintale after advertising that I was hiring on bulletin boards at the local mall, Makarere University, and online job boards. Young techies from all over Kampala came to interview. I met with them in the gardens of my home compound. As I looked over resumes and took notes, Sarah would come to offer drinks and tea. She knew the life I'd left behind in following her to Africa. She was excited to see that I was doubling down by establishing a business and embedding myself into the business environment.

Barbara was the second person I interviewed. She was the most professional and was experienced beyond her years. She was on time and well-dressed, annoyed to have to wait for a few minutes after arriving. Not because she was impatient, but because she thought *me* making *her* wait for her interview was unprofessional. It was the kind of no-holds-barred self-discipline the company would need. She wasn't going to let anyone slide and was willing to call out mistakes. A decade later, she's still in charge, with the same ambition.

"I like her. I definitely think you should hire her," Sarah told me, having overheard the interview. "She's not fooling around."

After interviewing more applicants, I found that there were diminishing returns. I was getting responses from people interested in the work but who weren't the right fit. Many of them didn't have the technical skills advertised. They were just looking for a job. *Any job.* In any market where unemployment is high, people get desperate. They apply for anything and everything on the off chance they find something. In Uganda, the employment rate was around 47% percent. I needed to try a different strategy. I suggested Barbara ask around at the University. There was a computer science program full of software developers looking for opportunities. They were inexperienced, but they had enough computer science skills that they could be trained. I thought back to the Facebook Garage and the emails I got from developers afterwards. I circled back to some who had reached out. The first on the list was Moses.

We started with a total of six, working from my offices in Mutungo. Even though I didn't know much about computer programming myself, my job was really to convince companies to give the team a chance at their projects. When it came time to do the work (building websites, mobile apps, and databases for our clients), it was up to the staff to deliver. For a while, this was a challenge. I wasn't skilled enough at computer science to do the projects myself. One of the earliest hires was the young programmer I met at the Facebook event, Moses Mugisha. If he couldn't join Facebook, he was determined to join the company that helped make the event happen.

Moses was barely in his twenties and, other than college, had little experience building software professionally. Yet he was a natural talent. Some people are at home in the language of computers and code without formal training. He was one of them. He taught me as much about working with software developers as Barbara did about managing them. He was also excited to take leadership on projects and teach others. Most rock-solid developers I'd met up to that point were distant loners content getting the job done on their own if necessary. He was different. Moses was selfless with knowledge, sociable, and eager to help others. The rest of the developers rallied around him.

Our team, made up of mostly Ugandan young software developers, would go on to support groups like Google, UNICEF, and the World Bank. The NGOs were always eager to help local businesses by nurturing local startups. For that reason, Appfrica was their natural ally. With UNICEF, our team followed their staff into villages to conduct surveys using mobile phones. Previously, the work of UNICEF staff in Uganda was limited to pencil and paper, which sometimes didn't survive the long trip through muddy roads and heavy rains. They were eager to go digital, so our staff helped them transition.

Google had different challenges. It wanted to extend its new mapping capabilities all over the world, including to Uganda. Our team joined their efforts to map the roads of Kampala. Other organizations hired us to digitize stacks of documents or to build websites and apps for mobile phones.

The prospect of time to work on individual projects and startups went over well with the staff. I found it was a big selling point in recruiting more experienced engineers who could get paid more elsewhere. There weren't other places in Uganda that were going to pay them to work on their ideas while offering them startup capital on top. Local businesses weren't interested in the ideas of individuals. That was something unique to my firm.

The ideas came immediately. One was a new spin on the call-center model, a joint project with a company with origins in India called Question Box. Question Box was a service sort of like 311, where human operators shared information with callers. In this case, our callers were far away, in villages that often took hours to reach. For the people living there, information about current events or prices at markets was hard to get.

The time and cost it took to travel to the city prevented them from getting essential information. Some items in the city markets cost more in rural parts. It cost vendors more to ship goods into remote regions with poor roads. Even after the goods arrived, the vendors knew they would sell less because incomes were lower in villages than they were in the cities. So even when goods were poorer quality, by the time they got to the village (often spoiled or soiled) they were more expensive. No matter how poor they were, the costs to get goods to the villages in the first place was passed on, trickling down.

It was expensive to be poor.

Our staff distributed the call center's phone numbers, posting them in markets and village centers, so people were aware the call line was operational. Anyone who dialed could ask the operator questions. The operators did their best to offer quality answers. If one farmer had a surplus of something like corn, and a different farmer called to find out where they could buy corn, the call center could connect the two. Our ability to match-make circumvented the expensive supply-chain villagers were used to relying on. With a service like QuestionBox, they could now buy from each other. It brought costs down for them, saving time and money.

In other cases, people called to stoke their curiosity. They just wanted to ask the questions they might ask in school, which many of them never had the opportunity to attend. Questions like: *Why is the sky blue? What time is it in London? How old is Michael Jackson?* The operators answered questions like this, day and night.

We were trying to drive down their cost of obtaining knowledge and information.

Another company we incubated, OhmSMS, notified locals when their power went out. In Kampala, blackouts and brownouts were frequent, and traffic was high. Imagine spending two hours in traffic trying to get home, only to arrive to a completely unlit house. The app they developed had users plug a modified mobile phone into an outlet at their home or office. As soon as it detected it was no longer charging, it texted the owner to let them know the power had gone out. It was a mild inconvenience, and a simple solution, but one that was quite useful in Uganda. Ugandan households lost a lot of food when blackouts left their fridges uncooled. Business owners needed to know when their computers, servers, and fax machines were off. What might be mild inconveniences in the U.S. could be major setbacks for consumers here.

A year after Appfrica launched, a venture capitalist flew to Uganda from his home in Ireland to meet with me. By then, the company had matured, and I was incubating several fledgling companies. The Irishman took particular interest in a company called Status.ug.

Status.ug was a social network built around the limited mobile phones prevalent in Africa. Unlike the smartphones commonplace around the world, which had apps that required the Internet and lots of data, we only had these basic phones. These mobile phones only offered the ability to talk and text. They were called *feature phones*. Because they were so boxy and heavy, they also earned the nickname *brick phones*. They had none of the scratch-resistant glass screens or colorful apps users had on the iPhones back home. They were more akin to the clunky cellular phones I remembered growing up in the late 90s.

To sign up to Status.ug, all one needed was a phone number. Eighty percent of the African continent had access to some form of mobile telephony. Rather than requiring a username, Felix built the system to simplify access to phone number and a personal identification number (PIN). This feature made it easier for Africans, who were more likely to log in from a mobile phone than they were from a computer. It was a text-only layer on top of social networks like Facebook, which made the platform accessible to people who otherwise wouldn't be able to use it. These were low-bandwidth areas; bandwidth-heavy products like Facebook struggled to be viable the same way it was elsewhere in the world. Facebook was exploding in popularity at the time, so a text-based solution to use the social network in low-bandwidth areas had the potential to be quite popular.

The startup's marketing collateral explained in detail:

> *To sign up for Status.ug all your group has to do is send an SMS to +256783XXXX27 with the keyword "signup" followed by the desired password. Once that happens, you'll have a platform that will work with Facebook, Twitter and our local portal, regardless of whether or not everyone has accounts on all of those services.*

> *To make friends on the service, just type "friend [phone number]" where [phone number] is the person that you want to be friends with. But that person needs to be a member of Status.ug as well.*

> *Whenever you send a message to the service preceded by the word 'status' you'll update the whole world!*

As a blogger, I acted as a sort of a business correspondent, covering the ups and downs of running a software company from Africa. In addition to information on my own company, I included news about companies across Africa as well. The company blog, which I updated daily, became a de facto source for journalists looking for stories.

Angela Benton, the editor of a popular blog called Black Web 2.0, covered Appfrica's entrepreneurs often. With her blog, Angela wrote mostly about the U.S. tech industry as it related to African Americans. In her search for new and different content, she came across our blog at Appfrica, which her editorial team took great interest in covering. Later, publications like the New York Times, the Economist, and CNN would write about our entrepreneurs after reading her coverage. This included Status.ug.

Ten thousand miles away, while Felix was working on Status.ug, a direct competitor was born that would scale quickly and become a behemoth. In 2007 WhatsApp founder Jan Koum left his job at Yahoo to spend over a year sabbatical traveling around South America. In January 2009, Koum, inspired by the release of the app store on the iPhone, came up with an idea to place visual alerts next to phone numbers on smartphones. The alerts were signals to users, to let them know if their friends were available or busy without having to call them to ask. The problem was that users had to remember to check them. WhatsApp had built something that worked technically, but it failed to change user behavior.

It wouldn't be until June of that year that the young company would find its path. Apple, the company that had inspired Koum to start his company in the first place, launched *push notifications* on June 17th, 2009. Push notifications were updates that automatically posted to the home screen of a smartphone to remind users of new messages waiting from a friend. Message alerts in the apps were silent and easy to forget. Plus, they were only visible when the user had the app open. Push notifications were the opposite. They interrupted the user's activity by making a sound or vibration to let the user know there was something new that needed their attention. Users no longer had to remember to check for status updates. Instead, notifications reminded them. Suddenly, the company found its way to change user behavior. The app exploded in popularity, growing to more than one billion users. The company later sold for 19 billion dollars.

The Status.ug app was similar to WhatsApp. The two companies were founded around the same time, within a few months of each other. The Status.ug tagline was even similar: *Tell the World What's Up!* Similarities between competing tech businesses wasn't at all uncommon in the startup world. That era of tech startups was full of innovative services that were copycats. Also-ran companies, most of which didn't survive:

SCVGR and Foursquare.

Twitter and Pownce.

Facebook and MySpace.

Sometimes only one company succeeded, sometimes both failed.

Entrepreneurs in tech learned not to worry about plagiarism or idea theft. Why? When everyone is dealing with similar problems, it is entirely plausible that different people will come up with similar solutions. Starting from second place could be an advantage for businesses, too. By following the innovators, they could learn from mistakes and adapt. Facebook learned from MySpace's missteps and became a much bigger business as a result. Google learned from Yahoo's mistakes. First movers didn't always have the advantage. Copying a good idea didn't mean the person copying had the right skills to turn that vision into reality. Execution was everything.

The inability to execute a good idea meant an entrepreneur had little to nothing. Ideas were everywhere; everyone had them. A great idea had no value on its own. Finding people who could execute ideas, and turn them into viable businesses, was the harder part of the equation. Talent was hard to find, hard to keep focused, and expensive. Startups had to put together the right teams, raise money, and go from idea to building products people could use.

What kills most startups isn't being too early to market, or too late, or failing to find investors or customers. The thing that proves fatal to most of them is the inexperience of the founder or lack of focus of the team. In the tech world, execution is all that matters. No one can use what doesn't exist. No investor is going to back a product if they don't have confidence in it. Sometimes that means you have to paint the picture for them.

When Appfrica found its first investor, I had more than just a vision to offer him. I had a handful of customers, staff, and momentum – what tech entrepreneurs call traction. This meant progress that showed a potential investor the business was headed somewhere with or without them. The investor could envision what was possible from what I'd accomplished already. He could envision what I was attempting to build, the change I wanted to see in the world, without necessarily having to be as convicted as me. As the entrepreneur, I helped *finish the picture* for him by getting as far as I could on my own and then seeking investment when I couldn't go any further. That came from doing everything I could to make the company work. I had to be sure I could always show traction. I had to push myself. In the case of Status.ug, it felt like Felix wasn't pushing. Instead, I was dragging him down a path he didn't necessarily want for himself.

Status.ug was crushed in its infancy. The founder, Felix, and the investor butted heads. Felix wasn't used to the pressures of answering to outside investors, a skill in itself. The pressure of delivering software on time and at a certain standard is tough on any entrepreneur, but it was a new expectation here. It required a focus on work that was obsessive and probably unhealthy. Tech never turns off, nor do customer demands. To succeed, there's a lot of pressure to keep everything going, particularly in an industry dominated by Silicon Valley. Many Americans sacrificed everything for work: free time, family, and sometimes health. At the time, some techies used drugs called *nootropics* just to keep up with the quickening pace.

Here, work was just work. It didn't define people. Friends and family were the priority. I didn't realize it then, but part of the problem was trying to force-fit my culture onto the team. I had become familiar with the demands of the tech industry and grew up in American business culture. I was trying to force my staff to code switch with me.

The investor wanted to see a faster rollout plan. He had agreed to fund the development of the app but only if we maintained a tight release schedule. In the end, it would be this tension between cultures that killed Status.ug. I was burning this twenty-something software developer out. I had a vision that he didn't. Status.ug would never mature beyond its early launch and its first few hundred users.

It was a valuable lesson I learned as an investor. The fledgling social network ended when the founder walked away. It didn't matter if I was a believer in an idea if the founder wasn't. An investor shouldn't want success more than the entrepreneur does for themselves.

* * *

In the tech world, there are what are called *moonshots*. Moonshots are business ventures whose success seems impossible, but are just possible enough to be worthwhile. Most people will find it hard to tell the difference between a moonshot and a business idea that's implausible. They can't see the world for anything other than what it is already. To them, trying to predict what *will* happen is in the realm of fantasy. Inventors, creators, and entrepreneurs are the opposite. They have already seen the future.

They have the vision for it. They have a different reality in their heads that they work to make real.

In popular culture, hackers know everything about software and the command line, working their way around digital dead ends to break their way into computer systems. In real life, hackers are insatiable problem solvers. Building software in Africa taught me how to be more than a hacker. I had to learn how to do it all, including solve the problem under the problem. Sometimes the problem was the computer itself, so I had to learn how to fix those too. The staff and I built computers and servers from scrap parts just so we could write software that ran on them. We didn't do it because we were geniuses, we did it because we had to. Our only resources were a hodgepodge of wires and scrap computer parts left behind by ex-pats who came and went before us. I couldn't just order a new part if a motherboard was fried because of a power surge. I had to figure how to fix it. My moonshot was a future where Appfrica manufactured electronics and computers locally. We were already doing a lot of hacking and tinkering with hardware to get software working. It was like wanting to be a race car driver in a place where there were no cars. You had to build the device so you could then become an expert in using it.

When I did try to buy versus build, it came at a premium. I knew how much more I was paying for computing equipment in Uganda because it was all imported. Similar to the problem of getting goods to villages, getting electronics to Uganda was expensive. Those costs trickled down. A $500 laptop in the U.S. could cost upwards of $2,000 in Uganda because of shipping costs, logistics, and heavy tariffs that came from customs. Often it was cheaper to just buy laptops when I was in America and then bring them back with me on the plane. The only other way to drive my operating costs down would be to make our own computing equipment locally. So that's what we did.

A new group of corporates who came to visit us had the type of money that could make this kind of moonshot possible. If we aimed for the stars, maybe we'd land on the moon.

"Our next phase will be to build computers. Hardware. Made right here from Uganda," I told the room.

I was sitting across from a delegation of Google executives. I was nervous. They were paying close attention. There were six of them. Their team was the size of our whole company. It always surprised people that I wasn't Ugandan and didn't have any Ugandan ancestry. These executives from Google were no different. They were as curious about my background and how I ended up in Kampala as they were about the company. They were there to vet us to make sure we knew what we were doing. They needed to see that we were large enough to handle the projects they might want to collaborate on. When companies look to make new investments, they conduct what's known as *due diligence* where they research a company, its staff, and its capabilities. This trip to Uganda and to neighboring Kenya was part of their diligence on software development firms active in the region.

"That's the goal anyway," I continued. "Every company starts somewhere. Right now, we're sort of like a house of ideas. When the staff isn't doing client work, we build software and mobile applications for African consumers or the businesses targeting African consumers. Apps like social networks, news apps, e-commerce websites, stuff like that."

"Well, you've made a lot of noise," one executive said. "We're impressed that we even heard about your company in Mountain View."

I'm sure he had a hard time deciding what to make of my ambition. Was I delusional about manufacturing hardware in Africa?

Was I just an unfocused kid with a loaded weapon? Either way, coming from Silicon Valley, he had probably seen it all. I'd developed relationships with Googlers, including their product manager for Sub-Saharan Africa. He had become an active reader of the blog, commenting often. I was pretty sure he had something to do with the team's visit.

Shortly after the trip, Google hired us again. Appfrica worked with them to translate their search engine into the locally spoken language *Luganda*. This process was known as *localization*, taking software and translating it to make it relevant in different regions of the world. We were the partner of choice for Google in Uganda. Google was investing a lot of its resources in figuring out Africa, and we were on a shortlist of companies they knew to contact.

What could make these six executives come from Mountain View to Kampala to meet with our team? Reportedly, a year prior Google had acquired an equity stake in a Kenyan company called Mobile Planet.

"Are they here to buy us?" Moses asked. "I'm not sure I'd even want to work for Google," he continued.

"Really?" I was at a loss. For me, the opportunity to work for Google was definitely a goal. The ultimate techie badge of honor. Google, too, was just emerging from its own startup status and into its role as a mature company, one of the world's most dominant. It still had its wow factor as a company that had actually achieved its moonshot vision to *organize the world's information.*

Moses continued: "We're doing something different here. *You believe in us.* You believe in our ideas. You invest in *us.* At a company like Google, no one will respect us. We'll get ignored. Our ideas won't mean anything. For us, Appfrica is more important than Google!"

It dawned on me that what he was saying wasn't even really about Appfrica. It was that I believed in them. I had a vision that was inspiring other investors to believe in them, too. There would be no more thoughts of acquisition, with Google or anyone else. Moses had both humbled and encouraged me. I was mistaken. My moonshot wasn't making computers. My moonshoot was taking what we started here in Kampala and expand it across Africa. So that's exactly what I set out to do.

#Abuzz

> *"If you want to go fast, go alone.*
> *If you want to go far, go together."*
> **—African Proverb**

On July 25th, 2015, Air Force One descended towards Nairobi, Kenya, where U.S. President Barrack Obama would keynote a conference, the Global Entrepreneurship Summit. For many, this was the apex. It was the culmination of years of building a culture of entrepreneurship and tech in Africa. Entrepreneurs from more than 120 countries attended, from all over Africa and the world.

Obama himself—the first sitting U.S. President to visit Kenya—was coming to acknowledge their work.

He began his remarks between outbreaks of applause and chatter. "All of you embody a spirit that we need to take on some of the biggest challenges that we face in the world, the spirit of entrepreneurship, the idea that there are no limits to the human imagination, that ingenuity can overcome what is and create what needs to be."

"Entrepreneurship creates new jobs and new businesses, new ways to deliver basic services, new ways of seeing the world — it's the spark of prosperity. It helps citizens stand up for their rights and push back against corruption. Entrepreneurship offers a positive alternative to the ideologies of violence and division that can all too often fill the void when young people don't see a future for themselves."

President Obama, former community organizer and U.S. Senator, born in Hawaii to a black Kenyan father and white-American mother, was more than just comfortable. In this room of African overachievers, rebels, code switchers, and rule breakers, he had set the mold.

* * *

When I started Appfrica in late 2008, the idea of a software company opening its doors to the public—a place where any tech entrepreneur in the city could come work—was still new. Kampala had several software companies, mostly making software for mobile phones far more pervasive in Africa than in the United States. Many of these companies operated with rigid styles of management that left no room for curiosity or experimentation. They didn't have open office work plans or flat hierarchies where everyone in the company had as much say as the CEO. They had a company owner, and below him or her, management. Below management was the staff. The farther away from the top, the less power an employee held. A random entrepreneur off the street couldn't just walk in with ideas. When entrepreneurs realized they could do just that at Appfrica's community workspace, it caused a stir.

Our doors were open. All were invited. At first, people would drop in because they were curious about the work we did. Our new office was about half a mile away in a shopping center in a much larger space. We had outgrown the guest house at my compound in Mutungo. My girlfriend Sarah could no longer visit during the day to bring over cookies and tea for the staff. The office was now too far away from home for her friendly drop-ins, so I hired a caterer who could handle our growing numbers. We were now around fifteen or twenty, not including the random entrepreneurs from around the city who came to work alongside us.

Our second office was on the second floor of a strip mall, with big open windows. It had previously belonged to a restaurant and was built to be as inviting as possible to pedestrians. People driving past could see in as we worked. We had an open office floor plan – everyone in the office could see each other. Software engineers sat on one side of the room, while our administrative and sales team sat on the other side. We had widescreen monitors where we played video games in our downtime or demonstrated our work for clients when they came for meetings.

The office was as out-of-place in Kampala as a whale would be in Lake Victoria.

Local people and foreign visitors would drop in and ask, "What kind of place is this?"

"Tech company? Here? Wow!"

"How can I work with you guys?"

"Here is my resume."

The local entrepreneurial community was buzzing with talk about this new workspace with great lighting and fast internet. It was towards the end of our second year in business that it dawned on me: although our office was useful, it wasn't necessary for our operations. Most days, I worked from my home in the hills of Mutungo. As the company got busier, I spent most of my time in meetings around the city or in other countries. Even my colleague, Barbara, who had solidified her spot as a crucial staff member, was busy with meetings around town. Keeping our office operational for the staff was becoming a nuisance. The developers had mobile hotspots that allowed them to connect to the internet from anywhere – hotels, pools, gardens, airports, or even at home.

One day, I walked into our office and found it empty save for the caterer preparing the daily buffet-style lunch. Everyone else was gone.

"Where is everyone?"

"They have gone," the caterer said, carefully placing cutlery next to plates.

"Everyone?"

I guess I couldn't complain; we were still in business and growing. Yet growth and success seemed to be happening independently of the office. Perhaps it was time for a change?

The next day, I asked a good friend named Teddy Ruge, "What do you think about this office? We don't really need it anymore, but it also seems to be popular with the community."

"Maybe it should *only* serve the community?" he said. Teddy was also a provocateur blogger who, somewhat like me, had become notorious for his scathing takedowns of the tech community, the developmental aid community, and the Ugandan government. He was a Ugandan-American who had repatriated to Uganda and cheekily referred to himself as 'an angry African'. He was also a designer and artist who helped train our staff. On top of all that, he was a former Olympic athlete who broke national records for Uganda's pole vault, high jump, and decathlon. Later in life, he transitioned to innovating with agriculture. He founded Raintree Farms, which specialized in moringa plant cultivation.

"Everyone knows where it is and a lot of people want to be here," he continued. "We should turn it into a place for everyone."

The only example we had of something like this in 2009 was Regus, a company in the U.S. that offered conference space and offices on demand. The concept of *co-working spaces* hadn't yet been proven. Senegal was probably home to the first co-working space in Africa, a place called Active Spaces. We were second. In neighboring Kenya, a company called the iHub had been announced but had not yet launched.

Over the next few days, Teddy and I laid out plans for what would become known as Hive Colab. Two other local friends helped us shape the vision for Hive: Daniel Stern (an American expat heavily involved in Uganda's business and political community) and Solomon King (another blogger who also operated a local software company). Later, a Senegalese entrepreneur named Mariéme Jamme also joined. Together we shaped what became Hive, Uganda's first innovation hub and over a decade later, its longest running.

It was Teddy who came up with the name. "This space is always active. Frenetic, busy, abuzz with entrepreneurs and ideas. Like a beehive!" By the end of the day, he had crafted the logo too, inspired by the hexagonal shapes in a bee's honeycomb.

Where do you go when you can't afford internet, reliable electricity, or an office of your own as you're struggling to build a business? This was the question I set out to answer when we finally rebranded Appfrica as Hive Colab in 2010. The name change was significant. Appfrica was a software consulting business and incubator that later evolved into a fund. I wanted to demonstrate that, as Hive, this physical space was no longer mine nor the company's. It was our gift to the tech community of Uganda. Also, we were sure to fit the name CoLab (for *collaborative lab*) in the title to signal that this was a space where anyone could come work on whatever project they wanted. I also wanted the new board members Daniel, Teddy, Solomon, and Mariéme to feel ownership over the space. They each contributed immeasurably to Hive's growth over the years.

Soon, co-working spaces, where users pay rent for a desk or smaller office inside a much larger professional building, became increasingly popular. In fact, 2010 was the same year WeWork was founded in SoHo, New York. Throughout the world, co-working spaces became the turn-key solution for startups, independent lawyers, and entrepreneurs of all types. None of them went on to be quite as prolific (or notorious) as WeWork, but each of these spaces has proved worthy of lasting as long and continue to thrive.

In Africa, co-working spaces like Hive were called *innovation labs* or *tech hubs*. They were more critical to the fabric of society than just serving as cheap places to work. They represented an entry-point to the business ecosystem of the countries they were in. They were hubs of activity for technologists, social entrepreneurs, governments, tech companies, impact investors and hackers. Some foreign businesses would even take up permanent residence in them. Doing so gave them access to a constant supply of young technical talent in countries where it was otherwise hard to find. Also, the hubs offered infrastructure – working water, office desks, copy machines, printers, laptops, mobile phone equipment, servers, etc. They were ready-to-go places to work. Instead of having to fly these things to Africa, or buy them once there, an organization working in Africa for any extended length of time could work from the hubs. The hubs also served as easily identifiable meeting spots and event spaces. They popped up in cities across the continent like Kamapla, Lagos, Addis Ababa, Nairobi, Accra, Dar es Salaam, Johannesburg, Blantyre, and more.

The other benefit of hubs was they served as points of trust.

Previously, when foreign corporates and non-profits came to Africa, their employees didn't know which companies or individuals to trust. Who should they hire? Who should they buy from? Who wasn't going to try to manipulate or scam them? Mistrust of locals was pervasive, mostly out of an abundance of caution. Public institutions and humanitarian organizations had strict guidelines on how they were allowed to spend money. They couldn't put their organizations at risk of supporting individuals who had bad reputations. Also, the Foreign Corrupt Practices Act meant that US firms had accounting processes to ensure every dollar was spent wisely. It was all too common that aid money ended up lining the pockets of local bureaucrats and politicians. Unfortunately, the mistrust for individuals at the top cascaded down to the people at the bottom. As a result, a culture of mistrust for African businesses became the norm.

Innovation hubs helped curb that. What they presented was a network of trust. The hubs were founded by known entrepreneurs, investors, and prominent leaders from Africa. These weren't random people; they were well-known and often highly regarded. They expected management to vet the people who worked there. As hub founders, our reputations were on the line for the experience we provided locals and ex-pats alike. Also, each of these hubs had donors who often supported them with grants or investment dollars. Getting through the vetting process that allowed tech hubs to receive philanthropic capital was no small task at all. Successfully securing funding was a signal that they were indeed trustworthy. It was a good sign for other potential partners and investors. Even if a visitor didn't trust the local tech centers, they could trust the financial institutions that supported them, groups like Hivos, Omidyar, Grameen, UNICEF, The World Bank, Microsoft, Sainsbury, Indigo Trust, and other corporate and family offices who partially funded the establishment of innovation hubs across Africa. Whatever their benefits, innovation hubs, collaboration labs, and community workspaces were here to stay. In 2009, when Appfrica was founded, there was only one such space like it on the entire continent. As of 2022, there are more than 600 in ninety cities and thirty countries.

The continent was indeed abuzz with entrepreneurs and ideas.

#Butterflies

"Ue o muite arukō namida ga koborenai youni."
—Kyu Sakamoto (Japanese musician)

In the middle of our flight from Lusaka, Zambia to Lilongwe, Malawi, one of the propellers stopped.

"Planes can fly just fine with one engine," I remembered my dad telling me once. He had been in the Air Force, and when I saw him while growing up, about once a year, he would take me to the base for air shows. Right as I was soothing myself with that thought, the propeller on the *other* wing stopped! Could a plane fly without both engines?

Panic.

We began to glide, slowly descending in the air. The twin silence of the engines haunted the cabin. Sarah wasn't bothered at all; she continued her nap. She was a humanitarian; trips on shoddy planes to cities with unpronounceable names were a part of her job. Moments later, the engines began to sputter and buzz back to life. The aircraft lifted, rocking its way through the sky.

"We apologize, the engine stalled!" the pilot shouted back. The only thing separating him from the passengers was a blue terry-cloth curtain. I considered pushing it aside to hit him in the back of the head. First, I'd have to let the blood rush back into my face.

Planes in Africa were often second or third generation, recommissioned from other countries after they were retired from their fleets. This knowledge did nothing to assuage my fears of flying. Over the years, I'd been on numerous planes where near emergencies were averted. On one flight, the landing gear was stuck, leaving the plane to circle in the air for what seemed like forever until the problem was fixed and we were cleared. It seemed like something odd was going on, but the pilot didn't share what had occurred until we were safely on the ground.

"We managed to get it un-stalled," was the highly detailed explanation he offered.

On another flight, from Atlanta to Sudan, the plane was struck by lightning. I could smell ionized air as all the lights in the plane lights flickered and went out. The engines went silent, and it felt like I could distinctly hear every sound made by every shoe, seat, screw, or insect onboard. The hair on my arms and the back of my neck stood up, and my stomach sank. *This was it* – my worst fear would become my demise.

There was an elderly Kenyan woman seated next to me. She had been terrified throughout the entire flight. With each bump from turbulence and each turn of the plane, she would grip the armrest. When the lights on the plane went out, we reached for the armrest at the same time. I turned to look at her; she was shaking.

I forced a smile and told her, "It's going to be okay."

We squeezed each other's hands until I felt her relax. Suddenly I didn't feel so afraid myself. I made peace with whatever was going to happen. Time seemed to evaporate as the plane careened along in the darkness, carried by momentum through the air. Then, abruptly, everything roared back to life. I heard the engine kick back on, the interior lights sprang back to life. Everyone sighed in unison. Some people cried. It has only been maybe three seconds, but those seconds felt impossibly long. The pilot came on the intercom.

"Ladies and gentlemen, sorry to scare you there. We were struck by lightning – that's not as bad as it sounds. These days planes are made with insulation and backup batteries for just these scenarios." I later learned that when a plane is struck by lightning, the electricity doesn't dissipate on its own. The aircraft has to *dump* the excess energy by shutting everything down and restarting mid-flight. Hence the brief blackout. What we had experienced in those terrible seconds of darkness where we literally flew through the sky like a paper plane was the pilots rebooting the electrical system.

On a flight from Entebbe, Uganda to Nairobi, Kenya, shortly before landing, the aircraft violently jerked to the left and the pilot rapidly ascended back into the air, pressing the passengers back into their seats and making my stomach turn. Nothing was said about what had occurred. Was he avoiding another aircraft? Was he fighting with some broken system? Something had to have been wrong. It was the only flight I've been on where I felt g-forces that strong. I never found out what the issue was. Instead, we landed and everyone went their separate ways, eager to be back on the ground.

In a different incident in Nairobi, I watched as one hundred people hurried from their gate, some in shock, others bawling. Pale-faced and visibly shook, damp with sweat from anxiety and terror, they rushed into the terminal from the tarmac. I recognized one of my friends in the crowd. A Dutch guy I knew from Kampala. I stopped to ask what was going on.

"Just after we took off, the plane's engine went out. We had to turn back. Just as the pilot was about to land, he aborted sharply and pulled back up into the air, shaking everything. Bags were falling out of the bins. People were vomiting. It was terrible. We had to circle a few more times until he was able to land. I've never been more convinced it was the end." His voice quivered as he choked back tears.

When I'm nervous on flights, I hum a song by the American R&B duo A Taste of Honey called *Sukiyaki*. The American version of the song was a reworking of a song released a quarter century earlier by Japanese star Kyu Sakamoto. The original, *Ue o Muite Arukō*, was written by Rokosuke Ei and composed by Hachidai Nakamura for Kyu. Ei had written the song about a lost love – not a woman but his home country Japan. He felt the country had lost its identity due to the overwhelming presence of Americans and the U.S. Military following World War II. It was a protest song, brilliantly masked as a love song. It was a hit in the Sixties, topping the Billboard charts with its haunting whistling chorus – one of the biggest international singles of all time.

In 1963, A Taste of Honey's lead singer Janice-Marie Johnson heard the song on the radio as a young girl. After her rise to fame from her own hit, *Boogie Oogie*, it was her idea to re-record Kyu's song as an R&B ballad. Rather than a direct translation of the lyrics, she wrote new lyrics. This led to many incorrectly believing the song had been translated to English. The reworked A Taste of Honey version, *Sukiyaki*, would also become a hit, charting at #3 on the Billboard Hot 100.

It's all because of you, I'm feeling sad and blue

You went away, now my life is just a rainy day

and I love you so,

how much you'll never know

'cause you took your love away from me,

Oh!

Most aviation disasters aren't caused by a single mistake, mechanical failure, or bad decision. When you study the history of air disasters, which I researched to help get over my own fears, you learn that most accidents result from a series of escalating mistakes. It is incredibly rare that one thing goes wrong to bring down a plane. Flying is statistically the safest way to travel. So much redundancy is built in to increase the options pilots have when the unexpected does happen. This amplification of small actions that compound to cause a much greater impact is known as the *butterfly effect*. Minor errors build on each other, snowballing, becoming bigger and bigger until they manifest as catastrophic errors down the line. In computer science, this is known as a *cascading failure*. Something as simple as a mechanic not noticing ice on the flap of a wing, or airline accountants attempting to save money by recommending fewer cross-checks, or a software system unexpectedly reversing commands sent by the pilot to the aircraft, can lead to a horrific air disaster.

On Spanair Flight 5022, investigators suggested a faulty air conditioning sensor delaying the takeoff of the flight was deliberately turned off by a single person, an air mechanic. When the pilot reported the issue before takeoff, he couldn't find an actual temperature malfunction, just a reporting malfunction, so he disabled the sensor. Investigators also noted that prior to takeoff one of the pilots failed to conduct a critical safety procedure. They didn't ensure the plane's flaps and slats were extended during takeoff, as was required under regulations. The flaps automatically retract when an aircraft goes to the gate for maintenance. It was resolving the first problem (the air conditioning unit malfunction) that allowed for the second problem (the failure to check the flaps) to occur. It also caused a third issue.

Planes are equipped with warning systems that, in any other scenario, would have alerted the pilots. It would have let them know the flaps were not extended. But this takeoff warning system was controlled by the same unit that powered the original air conditioning probe. When the mechanic switched that sensor off, he wasn't aware of the plurality of effect his actions were causing. 172 people were on board Spanair 5022. 154 died in the crash.

One small, seemingly insignificant action had profound consequences.

I hum the song to myself because of the way Kyu, the original performer, died. On August 12th, 1985, he was one of 509 passengers who boarded Japan Airlines Flight 123. The flight was doomed to become the deadliest single-aircraft accident of all time when it crashed into the side of a mountain. Investigators later discovered the plane had been improperly repaired years before the crash, an oversight that went unnoticed. For seven years, hundreds of thousands, perhaps millions of people had boarded that same plane, flown the same route, and they were just fine.

Small errors just built on each other, snowballing, becoming bigger and bigger. Eventually, the cascading failure materialized.

When the crash finally occurred, radio stations around the globe put both versions of the song, the original Japanese and the American R&B version, in rotation to honor his life. I don't hum the song because of Kyu's tragic fate, but in spite of it.

Many things had to go wrong for Flight 123 to experience its untimely end. But I think of how many people were working together, over seven years, to keep everyone else who boarded safe. I also marvel at how many things had to happen in perfect succession for the song Sukiyaki to even exist: World War II, Pearl Harbor, American occupation, the heartbroken Ei, a record from Japan topping the charts in 1963 America, Janice-Marie hearing the song as a young girl, her band having their own successful pop career and fighting a record label in order to release the song as an R&B single.

The song reminds me of how *unlikely* a cascading failure is aboard a plane. It calms me. It signals the statistical improbability that so many things will go wrong in the perfect order needed to cause tragedy. It represents the many times many little things do go wrong, only for it all to still turn out fine. I couldn't know how important these lessons would eventually become.

#Blankspace

"So, come on along..."
—Ebo Taylor and the Pelikans, Come Along

Between 2010 and 2013, you wouldn't have been able to tell I wasn't fond of flying at all. Appfrica was undertaking our most ambitious project to date. I wanted to scale our culture of openness and investment to entrepreneurs across Africa. The entrepreneurs of Uganda were brilliant. Many great ideas emerged from the company's twenty-percent innovation time initiative. I knew there was genius to be discovered everywhere in Africa.

We would go to as many countries as we could to find them. This was our moonshot.

"It's our job to help find and fund Africa's unknown talent – the future Mark Zuckerberg or Bill Gates," I told my team.

The problem in 2010 wasn't that it was particularly tough to find entrepreneurs and technologists across the continent. The problem was there wasn't much support for them wherever they were. In Europe and the U.S., technologists thrived because there were angel investors, venture capital firms, and private equity firms that all sought to capitalize on the brilliance of young entrepreneurs by investing in them. In turn, these investors got equity in the businesses started. There weren't enough investors interested in Africa. When those businesses went public or were acquired, the investors made their money back, usually with an incredible return. All of this required sufficiently healthy economies so the companies could go public, or it required larger enterprise companies looking to acquire these emerging startups. Throughout most of Africa, this economic picture was incomplete. Either there was poor economics, too few large corporations on the hunt for acquisitions, or basic infrastructure challenges. Even the smartest person in the world isn't going to accomplish much on their own. They need an ecosystem, networks of support.

I had allocated money from our balance sheet at Appfrica to establish an investment fund and established a partnership with the various stakeholders, including the U.S. Department of State. It was what the staff at the State Department referred to as a *public/ private* sector partnership. As a for-profit entity, Appfrica could do things they couldn't, like invest, while as a public entity, they had access to resources that we didn't.

What emerged from our collaboration was a campaign to visit as much of Africa as possible to hold events, workshops, and conferences where we'd invite local entrepreneurs to meet with us to share their work and ideas. They could also compete for investment, upwards of $30,000 as seed funding for their various start-up companies. Our process for picking the best of the applicants was like a mix between Shark Tank and American Idol, with the rigid investor panels of the former and the open invitation aspect of the latter. This was to ensure the money we were investing was being spread objectively and didn't just go to people from the biggest and wealthiest countries. Our secondary goal was to spread the economic impact as far across Africa as possible. This also met the State Department's goals.

"Diplomacy through capitalism," I joked.

The State Department underwrote many of these events, so each served a dual purpose: to find emerging innovators, and to connect them with the civil servants who might consider hiring them as consultants or vendors. We also established relationships with press and media in each country to highlight their individual stories. I didn't have enough money to invest in everyone we met but the ones who walked away empty-handed might benefit from any media attention we could direct their way.

"We're going to canvas the continent," I said at a kickoff event we held in Kampala. "I want every entrepreneur in Africa to feel like they've got their *twenty-percent time*. Wherever they may be."

* * *

In Harare, Zimbabwe, we arrived at its jagged city skyline and blossoming jacarandas to rooms full of developers eager to have a voice. For many, it was the first time they were interacting with investors directly. Zimbabwe was still reeling from two crises: a compulsory land redistributing program that took farms from foreigners (mostly whites) and the subsequent financial crisis that resulted in catastrophic hyperinflation.

In Lagos, Nigeria, we were welcomed by CcHub founder Bosun Tijani. Now one of Africa's largest innovation hubs, in those days, CcHub was still fledgling. In 2019, he acquired the iHub network in Kenya, uniting the tech communities of West and East Africa.

In Gaborone, Botswana, where the ends of the Kalahari Desert gave way to lush greenery at the edge of the Okavango River, we stopped at the Sun Hotel, where we met more eager hackers, tinkerers, and techies. Botswana had a growing economy, one of the most competitive banking systems in all of Africa, and was beginning to release barriers to foreign investors. This meant the market was becoming viable for entrepreneurship in a way that would not have been the case years prior. It was a country realizing the value of its own human talent. We were there as allies to help them invest in that talent.

Kigali, Rwanda was home to one of the most aggressive, country-wide expansions of information technology infrastructure in Africa. There, the challenge was less that the government didn't know it needed to support the business community. Rather, they were executing on a decades-long plan. They wanted to lift as many people out of poverty as possible through government-funded projects in infrastructure. It was a top-down model that previously worked for China and Singapore.

In Nairobi, Kenya, our staff danced in nightclubs and ate game meat at Carnivore, a staple restaurant for Nairobi tourists. The next day we hosted working sessions and events at the iHub, one of Africa's more prominent innovation hubs and the largest in Kenya. Kenya was home to one of the most vibrant tech ecosystems in all of Africa. It had a thriving economy thanks to its strong financial institutions, telecom industry, a port in Mombasa, and the country's position as the nexus to all of East Africa. There were even more entrepreneurs and software developers here than in Uganda. Here they had so much access to other opportunities that it was hard to fill the room. The entrepreneurs of Nairobi were used to people competing for their time and talent. They had options.

At the embassy in Antananarivo, Madagascar, we were welcomed by diplomats who shared the country's unique challenges. There was a large skills gap and limited resources for public education.

In Bamako, Mali, we held lively sessions at the Radisson Blu. Mali was among the poorest countries in the world. Most of the country's economy was dependent upon gold extraction and agriculture. Still, the spirit of tech entrepreneurship was alive and well here, too. Around fifty hopeful software developers, women and men, showed up to meet us.

In Mozambique, the team drove along Avenida de Marginal, following the coastline to Universidade São Tomás de Moçambique in cosmopolitan Maputo. We learned one of the barriers to the economy in Mozambique is that land was not for sale; it could only be leased. This discouraged foreign investors from developing properties or investing too heavily. With no development, there was no job creation and few consumers – therefore, no viable market for software developers.

In Accra, Ghana, we held an event keynoted by the Mayor of Accra himself, Alfred Vanderpuiye, at the Kofi Annan Centre of Excellence in ICT. Ghana's economy was thriving and growing. The infrastructure and education system were better than Uganda's. For the Ghanaian events, hundreds showed up. Years later, one of the companies we were able to support there, Farmerline, remains one of the fastest-growing technology startups in Africa.

In Dar es Salaam, we were at the Tanzania Commission for Science and Technology (TANZICT) with a full house. The economy in the country was strong. Education and access to stable electricity and IT infrastructure meant it was producing a healthy supply of young technical talent.

Sandwiched between Mozambique and the island of Madagascar, in the nation-state island of Comoros, we worked with the diplomats of Moroni to discuss what, if anything, could be done there. Comoros is known mostly for being a loosely regulated tax-haven. It's one of the world's poorest countries, with poor education systems, and few natural resources.

In Uganda, since we were already based there, Teddy convinced us to take our campaign to the villages of Masindi. We organized our events outside in open tents along a dusty, grassed field where girls performed traditional song and dance. In the distance, boys ran back and forth, playing football.

In Johannesburg, South Africa, we socialized with venture capitalists and tech evangelists at The Forum, a lavish five-star venue accommodating upwards of 800 guests. In Capetown, South Africa, we partnered with Google and its affiliated fund, Umbono, for a lively session hosted by local tech heroes and investors like Nic Haralambous. The State Department also invited our team to Durban, South Africa where we were speakers at the United Nations Climate Change Conference (COP 17). In Dakar, Senegal, we invited local entrepreneurs and technologists to Ecole Supérieure Multinationale Des Télécommunications (ESMT).

Ethiopia previously had a strong economy and still had strong institutions and a government actively courting investors, but over time, everything had slowed. Inflation was rising and unemployment was high. Still, entrepreneurs came out in droves to an innovation hub called Ice Addis in Addis Ababa.

Lusaka, Zambia was rapidly developing and courting a lot of foreign investment after turning its economy around following a crash in the 1970s. Entrepreneurs flocked to meet us.

Luanda, Angola featured just one of the fastest-growing economies in Africa; it was one of the fastest-growing in the world. Angola was resource-rich with diamonds, gold, oil, and copper. In 2010, it was ranked as the #1 oil supplier to China. Despite that, more than half of the population in the capital of Luanda still live in dire poverty. For the rest, the economy was booming. Construction was happening everywhere, erecting high-rise luxury hotels, palatial homes, and skyscrapers. It was ranked as the most expensive in the world for tourists and expats. Were there tech entrepreneurs? Sure, but they were mostly targeting the booming industries there—oil, banking, and supply chain management.

In Kinshasa, Democratic Republic of Congo, our team was hosted by Institut Facultaires des Sciences de l'Information et de la Communication (IFASIC). Formerly Zaire, it was the second-largest country in Africa. Kinshasa was impressively developed and urban, with a population of 11 million. That year, 1,500 miles away in the provincial region of Kivu, M23 rebels were waging an assault on the local capital of Goma. The most prominent challenge entrepreneurs felt here was that international investors didn't differentiate between the war-torn areas and the more affluent parts like *le ville basse*.

They stayed away from it all, unable to see past the headlines about civil war. They couldn't get past the *Congo* part, unable to differentiate the Democratic Republic of Congo from the neighboring Republic of Congo. *Heart of Darkness* is all they remembered; a phrase bestowed on the region by Joseph Conrad's 1899 novel. In the book, the protagonist Marlow tells others that he's fascinated by the "the blank spaces" on maps—one of which was pre-colonial Congo. In the narrative, Congo is described as a place of darkness and horror.

I too was fascinated by the blank spaces on the map, places not known for wealth, technologists, or innovators. What I found was resilience, brilliance, and the aspiration of entrepreneurs all over the continent. In our travels, Appfrica's staff visited over half the countries on the continent. We found the blank spots on the map weren't dark at all.

In fact, they were quite bright.

#Albertine

"Over the Mountains of the Moon,
Down the Valley of the Shadow, Ride, boldly ride"
—Egdar Allan Poe

The ledge was coming up fast.

I was facing the edge of an open abyss fifteen feet below. It stretched for what seemed like an eternity in either direction before dropping hundreds of feet into a deep valley. My grip had slipped from a tree root, leaving me sliding down over the wet, mossy forest undergrowth, right towards the hungry ravine. The forest floor was thick with tree roots, foliage, and weeds that grew so tightly they looked woven. I searched for another root – *anything* to cling to.

My left hand tightened around this new root while my right hand grasped the strap of the expensive Canon camera that nearly slipped from my hands as I fell. I abruptly jerked to a stop. I gasped and pulled on the root. I let out a sigh of relief, briefly resting and staring up at the sky, trying to avoid looking down.

"Jon!" Sarah saw me stumble towards the cliff and shouted after me. "Be careful!"

The panic left her voice when she realized a near disaster had been averted. She was worried for me, but we were all in the same perilous position. We were at a thirty-five-degree incline clinging to the side of this steep, unforgiving valley in the Kigezi mountains. There was nothing to catch any of us if we happened to tumble to the ledge, other than the rocky woodland at the base. We had no safety gear.

Safety here meant not screwing up in the first place.

"I'm alright..." I called back panting, completely winded.

We were there to follow, *trek*, a family of mountain gorillas. Gorillas were endangered, with less than one thousand left in existence. This was the only place on earth to find them. Monied tourists like us paid to see them in their natural habitat. The proceeds the parks earned from trekking were used for conservation efforts, to keep the lands free of poachers and pollution.

Trekking is not for the faint or feeble. It can be a non-stop assault on your physicality, both aerobic and anaerobic, as you climb, pull, push, hack, and claw your way through a rainforest that was called *impenetrable* for a reason. Sarah and I had prepared for the trip by doing mile-long hikes around Mutungo Hill every day for a month. Now on our trek, I was discovering that it was not nearly enough preparation. It had only been thirty minutes. The ranger turned to remind us that it might take up to eight hours!

The hike to find one of the few gorilla families left alive required ascending the steep face of a mountain, at times requiring equal parts hiking and mountaineering. A handful of porters trailed closely behind at our every step. They sometimes are called carriers because they carry your backpacks and other gear. Their bodies were trained for this, making the long hike up and down the mountain daily. I decided they were called carriers because if you passed out (or died), they are the ones who carried your limp body back to camp at the mountain base.

The intimidating sounding Bwindi Impenetrable National Park, where we were, is in the southwestern-most part of Uganda, bordering Rwanda. The park is one of the most famous National Parks in Africa as one of only three natural homes for the gorillas. It's also one of the most ecologically diverse forests in the world, known for hundreds of plant and bird species contained within its lush, foggy rainforest. At times, it is dark, with sunlight barely peeking through small gaps in the Ceiba and Mahogany trees above. The canopy is so thick that helicopters flying overhead cannot see a single soul moving on the ground below.

The park sits along the Albertine Rift, a mountainous range of terrain that stretches from Lake Albert in the north of the Democratic Republic of Congo, where it gets its name, down to the southern border of Tanzania. The Albertine itself is part of an interconnected system of thousand-mile-long *rifts*, fractures in the earth's crust that cause earthquakes and volcanoes. Think of these rifts as the figurative seams of Africa, where the continent is literally being torn apart.

Sarah, her mother and father, and I had made the journey there with our park rangers a few days prior from Kampala. If the continent-destroying Albertine Rift sounds terrifying, driving it was worse.

On the way, we took the mountainous route, driving four hours out of the way from Kampala to a place called Fort Portal. From there, it would normally be eight hours to Bwindi. Our guide took his time explaining the Ugandan countryside, telling clearly rehearsed stories about each landmark. He probably made the drive multiple times a month, taking tourists back and forth. Traveling this route, we passed through parts of the Rwenzori Mountain range in the westernmost part of the country, dubbed the Mountains of the Moon.

The terrain is easily excitable, rising steeply and dropping sharply without warning. The roads are narrow and rugged. Through the mountains, even though the roads can be traversed in both directions, they were barely the width of one vehicle. They spiraled up and down the mountain's ridges and hills. The way the earth curved made it impossible to see around corners.

Still, our driver was unwavering, rounding corners at speeds that made my gut sink. When at an impasse with an oncoming vehicle, he sped up, driving directly at it, either veering towards the vertical mountain wall to our right or towards the thousand-foot drop on our left. At times I'd have sworn we were spiraling up this mountain on two-wheels...because the other two had no ground to tread! I closed my eyes and tried to avoid thinking of our four-wheeled van tumbling down the cliffs.

This is insane.

When I was anxious on turbulent flights Sarah would tell me, "Don't worry. Think of it like driving on a bumpy road." In this case, we were *on* the road. The road was the problem. At times there was no road!

We were driving in a 4x4 Toyota Land Cruiser made for trips across rough terrain. It was perhaps the most popular Safari vehicle all over Africa. Boxy and stocky, perfect for driving through volcanic effluvia or unexpected showdowns with a combative boar. The driver told us it handled water well too. That came in handy as we drove through water that reached as high as the passenger windows without stalling. The roof opened upward, swinging back on scissor hinges that gave enough room for tourists to peek out for photos, while still offering overhead protection from the elements.

The journey is more intense when you travel this route, but it was worth it. In the span of a few hours, we passed through what seemed like endless biomes. Marshland. Swampland. Mountains. Plains. Desert. Lakes. Farmland. Traveling north, towards the border of Congo, we passed through a volcanic region with active vents that emerge in marshy, bubbly, molten bog. Thick, boiling, sulfuric liquids of all colors made me think of the primordial origins of life itself.

Uganda is the most naturally beautiful country I've ever traveled across, and I've been to 55 countries. It's not beautiful because of any beaches, or clear water, or cool sand, or resorts that stretch for miles. There isn't any of that. It's beautiful because it's like a road trip through time. It's beautiful because of the untouched vermilion landscapes that seem impossibly old, holding secrets of the past I'd never learn. It's beautiful because it's the pearl of Africa.

Our trip to Bwindi took nearly a week, far longer than usual, because we took the Safari route. This meant staying overnight in remote lodges and game parks, deviating numerous times to visit some of the many amazing parts of the country. Mukono, Jinja, Ggaba, Mubende, Kibale Primate Lodge, Kyambura, Flamingo Lake, Mpanga Falls, Murchison Falls. Finally, we made it to Bwindi. We spent the night at a lodge near the base of the forested mountain we'd be hiking the next day. Shortly after dawn, while the sun was still rising, we were ascending the mountain.

"These mountains have lessons to teach," our ranger said as we headed out. "Be a good learner. Poor learners do not come back."

Our family had opted for a private tour, so we were the only people in the group. In addition to the four of us, we had a ranger leading the way, followed by four porters who each carried our respective bags and gear for the long hike. Behind the porters was one more ranger closing the rear. The rangers were essentially experienced park guides who knew the terrain. They could identify the various gorillas by name, they knew the weather patterns, and they knew most of the people in the surrounding area including in the farming villages nearby. You could tell them apart because they were the ones in fatigues. And they had guns.

"They are for the gorillas, not for *guerrillas!*" our ranger told us, chuckling heartily. He looked back at us, no longer laughing. "Mostly."

Bwindi became infamous in 1999 when a group of tourists were ambushed by guerrillas called the Interahamwe. The rebel group had escaped into the Albertine region following the Rwandan genocide in 1994. They took to the mountains where they hid from pursuing Rwandan military forces.

Once there, they followed the rift's path through Rwanda, Uganda, and the Democratic Republic of Congo. They navigated from Rwanda into the DRC where they traveled miles north into the mountains, eventually crossing into the Ugandan border. The Interahamwe would later state they targeted Bwindi because they knew it was highly touristed. The success of the 1988 Michael Apted and Sigourney Weaver film *Gorillas in the Mist* had caused a huge spike in foreigners from Europe and America interested in trekking gorillas.

These rebels were seeking to destabilize Uganda's economy by carrying out an assault so horrific they hoped no tourists would dare visit the park again, thereby depriving Uganda of valuable tourism revenue. The Interahamwe were still bitter about the outcome of the genocides in Rwanda years prior. They were enraged when Britain and America had not backed them during that conflict. So, they kidnapped fourteen tourists who were trekking Bwindi along with their Ugandan game warden. Then the rebels doubled back towards the Congo side, forcing the tourists to make the exhausting hours-long hike through the mountains with them. The ones who struggled to keep up were slaughtered or tortured. Eventually, the rebels released six of their hostages, but only after they raped and murdered one of them and two others escaped. They butchered the rest with machete and clubs. In all, two Americans, four Britons, and two New Zealanders were slain.

Of the six released, one happened to be the French Deputy Ambassador to Uganda, whom the rebels told their motives. They wanted to ensure their message got heard and their aims were known to all. It was also probably not lost on them that the Hutu and the French had long been allies.

During the 1994 genocides, United Nations Peacekeeping forces led by the French launched a mission to evacuate expatriates, mainly French and Belgian citizens, from Rwanda. The Rwandans who tried to come along were physically forced off escape vehicles and left behind. In some cases, spouses and children were torn from the arms of family members. The evacuators knew those left behind would likely be executed but did not want to provoke tensions by appearing to favor either side of the conflict. They neither fought with, nor acted against, their former allies. It wasn't yet clear if America or Britain would be forced to act, or which side they'd be on if they eventually did.

Instead, these and other nations chose to take no side in the conflict. They stood by and observed the assault on Tutsi and other minority ethnic groups. It's estimated seven out of every ten Tutsi were killed – an estimated one million people. These actions, *or inactions*, of the UN, French and International community were dramatized in another famous movie, *Hotel Rwanda*.

"This we do not speak of," the ranger said in a heavy tone when I asked him about the incident with the tourists. He used his machete to hack a trail through the underbrush, "That was long ago. In over ten years, we have only shot poachers. No tourists. No gorillas. No *guerillas*. You are safe in Bwindi."

That's good, I thought to myself skeptically. My lungs were burning. I've been prone to asthma attacks since I was a child. As an adult, I'd mostly grown out of them but now that fact was being tested, too. I was drenched in sweat. The ranger warned us not to drink too much water since we didn't know how many hours were left in our journey. *Hours!?* It had barely been forty-five minutes.

As I contemplated whether or not I was up for the trip, the ranger turned again and motioned with his finger for us to lower our voices, "We have found them...or shall I say they have found us!" He chuckled, returning to good spirits. He and the other ranger rushed ahead and pointed out the path we would take, heading towards the steep valley nearby.

"Tugende! We go!"

I watched as we approached a quiet family of gorillas. They were in a world of their own, completely ignoring us as we approached. This was their *room*; they were comfortable. We were now in a clearing that left them as exposed to us as we were to them. They were the mirror image of our family – a male silverback, a female, and two children juxtaposed with Sarah's mom and dad, Sarah, and myself. I took a few photos, careful to turn off the flash so as not to startle them. I did this with one hand, so I didn't slip again. We sat there watching them for an hour. We each clung tightly to our roots, carefully taking in the lessons this mountain had to teach.

#TonicsAndGin

"Guns, germs and steel."
—Jared Diamond

"One hundred and three degrees…" The doctor masked any concern with a blank face.

At dinner that evening, a wave of chills had washed over me. It took me a while to realize that it wasn't an air vent blowing aggressively. In Kampala, the restaurant more than likely didn't even have any air conditioning. Beads of sweat began to form on my brow followed by the worst headache I'd experienced in my life. At first, I ignored it, thinking the wooziness would pass.

We had been eating with a collection of friends, other expats, whom we met with frequently to share news, gossip, and talk politics. Our friends in Kampala were journalists, bloggers, software developers, graphic designers, diplomats, financial consultants and an ever-growing eclectic mix of people. Some were Ugandan or from other parts of Africa. On any given night, we'd all meet for big social dinners to chat, drink, and laugh together. Eventually, they too noticed something wasn't right with me.

"Are you okay?" my friend Teddy asked.

The sweat beading through my shirt was forming big circles of wetness around my pits. By this point, the chills had become unbearable. "No, I don't know what this is, but it's bad."

"We better get you home," Sarah said. She rushed to help me up from the table. We said our goodbyes and paid our portion of the meal before departing. I was able to stumble my way to a carshare before passing out in the car...

I awoke to Sarah shaking me.

I was in our bed, sheets drenched, sticking to my skin. I winced from the throbbing in my head. It felt like someone was hammering hot steel into my temples. Apparently, she had helped me out of the car, into the house, and into bed. I still don't remember this but, somehow, she got me from the car to the bed. We were at home already.

How much time had passed?

How did we get here?

How did she get me here by herself?

"Jon, we have to go. Now! You're burning up. We need to get to the hospital!"

I had covered myself in blankets. I was clinging to them like a newborn. "I....can't... cold..."

"That's the problem. You're not cold! Your temperature is one hundred and three!"

* * *

We made it to the International Hospital of Kampala (IHK) in Namuwongo around midnight. Apparently, after dinner, I was able to get to the car with Sarah and when it was time to get out, she says I was mumbling but still able to walk on my own. I got myself into bed. On the way in, I stumbled and vomited in front of the gate outside our compound. At first, she thought I'd sleep it off, but after checking my temperature, she got concerned. When she woke me the second time, I was barely able to put my clothes back on myself. I was definitely too weak to stand, so our live-in guard, Godfrey, assisted her in getting me to the car.

Now at IHK, the expat hospital, I was in a bed where a doctor examined me. She knew what it was immediately, before even beginning her examination. She confirmed, but had identified it as soon as I walked in.

"He has malaria."

Malaria is no joke. It kills over half a million people a year, usually the very poor who can't afford treatment. It's a known illness carried by female mosquitoes who carry plasmodium parasites in their saliva, injecting them into the blood of the victims they bite. Once in the system, these parasites lay eggs and begin to multiply, then they go on the attack against healthy red blood cells in your immune system.

"He's going to have to stay, at the very least, overnight. We need to keep an eye on that fever," I overheard her say to Sarah. "It may even be a few days."

I could hear them talking, but only in the same way you recall voices from a dream. Distant echoes. The only thing my eyes could fixate on was the slow drip of the bag hanging overhead that was pumping fluids into my veins.

Sarah was horrified. I had come here for her. I truly hoped she wasn't feeling responsible, but everything I knew about her told me she did. *Get better – for her*, I thought.

Before you can move to a country like Uganda, or even visit, you have to get all kinds of vaccinations and shots. When you do, you get what is called a *yellow card* – think of it as a passport but for doctors. It lists the dates of your vaccinations and when those vaccinations will expire. Upon entry into a country for the first time, the immigration desk will review your passport and your yellow card. Mine read:

INTERNATIONAL CERTIFICATE OF
VACCINATION OR PROPHYLAXIS
AS APPROVED BY
THE WORLD HEALTH ORGANIZATION

MAR 1 9 2008	*Diptheria 0.5 ml/Tetanus*
MAR 1 9 2008	*Hepatitis A #2*
MAR 1 9 2008	*Hepatitis B #1*
MAR 1 9 2008	*Polio IPV 0.5 ml (booster)*

MAR 1 9 2008	*Oral Typhoid 4 Caps (5 yrs)*
MAR 1 9 2008	*Influenza 0.5 ml*
MAR 1 9 2008	*Menactra. Meningococcal (Groups A, C, Yand W-135) Polysaccharide Diptheria Toxoid Conjugate Vaccine*
2006	*Hep A #1*
2006	*Typhoid Vi*

Yellow cards are mostly handwritten or stamped. Since there was no international medical record database at the time, this yellow card is all you got. Don't get it wet, lose it, or forget it when you go to see a doctor abroad. Remember the first rule of the Impenetrable Forest: *Safety is not screwing up.*

Life in Africa is life with no guard rails. There are medicines that reduce the risk of contracting malaria, but there is no preventative vaccine. Also, the medicines that do exist are meant to be taken for two months at a time, max. They are great for tourists visiting only for a short period but inadequate for anyone staying longer, and especially useless for the 1.2 billion Africans who live there.

Also, these recommended drugs have their respective side effects:

Quinine, coupled with Doxycycline, are like the buddy cop pair of malaria treatment. For some reason, Doxy, as they call it, isn't effective on its own. It needs it a partner, Quinine (or Artesunate), to really get to work. Side effects can include abdominal pain, sensitivity to the sun, diarrhea, deafness, blindness, and disturbances in heart rhythms. Another medicine, Malarone, consists of atovaquonbe and prouanil. It's more of the same awful side effects but less effective than Doxy.

Mefloquine (also sold under the brand Lariam) is meant to be taken before exposure or at least one week after you think you've been exposed to malaria. Its side effects include vomiting, diarrhea, headaches, and possibly an outbreak of rash. It can also cause, depression, hallucinations, anxiety, seizures, and neurotoxicity. Some people who have been found to have overused mefloquine have lucid hallucinations, some even committed suicide. This earned it the nickname *crystal mef* amongst expats.

Prior to the discovery of quinine, Africa was rumored to have its own natural immune system. Slave traders and imperialists still came to Africa, but the environment was so harsh, they suffered catastrophic deaths from illness. Their main losses were to the environment itself, before fighting anyone. A lot was extracted—slaves, gold, and other resources—but no European or Westerner desired to stay in Africa longer than they had to. They were ill-equipped for the continent's mysterious diseases and infections. It was so effective that Europeans arriving by boat dubbed it *the white man's death*.

Quinine changed that.

Initially, it was discovered a world away by the indigenous people of Peru, the Quechua, who would grind up the bark from cinchona trees with sugar water to offset the drink's bitter taste. It was a medicine they used, essentially, as a muscle relaxer. By learning to extract the medicinal qualities from this tree by putting it in water, they inadvertently invented *tonic water*.

Quinine had a long history through the ages, as far away as Rome where it was used to treat malaria as well. The Roman Empire at its peak stretched into Africa. It wasn't until 1820, though, when two French researchers, Pierre Pelletier and Joseph Caventou, created the form still used today. They also gave its modern name, derived from the Inca word for *holy bark*. The discovery of this more potent form of quinine equipped Europeans, South Americans and North Americans with the defense mechanism they needed to survive for long periods in Africa. Quinine was also effective in India, where it was mixed with tonic water to trick British soldiers into taking medicine that allowed them to not die from malaria. The discovery of potent quinine paved the way for the colonization of the African continent and Indian sub-continent. In Congo alone, it was quinine more than any other ally that enabled King Leopold II and his men from Belgium to colonize the country, slaughtering more than 10 million people in the process. It was a horrific kind of cascading failure.

Mefloquine didn't have a legacy like that, but it held its own horrors. In August 2002, authorities discovered the body of a young Cambridge University student named Vanessa Brunt. Her parents would later state that she suffered from a profound period of mental illness that lasted two years, beginning with a semester abroad in Asia where she had been prescribed Lariam as a pre-emptive measure against malaria. Her parents blamed the drug, remembering that it was only weeks after beginning Lariam that their daughter changed, saying she became physically and mentally ill. "Haunted," they said.

Another man hung himself in his room, where the only substances found were Lariam and alcohol. In fact, dozens of suicides have been linked to the drug. The story is mostly the same as Vanessa's. Everything was fine, spirits were high with nothing abnormal to report, and then came this drug. One Frenchman was reported to have died as the result of multiple self-inflicted stab wounds made after taking the drug over a prolonged period. Others died from cardiac arrest. Far more reported lucid dreams that spiraled into vivid nightmares that plagued them for months.

Is Mefloquine confirmed to be the gateway to psychosis or suicide by the medical community? No. It's been available since the 1980s and of the millions who've taken it, these cases might be considered outlier scenarios. Yet, while there is no clinical proof of causation, the drug has been suspiciously linked to mental illness and breakdowns. As expats, you believe other expats. Everyone I knew had a story about Mefloquine. The people I stood in a circle talking to Stephen with had their own stories. The consensus was: don't touch it if you can avoid it. It may have been mere gossip, but I remembered that.

The best protections against malaria were simple. Using bed nets, mesh material that hung over beds to trap mosquitos. Keeping a safe distance from standing water, where mosquitoes gather, especially at night. And finally, staying away from dense forestry. Like the mountains, I had spent days in earlier...

Ah ha!

Bwindi still had its lessons to teach.

Act #3

Askari

#TheKampalaReport

"Okay, we're running for our lives."
—Solomon King, Ugandan Activist

The tear gas canister hit him in the face. A bright explosion of red mist sprayed over everyone standing nearby. The musty stench of sweat and blood hung in the air. He crumpled to the ground and didn't move.

Men nearby hurled anything they could grab. Police with riot shields tightened their formation. Rocks. Bottles. Cans. Books. They grabbed at the guns and batons of the policemen, trying to wrest them from their grips. Gunshots whizzed past their heads, occasionally connecting, sending men flying backward – they then lay motionless.

Red dirt swirled everywhere. A shed near the advancing police brigade burst into bright orange flames and growled aggressively. A woman ran through the chaos with her infant. She screamed for someone to get her child to safety. *Bam!* Her world shrank to the size of a pinhole and spun. She found herself looking up at the sky from the ground, head throbbing. She struggled to breathe. She coughed and clawed the dirt looking for her child. A man in police garb standing over her drew the butt of his gun back and struck her in the face again. Then he punched her a few times and slapped her, his arms flailing widely. She fell back onto the ground and turned as something caught her eye. She saw her child, glass-eyed and motionless. Then she saw the entry wounds. The man wiped her blood from his hands and walked away. Sobbing, she crawled towards her lifeless infant lying in the bloody dirt.

* * *

This riot in Lubaga, Uganda was the culmination of events that threatened to push Uganda to the brink of civil war. After a re-settlement agreement was established between the President and King years ago, Lubaga had become the epicenter of what's known as the Buganda Kingdom. The Buganda Kingdom is more of a concept than a place. It refers to the Baganda people and wherever they live. When their king was banned from entering one of Museveni's political rallies, for fear that he'd incite violence, the Kabaka became outraged. He demanded his traditional powers be recognized. He demanded to be able to freely traverse Kampala. The President denied him again. That's when the king did exactly what the President had feared. He called for his people to retaliate.

Burn it down.

The evening of September 10th, 2009, I was anticipating the memorial ceremonies for a different tragedy: September 11th, 2001, when four commercial planes in the United States had been turned into missiles and flown into buildings. An attack that rewrote history.

I didn't have television or radio at my home on Mutungo Hill. It wouldn't have mattered anyway; the Ugandan government demanded the radio stations be shut down. It was a crowd control tactic often used in Africa. They had learned this from Rwanda in 1994 when genocides claimed the lives of nearly one million people. There, radio broadcasters were blamed for instigating violence, calling more and more people to the streets as tensions between ethnic groups rose. It was a double-edged sword. African governments had learned that taking over radio stations was a way to control the masses during a crisis, but it also showed them they could control the masses whenever they wanted. If need be, they could invent reasons to take over a station, which they often did. When they did, they could change the national story to whatever they needed it to be. Therefore, the media couldn't always be trusted. Instead, the first reports of the riots came to me via text message and relatively new tech startup called Twitter.

A friend of mine, a young Ugandan blogger and photographer named Solomon King, would later rise to prominence for reporting the violence that was unleashed that day. He was near Lubaga when the riots began, when the mother and her infant child were shot, an act that ensured nothing would be resolved quickly. Initially, he stopped to take photos. He stood in the streets tweeting reports of the unfolding incident to those of us following him online. Then it became clear that he should not be reporting – he should be running. He turned and sprinted nearly a mile until he reached a safer area. Breathless, he paused and began to tweet again.

Across town at my house in Mutungo, I was on my laptop. I didn't see Solomon's message until a few hours later when I opened my laptop and saw my timeline on Twitter explode with reports about what was happening. The riots had now been going on for about 12 hours. Solomon was tweeting from what we called *the red zone*. When they began their coverage, international news outlets were citing reports that came from Solomon, myself and a handful of others. We had become defacto correspondents, giving our moment-by-moment updates to the world's newsrooms, informing them of what was happening in Uganda.

Text by text.

Tweet by tweet.

International news outlets were looking to us for information. Local news had been silenced by the government. Other Twitter users in the city were the only sources of information we could rely on. We helped each other, using text messages like short-wave radio. Those of us at home on our laptops followed along with reports on Twitter about what was happening where. We'd then use Google Maps to navigate those still in the field around the trouble areas.

I'm at the corner of Port Bell road and Wampewo Avenue. Do I turn left or right?

Left! They are right behind you!

No stop… wait… Okay, you're clear! Run! Run!

That night I also wrote about the day's events on the Appfrica blog:

Yesterday around 2 p.m. riots broke out in specific regions of Uganda's capital city Kampala. If you lived anywhere else in the world, you probably didn't hear about the story at all.

The American press didn't pick up the news until there were reports of a U.S. celebrity who needed evacuation. Gospel singer Kirk Franklin and his caravan were ambushed on the way to the airport after meeting with the Vice President of Uganda. "Rioters block U.S. singer Kirk Franklin" one headline read. A military detail had to help the singer and his entourage escape their buses, rushing them into Nansana Police Station as the rioters closed in.

Other than hubs of military presence throughout the city, signs of the riots were contained to specific areas. My house overlooked the city. In the distance, I could see smoke rising from the direction of Lubaga. Around 8 p.m., the cellular networks began to buckle. There were unsubstantiated reports of a media blackout. My phone retained its coverage and I still had Internet access so I dismissed it. I worked like a switch operator, reading and relaying information as fast I could. At times I sent messages from both my iPhone and my cell phone, swapping between the two as needed. Then I repeated whatever was happening around the city for my online audience abroad.

Sarah and I locked the security doors at our house. We sat on the couch with our laptops watching messages from our friends around the city. They shared updates and photos from the riots. That night, we gazed out our window and held each other, watching for any sign of disturbance. In the morning, the reports began to flood my screen again. This time, though, the riots were shifting, moving through the city and closer to our location. Even though I let the staff at Appfrica know that they had the day off, many of them stayed at the office. Some lived in the areas the riots had torn through. For them, staying at the office was safer than going home. It was also more entertaining. At least the office had working power and internet.

Sarah was concerned. "What should we do? Should we call the Embassy?"

"I guess. We don't know how long this is going to last or how bad it's going to get. They can't send anyone if they don't know where we are."

When you live as an expat, any time shit hit the fan, you wanted the American embassy to have a record of where you were. Supposedly they already did. When you arrive in-country you're encouraged to go to them and give them your name, phone number, and your address as well as the contact information of loved ones. However, that information likely sat on a shelf somewhere that no one ever bothered to look at until they were trying to figure out where to ship a corpse. Also, you may have moved or changed phone numbers. The way Kampala's roads were oriented, with choke points into and out of town, the riots had moved into areas that completely cut off our ability to escape by car.

We would need to be evacuated by helicopter. Luckily, we lived on one of the tallest hills in the city. If that ended up being the case, it was the perfect place for a helicopter to land.

She pulled her cellphone away from her face, "They have our info now. They said that we shouldn't try to leave at all. Just stay in the compound and keep the doors locked." She feigned reassurance: "We're going to be okay."

I didn't know if she was talking to me or herself.

"Let's hope so." My laptop was full of images of a Kampala at war with itself. Requests for interviews from publications like the

BBC and Guardian poured in. "My friend Solomon is actually closer, talk to him," I told them. "I'm just the messenger."

"Well, thanks for keeping us up to date. Y'all bloggers and Twitter guys are invaluable to us right now," a reporter said over the phone.

"Thanks. I just hope the networks stay up today."

* * *

To understand what sparked the Lubaga riots, I first need to explain a bit of Ugandan history.

The earliest known inhabitants of Uganda were the Bantu-speaking people who had migrated for thousands of years around the continent. The lands that would later become Uganda shows a record of human activity as far back as 100,000 years. As generations passed and the migrations slowed, a portion of these people settled there, cultivating it through agricultural and pastoral gathering. As the clans multiplied, ways of organizing and maintaining order were needed. A form of governance was adopted where clan chiefs were the authority at a village level and powerful leaders were appointed above them, presiding over multiple villages. Different ethnic groups emerged. These groups—the Hutu, the Chwezi, the Hima, Tutsi, and Bito—vied for control over each other until the Bito group emerged victorious. They then established a far-reaching kingdom called Bunyoro.

Other large kingdoms were established, like the Haya kingdom to the south near what is now Tanzania. The Buganda kingdom emerged in the northern part of what is now Uganda. The Bunyoro kingdom grew to be so mighty that when its Prince traveled to Buganda in the 15th century, he usurped the throne.

He became what would be the first Kabaka of the Buganda kingdom, unifying the people of Buganda and Bito. As a result, the Buganda kingdom grew in strength and importance, eventually eclipsing and assimilating all other kingdoms. By the 19th century, the Buganda Kingdom consisted of millions, with armies comprised of hundreds of thousands, sometimes for a single mission. The Kingdom was well organized and protected. Towns and roads were meticulously carved from the forests, with miles-long walls surrounding their towns. The kingdom continued its growth until the mid-19th century when American, Egyptian, British, and Tanzanian traders took notice.

It wasn't long before the conflict with these foreigners began. After years of war and infighting, the British emerged victorious and began the occupation of the once mighty kingdom. For the Bugandans, it was a self-inflicted wound. Those among the Buganda who converted to Christianity and sided with British colonists effectively brought the Buganda kingdom down from the inside. It would remain under colonial rule for nearly 100 years.

On October 9th, 1962, Uganda was granted independence from Britain. At the time, Queen Elizabeth II of the United Kingdom also held the official title of Queen of Uganda. Following independence, Uganda was left to self-organize again. Elections were held that resulted in a Prime Minister named Milton Obote. President Edward Muteesa II, who represented the Buganda Kingdom, was the new Kabaka. The two were to share power: Obote as leader of the newly formed country, while Muteesa was given authority to honor the Buganda kingdom that the British dismantled so many years ago.

Obote was widely seen as a weak leader. Only a weak leader would agree to a power-sharing agreement at all. A strong leader would dominate. Meanwhile, traditionalists did not respect the authority of the British or Obote. They saw him as a puppet, a tool of the colonizers.

The Kabaka became meddlesome and bitter about the arrangement. His people were resentful that the country was electing to maintain the British-style system of government imposed on them. It was perhaps inevitable that the Kabaka would attempt to depose Obote. He tried escaping by scaling a wall and fleeing on foot. He made it out of the country and eventually died in exile. Ironically, he died in Britain—the imperialist country he despised. After this failed attempt at a coup by Muteesa, Obote would suspend the constitution, abolish the traditional kingdoms and all their powers. He made himself President. The General who successfully helped him stop the Buganda king's coup attempt was a man named Idi Amin.

Obote didn't know it, but he had set the stage for his own demise as President. Having abolished traditional powers, when a second coup happened, he had little support from the country's people. They were Ugandan but most still identified by their ethnic group and still respected the political power of traditional kingdoms. Also, Obote's increasing loyalty to Britain made him unpopular. The British were seen as horrible oppressors who dominated the country for a century. Why was their President appeasing them? This also turned Idi Amin against him.

The next coup happened while Obote was at a conference meeting with the Commonwealth Heads of State in 1971. Idi Amin's men stormed his offices and demand the military pledge loyalty. Amin, recognizing the need for the ethnic groups, held an elaborate funeral for Muteesa when he finally died. For the first time, this allowed him to secure support from both the Buganda traditionalists and widen the Ugandan public at the same time. They were happy to see Obote go.

They couldn't have known what horrors were in store.

Once he took power, Idi Amin ruled harshly and vengefully. First, he purged Obote's soldiers in the thousands. Then, he targeted political opponents who were loyal to Obote or related to him by ethnicity. Then he targeted anyone who critiqued him – outspoken foreigners, lawyers, students, anyone who presented a threat. It's estimated that during his eight years in power, Amin had anywhere between 300,000 and 500,000 people murdered and their bodies dumped into the Nile River.

Amin then waged a short-sighted economic war against foreigners who ran the country's business sector. His exile of the Asian population, attempting to redistribute their wealth and businesses, crashed the economy. Along with the economy, support for Amin plummeted. He had caused his own undoing. He was soon ousted by military coup. Ironically, it was Obote who returned to replace him. He was elected President once more.

This time a new challenger, also a General, claimed that Obote was unjustly installed by friends through a rigged election. Many who agreed waged a war against his illegitimate Presidency. That war, the Luweero War, would last nearly five years and claim the lives of another half-million people. One of the men who led this opposition to Obote was a young Yoweri Museveni, the current President of Uganda. However, it wasn't Museveni who would depose Obote.

The war between Obote and Museveni was so costly that two of Obote's other commanders turned on him. They were sick of the bloodshed and the disruption he was causing. They ousted Obote to end it all. Once again, Obote had to step down in shame. Yoweri Museveni would use the confusion and lack of leadership to successfully take the Presidency for himself on July 27th, 1985. He has been President ever since. Recognizing the importance of Buganda, rather than trying to end the Kingdom altogether, Museveni sought to control it. The coalition government that balanced the Presidency with the traditional King returned in 1993. Though Buganda's King, the Kabaka, would again hold no real political authority, the sway the Kabaka held over his ethnic people was palpable.

* * *

It was this history that culminated in the events that took place on September 10th, 2009, when my friend ran through the streets with his cellphone; half-reporting, half-surviving. Tensions between the President and King led to the eruption of violence that gripped Kampala. How the Kabaka is treated plays a critical role in keeping peace in Uganda. A significant portion of the population, the poor and resource-starved villagers and farmers of Uganda, still support their ethnic leaders, often above the President. They were ready to fight for their king as much as they would have three hundred years ago.

As long as its affluent citizens enjoy the status quo, the poor have nothing to lose by voicing their displeasure when they feel their traditions aren't being respected. For them, a return to tradition would give them more of a voice in society. Additionally, Kampala now sits in the heart of land once considered sacred to them. From the perspective of the Baganda, the city is just leasing the land from them. A lease they can revoke at any time.

The only thing that kept these tensions from rupturing had been the symbolic powers Yoweri Museveni restored to the king. Museveni had come to power as the result of a bloody five-year war and didn't want to return to violence. In return, the king (now Ronald Mutebi II) agreed to make no attempt to depose Museveni. He also agreed not to call on those loyal to him to rise up against the President. Museveni and Mutebi II mostly respected this agreement with each other.

That is until they crossed each other.

For nearly two years leading up to September 10th, 2009, Mutebi II used his position to criticize not only Museveni but the whole of the Ugandan government. Some saw it as him trying to drum up another populist movement, potentially to stage another coup. Recognizing this possibility, Museveni claimed he wanted to de-escalate the situation by preventing Mutebi II from visiting areas of the Buganda Kingdom. The restrictions imposed on Mutebi II were only meant to be temporary.

However, Mutebi II saw them as an attack on his authority as king. He demanded the visit take place in spite of Museveni's wishes. Museveni insisted that it not. He had the king arrested. The two immoveable bulls bumped horns once again. This time tensions spread to the streets. The king's followers revolted and the conflict sent Kampala tumbling into chaos.

#TheBeautifulGame

*"Some people think football is a matter of life and death.
I assure you, it is much more serious than that."*
—Bill Shankly, legendary Liverpool manager

In one of the busiest markets in Chennai, India, people come to buy everything from saris to gold, housewares, and furniture. It's a typical market, as found in most places around the world. In fact, if we were to go back several hundred years, we'd find that much of the world's commerce occurred in places like this. Chaotic, cramped, loud. A sea of people and the unseen connections between them. The person on the street who's pick-pocket-ing discreetly; the people who once knew each other but who no longer speak on friendly terms; the merchant who purchases his goods and then quietly crosses over to the next market to resell everything at marked-up prices.

That year in Kenya, I had a conversation with a friend, a journalist, working for the New York Times who shared this memory of when he was a boy staring at the markets in Chennai. He wondered what the connections were between the masses of people before him.

"We know they're there, but these connections are difficult to see," he told me.

When the average person thinks of *apps*, they think of tools that let them connect with their friends, post funny videos or find a decent restaurant. I was focused on using the same technologies in different ways. Instead of connecting people with friends, I wanted to help refugees connect with missing family members, or share videos of an unfolding crises, or the pathway to safe zones during riots. Disaster response, community activism, election monitoring, and citizen journalism—these were the uses of social media I was concerned with. I built tools for data collection, mapping, curation, and visualization. I took these hidden connections between people, places, and things and made them visible. *Mapable*. Lessons I had learned from the Garmin. More importantly, these products would be used by first-response organizations to facilitate their own work. These apps made it possible for tasks to be distributed amongst the many but carried out by few. This empowered small organizations to accomplish big things. When done well, people all over the world could solve problems together, from wherever they were. It was micro-tasking.

It was a bit like watching a soccer match.

The players of both teams are constantly moving in many directions, but collectively they have one goal. Win the game. To achieve that goal, the players must perform smaller tasks, often deviating from plays carefully orchestrated by a coach before the game. Spontaneous acts are sometimes needed for the sake of the team. For this reason, and others, soccer is referred to as *the beautiful game*. Players work together and, at times, individually. They play in unison and dissonance, working together and against each other, quickly and slowly. This is what *radical collaboration* looks like. In data science, the math behind this type of network of transactional action and interconnected relationships is what we refer to as *graph theory*. This refers to the understanding of how networks work and how the actions within them also work.

I built tools for what I called radical collaboration. Collaboration by academics, volunteers, and activists to solve problems at a large scale. Like soccer, this type of collaboration was far more complex than it appeared on the surface.

It too was beautiful.

* * *

In December 2009, I met with a company with Kenyan origins called Ushahidi. Given our mutual interest in business in Africa and technology, it was a dream collaboration. The company combined data, tech, and humanitarian work into a single software platform. Ushahidi was founded by code switchers, all active bloggers who knew each other from different circles in activism and tech. They primarily interacted with one another online. Being visible in the African tech ecosystem, they already knew who I was. It turns out we admired each other's work from afar.

We knew about each other through the conference circuit, where we had all been invited to speak about our work with tech across

Africa. One of those events, where many players in Africa's tech ecosystem first met, was actually organized by Google. It was held at the company's Mountain View campus in California. The event was spearheaded by a consultant named Kaushal Jhalla, who had roots in Kenya. I assumed he was from one of the Indian families who were native but had been expelled. The event was called Barcamp Africa. The idea was to hold a conference about African tech but to have Google host. These were conferences with a collaborative agenda that was only outlined once people arrived. Barcamps were very fluid and reactive to whoever was in the room. The idea was to offer a one-time experience that could only be created by the people who were there.

Most people in Silicon Valley assumed Africa was devoid of progress. To them, it was a place for philanthropists and charities, not software developers. They weren't eager to talk about its contributions to tech, if they knew of any. They had no idea about the innovations emerging all over the continent. Kaushal's calculus was that a conference with free food and drinks, hosted at Google HQ in San Francisco would be attractive. If not, the appeal of the popular Barcamp format would be. It was at Barcamps like this one where *#hashtags*, now so pervasive on social media, were conceived. If hashtags could take off at Barcamps, so could African tech.

It was at events like this, in Africa or elsewhere, that the bonds between the individual champions of the African private sector would form. The rest of the world wasn't taking Africa seriously. It remains an attitude that wasn't uncommon in Silicon Valley at all. Nonetheless, Barcamp Africa was an incredible experience. It was hard for people to be dismissive when it brought people in African tech together to speak for themselves.

* * *

"We need people who have experience with tech and experience working in Africa, with African software developers...that's a very short list," Erik said over the phone. We kept in touch after meeting at an event. He had heard about what Appfrica was doing in Uganda and I had heard about what Ushahidi was doing in Kenya.

I initially got on his radar because of the role I played in reporting the Lubaga Riots. I had unexpectedly created a great case study for their disaster software. At the time, Ushahidi was still trying figure out the best way to respond to crisis events. In posts on my blog, I drew comparisons between their platform and what tech activists were doing in. They read it and wanted to meet. When he called, it was to ask if I'd join their company in some capacity. I agreed, on the condition that I could keep Appfrica running in tandem. I didn't want to leave the company I'd started, plus I thought the team in Uganda could be extra capacity for software development if we ever needed them.

Ushahidi itself was a company born in response to violence. The company made software that was created to help citizens displaced during the 2007 Kenyan riots. The goal was to allow citizens to report what they saw in real-time using their cell phones. The software would collect these reports and organize them based on urgency and map them based on the person's location. Waypoints told the story of human suffering and triumph, a richer purpose than where a memorable pub was located. In 2007 this was not only a novel use of location technology, it was the blueprint that changed the way data and maps could be combined. They pioneered the use of digital maps to navigate the infighting that plagued Kenya at the time, violence that nearly tore Kenya apart.

The original catalyst for the company was a lawyer from Nairobi, a woman named Ory Okolloh. In 2006, Ory became the founder of Kenyan parliamentary watchdog site Mzalendo which in Swahili meant *patriot*. That project was aimed at increasing government accountability through the systematic documentation and release of proposed legislation, speeches from officials, standing orders, and more. She was a defiant, confident, and inspiring woman who demanded transparency and fairness from her country's elected officials. She had earned an undergraduate degree in political science from the University of Pittsburgh and later graduated from Harvard Law School. She was also an active and prominent blogger with her site Kenyan Pundit which, coupled with Mzalendo, became the nexus for journalists, activists, legal experts, and other bloggers concerned with the politics of East Africa. Even though Erik represented the organization, it was Ory who embodied what the company would become.

If Erik was the face of Ushahidi, Ory was its soul.

In late 2007, as tensions in Kenyan politics began to erupt, she was concerned about a country on the brink of combustion. She proposed an idea on her blog:

"Google Earth supposedly shows in great detail where damage [from the riots] is being done on the ground. It occurs to me that it will be useful to keep a record of this...for the reconciliation process to occur at the local level, the truth of what happened will first have to come out. Guys looking to do something – any techies out there willing to do a mashup of where the violence and destruction is occurring using Google Maps?"

A few days later, that message became the rallying call for technologists. A handful of people came together in response. Ory was joined by Erik Hersman, Juliana Rotich, David Kobia, and Daudi Were, who convened to establish Kuona.com, a platform that would change Kenya and later the world. The rest is history. Well...maybe in some alternate universe. In this universe, the domain Kuona.com was taken. Instead they went with the far harder to pronounce Ushahidi. It was a word that meant *testimony*.

The platform had the ability to capture and share first-hand accounts of sometimes tragic events in hard-to-reach locations. The company would soon find backing from one of the world's newly minted billionaires, Pierre Omidyar, co-founder of eBay. He set out to use his newfound wealth to support the use of technology for humanitarian causes and investigative journalism. In addition to his role as a major financial supporter of the company, he later went on to found First Look Media. First Look was the publisher of *The Intercept*, which employed journalists like Glenn Greenwald, Laura Poitras, Jeremy Scahill, Dan Froomkin, John Temple, and Jay Rosen. Omidyar funded other civic organizations through his company Omidyar Networks, which was like a hybrid humanitarian organization and venture capital fund. It was his desire to leverage capital for philanthropic change. He was a rare investor who gave us the space we needed to innovate. A more capital-focused investor would have been looking to profit out the gate. A pure philanthropist would have ignored the business opportunities completely. In Omidyar, Ushahidi had found the perfect funder, someone who appreciated both.

"We do what the Red Cross should be doing," Erik would often tell me. He loved to point out that the developmental aid organizations that made up the status quo were clueless.

Ushahidi's tools enabled people to share ideas, thoughts, messages, feelings, fears, concerns, images, and videos, mostly during times of crisis. They allowed people to locate each other and avoid areas where there was potential trouble. They could do this in real-time across borders and languages. If you've used the internet, you've likely come across some form of tasking platform where your tiny actions combine with the tiny actions of others to enable much more powerful work down the line. It was like the work Leila was doing with Samasource. Soon, a new term emerged for micro-tasking that evolved beyond work for business, work harder to define and coordinate, like managing volunteer efforts after an earthquake or riot. The term was *crowdsourcing*. Whereas micro-tasking distributed small tasks that were clearly defined, crowdsourcing was more about distributing multiple assignments to individuals who had to cooperate to get them all done.

Think of the *captcha* that you use to log into your favorite websites. Typing those garbled letters into a box with the prompt "type what you see here" over the past two decades has laid the groundwork for powerful computer vision algorithms. By associating what you type with infinite versions of each letter, these algorithms now allow printers to scan documents and turn them into typed documents. Or the algorithms can scan them and read them back to you.

If a Google technician walked up to you in the street and asked you to read the letters off a mangled business card because it would help him out at work, would you do it? Probably not. By breaking the work into smaller tasks that were unnoticeable and convenient, they made it possible for little bits of work by millions around the world to consolidate into advancing their products. Small contributions added up to something bigger. This was the same concept we used at Ushahidi to solve large scale humanitarian problems.

Ushahidi's software allowed for the remote guidance of first responders – aid workers, clinicians, even the military, by helping to improve what they called *situational awareness*. For instance, following the devastating earthquake in Haiti in 2010, the electrical grid and communication networks in the country were down. Previously, when first responders arrived at an unfolding tragedy, they had limited ways of getting information. They might be assisted by military satellites that helped show damage to the terrain and landscape or other tech that could say analyze the integrity of the outside of a building.

What they couldn't know was the emotional or mental state of the people inside that building. Were the people in there angry? Were they distressed and overwhelmed? Was someone dying? With our platform, the military was able to not only view the first-hand accounts of people in the building, but gain a sense of what they were walking into before they entered. We could map the concerns of people and, if necessary, reach back out to communicate with them. Disaster response went from one-way communication to two-way communication. Ushahidi called those first-hand accounts from people in crisis *testimonies*.

In the platform, they appeared as red circles, dots of varying sizes on topographical interactive maps. The sizes of the dots represented the number of testimonies from people who were there. They were like the waypoints I had left across Europe, only now I could see them. The color of the dots designated categories the reports belonged to like: *injury, casualty, needs water,* or *missing person*. At Appfrica, I had worked with Google on a relatively new product, Google Maps. Ushahidi supercharged Google Maps with information relevant to first responders responding to human need.

We weren't the only company good at crowdsourcing. It was a big trend in the tech world. Crowdsourcing allowed for the distribution of complex work amongst people who could be located anywhere in the world. The work happened in whole, or in part, in digital spaces. Instead of using industrial power to solve problems, crowdsourcing relied mostly on the cognition of humans. Companies like Yelp used crowdsourcing to turn masses of people into restaurant critics. Zillow transformed users into a panel of opinion on the quality of neighborhoods around the country.

Kickstarter encouraged millions of people to contribute small amounts of money to ideas that they loved, providing creators with the capital necessary to make them.

The use cases were endless but the dynamics were the same. First attract users with a unique app, then sell their data to advertisers who paid to target them. This allowed these companies to reach people at a scale and in a manner the world had not seen before. We were a bit different. As a non-profit, Ushahidi was never concerned with a business model. We had the benefit of innovating for innovation's sake. We also had the benefit of what felt like overnight success. For a time, it seemed like I couldn't go to any technology conference in the world without hearing crowdsourcing and Ushahidi referred to in the same sentence. At Clinton Global Initiative, TED, World Economic Forum, Personal Democracy Forum, Disrupt, Next Web, South by Southwest, at events all over the world, large and small, we found our way in the room. We became the subject of best-selling books and were invited to appear on morning news shows. In 2010, at the height of the organization's fame, *The Atlantic* named it one of their "Biggest Ideas of the Year."

We were young, brilliant innovators bringing the best of Silicon Valley-style tech to humanitarian efforts around the world. We also brought the kind of empathy and understanding to tech that often comes from humanitarians. We understood the challenges intuitively. Living in Uganda and Kenya, we experienced the other side of catastrophe every day. It wasn't just abstract theory for us. Every great inventor starts by trying to solve small problems that are personal. We were solving our own problems. We had to.

Every other month there was an article about our work in major media outlets: CNN, BBC, NPR, The Economist, TIME. The White House honored us on multiple occasions for our contributions to the humanitarian sector. Our team members gave TED

Talks watched by millions. People were eager to support a success story from Africa, especially one about this group of mostly homegrown technologists who emerged from Kenya. Before companies like Ushahidi, the official reports that mattered during a crisis were from large institutions. After Ushahidi, it became about citizens' first-hand reports. We were invited by journalists from across the planet to give lectures and lead workshops on the uses of crowdsourcing, GPS technology, and data.

Years later, in 2011, I received an internal memo that our organization had been shortlisted for the Nobel Peace Prize.

"Holy Fuck!" was my eloquent response.

We didn't win, but to be nominated was humbling. We were doing work that mattered a great deal. The recognition gave us that much more passion for saving lives with our software.

The ability for people to self-organize and challenge power was typically limited by their location. Individual dissidents who posed a threat could be found, jailed, or killed. Activists gathered to riot could be scattered with tear gas. Political rivals could be assassinated. With crowdsourcing, mobile phones, and the Internet, these activist movements were able to transcend the location of individuals. Their movements could now be everywhere at once. Once transmitted, data took on a life of its own. It could meander its way around the world in seconds. It was a river of information, impossible to contain.

#ShortCode

"Haïti chérie, ton sang est dans la diaspora
Regarde le pays agonisant qui va porter
le deuil pour toi? Ouille!"

—Dey, a song by Haitian singer and
actress Marie 'Toto' Bissainthe

Fabiola Dabrezil was walking along the uneven road that led from the center of town, down the hill. The road twisted from right to left to right again before ending near the stretch of houses and her home. It was after school and often her responsibility to ensure her brothers and sisters made it home safely. She went to the market on the edge of town to fetch the ingredients that would be used for dinner. If her mother wasn't home by 5 pm, it was her job to start dinner and feed her siblings. Her father always worked late, usually not returning until dark. She wasn't yet a woman, but that did nothing to stop the gaze of men whose heads turned as she walked, tracing her body up and down. Every now and then, they would stop her to comment and jeer...

You must be a good student.

Would you like to marry me, girl? I can be a good husband to you!

You've grown, Fabiola. I can't believe it. Come. Let me look you up.

I will give you fifty dola oos for one hour!

She tried to pay them no attention, hurrying past with her head down, items from the shop held tightly against her body. She walked past their lustful beckoning, the liquor on their breath, and the women who watched from afar but who said nothing. She walked as cars and buses whizzed by, the occasional teenage boy hanging from their windows shouting, "Vouzan! Vouzan!"

She walked as the heat worked up a sweat on her back and temples, her ebony skin combusting in the sun. The world for a girl like her growing up in Haiti could be intimidating, but this was as it was every evening. There was comfort in the discomfort of this busy town full of poor and wealthy, foreign and local, righteous and wicked. There was comfort in the constant hum of traffic. Behind her, kids shouted as they walked the same route she did. She found that comforting as well. There was even comfort in the weight of male gazes that gradually settled on her as she grew into a woman.

As she walked, something disturbed her comfort. Her heartbeat outpaced her quickening breath. She paused her stride and noticed the world that was previously alive with lecherous men, rowdy boys, judging women, and the other norms of the city were still. Everything had gone quiet. Her legs were no longer moving. She turned back to the building she'd just passed. It danced like grass on a breezy day. The road around it buckled and broke into pieces. She looked to the distance. The town had not gone quiet at all; it was being swallowed by something colossal and oppressive.

Fabiola screamed as the comfortable sounds of the city cracked and the earth shook. She turned and ran the only route she knew, down the hill, to the road that twisted from right to left to right again before ending at the stretch of houses and her home.

* * *

The earthquake hit Haiti at 4:48 pm local time on January 12, 2010, just outside of Port-au-Prince. It was a 7.0 magnitude quake that devastated the city and surrounding region, killing approximately 300,000 human beings. It was followed by aftershocks and a tsunami that caused even more damage. Over a decade later, the country, its people, and government are still recovering.

The earthquake came just as I was getting settled into my new official role at Ushahidi. We made software that allowed remote direction of first responders through digital maps and cell phones. Imagine an app like Google Maps or Waze but instead of reports of traffic incidents, the maps would dynamically populate with reports of crisis, incident, or crime. These reports came from people who had directly experienced the event. In the case of the Haiti quakes, through a series of partnerships, our maps were being populated in real-time from the victims, their family, and their friends.

The work was simple, but exciting. Wherever there was a major disaster, we were among the first organizations contacted. Sometimes we weren't even involved directly, but our data centers would send us alerts that our code had been downloaded by others and deployed to respond to some far-away tragedy we weren't even aware of.

While I was with Ushahidi, I was moonlighting. I still had to manage my staff at Appfrica in Uganda. In the months prior, the folks at Appfrica had been asked to work with aid workers to establish cell phone networks at refugee camps in the northernmost part of Uganda in a town called Gulu. Their work would become pivotal to Ushahidi's response to the quake in Haiti.

Gulu was the home to large groups of people displaced by political unrest in Democratic Republic of Congo, Rwanda, and other, less stable, parts of Uganda. They came seeking asylum but since they lacked proper identification, money, family, jobs, and other resources, the Ugandan government put the refugees in camps far away from the major arteries of the country. This continued until the asylum-seekers could either be routed back to where they came from, or to some other country entirely.

The refugees arrived with nothing but the clothes on their backs and their mobile phones. One thing most Africans kept was some type of mobile phone. In many parts of Africa, the price to receive a phone call was practically zero. When these displaced people had no money to refill their mobile carrier plans, they could still receive phone calls from all over the world. Even if they had no home or money, their mobile phones were essential. It was their only way to stay connected to family members who might also be displaced or who lived abroad. This worked as long as their phones did. The biggest commodity in refugee camps after the phones themselves was the electricity needed to power them.

The cell phone towers worked using software and technologies put together by an organization called FrontlineSMS. It was their expertise doing this cell tower work in infrastructure-starved Gulu that made their work highly relevant in Haiti, which had had its own infrastructure decimated by the quakes. Frontline became the missing link that Ushahidi needed to be useful in areas where there was no mobile coverage. Recognizing the rising population of the camps, the abundance of cell phones, and low coverage in the area, the team at Frontline worked to extend coverage using unorthodox means. It was too expensive to put new cellphone towers in these areas. For one, the refugees were coming from different places, and not all their phones could use the same mobile carriers. Cell phone companies made money by leasing or selling their equipment to other mobile carriers. For multiple carriers to agree to share infrastructure costs would require areas where users were in close proximity.

In a refugee camp, people came from all over the continent, but the fact that so little money was being spent by these users in the area presented a problem. Who would pay the cell phone companies? Even though inbound calls were free, outbound calls had a cost. In fact, they were expensive. Most cellphone carriers in Africa made money when users called out, unlike in the U.S. and other countries where both callers pay to connect. With poor refugees, this wouldn't be possible. So, the economics of a major telecom serving refugees by building new towers wasn't attractive at all. From their perspective, there wasn't enough money to be made.

The team at Frontline proposed a solution: "We can use cheap computers and open-source software to create what is essentially a pirate cell phone network. If we marry that with line-of-sight wifi dishes, we can help direct their calls over long distances. It'll increase mobile coverage for the camps, at much lower costs."

It was called a pirate network. Using makeshift cellphone towers cobbled together from spare computer parts, these collaborations between Frontline, Ushahidi, and Appfrica served as the inspiration for another collaboration, dubbed Project 4636, in Haiti. Project 4636 would go on to be cited in many academic and government journals for its role in innovating disaster response in remote places.

In order for our team to get messages to map, analyze, and route back to first responders, we needed a way to receive data. We usually relied on cellphone networks but in Haiti most were down. We needed an alternative network to get the messages flowing again. The software was born from widescale human crises and breakdowns in civil peace. By design, it was made to help with disasters. The Haiti earthquake was by far the most devastating call-to-action we had faced to date. Yet here we were working shoulder to shoulder with the U.S. Army, Red Cross, and other humanitarian organizations to help orchestrate their response.

Some organizations challenged the accuracy of the data the platform collected. It was a valid concern for any company involved in the lives and well-being of other humans. Following 4636, a curious employee at the European Commission's Joint Research Centre plotted Ushahidi reports against satellite maps of building damage and concluded that our crowdsourced data actually did correlate with the satellite imagery. This was a moment of validation from the highest authorities in the world. Our platform had serious merit, now. Prior to that report, we were an easy target for critics and skeptics. They pointed out that anyone could put data on a map, and that doing so didn't make what we did useful, accurate, or interesting.

We were, at times, defensive. We argued back that we were tapping into unreachable populations and shifting paradigms of trust from unreachable institutions to individuals. Was crisis mapping always going to be useful? Not in every scenario. But what tool is always useful? You need it when you do and put it down when you don't. What the ECJRC study did was give our methods credibility in a community of hardline statisticians, risk assessors, and government organizations around the globe. It was the co-sign we needed from an institution that was essentially saying, "Hold on, maybe these African kids are on to something!"

My responsibility at Ushahidi was to build systems that addressed how much people should trust the data our software contained. In order to process the torrent of real-time feeds from mobile phones, I needed to analyze and verify the accuracy of what was being reported. There were three areas of credibility to solve for: statistical, programmatic, and logistical.

To address statistical concerns, I spent a lot of time working with research institutions and universities. Prior to the pervasiveness of artificial intelligence, I relied on peer-reviewed studies from computer scientists working on the frontier of machine learning. With programmers, it was all about writing and releasing good code that could be easily run and vetted. For our partners, it was about ease of integration with the tools they already used. I suggested that we move away from frameworks that limited the sophistication of our code. We needed to move towards best practices with streaming real-time data like Twitter and Facebook were doing. In the early days of the earthquake, we were seeing hundreds of text messages per second and thousands per minute. If our goal was to process that kind of information, we needed more computing power at our disposal. We would need maps that were as fast and efficient as Google's were.

Major humanitarian crises were the canvas, our job was to complete the picture for first-responders.

It was nearly 48 hours into our initial response to the fallout in Haiti. I was far away from the rest of the Ushahidi team, at my home in Kampala, banging away on my laptop coordinating a team of digital volunteers spread all over the globe. From there, Nairobi, and elsewhere, we coordinated people who were on the ground in Haiti. We worked together to fix software bugs and build new software features that were needed in the moment. It was evening local time, 10,000 miles away where I sat near overwhelmed at my desk, near tears. I struggled with the weight of lives hanging in the balance while struggling to remember basic computer science. I was entirely self-taught. I was used to improvising, hacking, figuring things out. Hacking. In this case, the wrong move cost valuable time that might lead to an errant real-world decision – a cascading failure.

I felt we were moving too slow, not capturing or delivering data fast enough to the people who needed it in Haiti. My imagination ran wild.

People are dying.

· *Are we making the right calls?*

Are they dying because of bugs in our code?

If my next code merge doesn't work, will that be the difference between an emergency worker finding someone trapped in a collapsed building or a person's last breath?

As I reviewed the lines of code contributed by our staff members, my fingers trembled. There was so much pressure. I wasn't even the person on staff responsible for the most critical work and I was still stressed. We worked 18-hour days those weeks. I was sure to place my mobile phone under my pillow when I slept in case I got an urgent call from Haiti or the U.S. where there was a six-hour time difference. We had to be the experts, the champions, the cautious and the risk-takers all at once. It was a Sisyphean task, processing a data set that grew by tens of thousands of messages every time I hit refresh. We were swimming in data. Perhaps more apropos, drowning in it.

Drowning in rivers of data.

The solution we put in place in response to the Haiti quakes was a collaboration between our company and others, including Haitian tech companies, the U.S. Army, non-government humanitarian organizations, the U.S. Department of State, local Haitian telecommunication companies, and radio stations. We all helped each other respond to the mass destruction and carnage in Haiti. Meanwhile, from thousands of miles away in Kenya and Uganda, we watched the dots on the map move in unison. It reminded me of the game that in Africa we loved so much. Soccer.

The beautiful game.

Desmond Tutu once referred to soccer as bigger than religion for Africans. On our laptops nested in the suburbs of Nairobi and Kampala my colleagues and I played our small part by helping write the digital playbook the first responders in Haiti were putting to action. It was radical collaboration at its finest. We became part of something bigger than any sport, technology, or company.

The earthquake itself and the aftermath — aftershocks that rocked the region again and the tsunami that broke after the quake — would go on to claim the lives of between 200,000 and 300,000 people. In an unclassified email sent shortly after the earthquake, U.S. Department of State employee Katie Stanton wrote:

> *"Working with the US State Department they were able to get the 4636 number that had previously been used for weather infor-*

mation in Haiti [...] The team launched the SMS-based emergency information system with the support of the Thomson Reuters Foundation and technology disaster relief organization inSTEDD five days after the quake. The handful of radio stations still operating in Haiti at the time helped spread the word, bringing attention to how our emergency short code could be used. People could text to report where they were, who they were looking for, or if they needed help [...] The US Department of State helped publicize the number, announcing it via their official Twitter account and elsewhere."

* * *

I met VP of Search Products of Google, Marisa Mayer, at a conference in Long Beach prior to her becoming CEO at Yahoo. Along with executives at Facebook, Mayer expressed support for our company. I saw her chatting with a group of attendees and walked up to introduce myself.

"Oh! Ushahidi! Love Ushahidi. You guys do great work," she said. "You've started a big conversation about what more we could be doing around disaster response."

Both Facebook and Google had recognized the opportunity that humanitarian response and community organizing represented for their own growing businesses. Google, to differentiate itself from Microsoft, prided itself on supporting the open-source code community we were members of. We would meet with them and other large tech companies on more than one occasion to share ideas, advise, or collaborate with their engineers. When you have billions of people using your apps every day, your platform becomes a proverbial town square for software companies everywhere. Doing nothing during these urgent human-scale disasters was a corporate risk. No company wanted the PR of appearing to be indifferent to a crisis. *Doing more* meant changing their products.

The crisis alerts you now receive when you are using Google or Facebook about school shootings, floods, hurricanes, and other tragedies, evolved from the discussions with teams like ours between 2009 and 2012. In fact, people in our volunteer community would go to work for both companies on things like crisis mapping, public alerts, and localization. Prior to that, the only organizations concerned with breaking news about crisis events were journalists. Companies like Ushahidi and Frontline had made it impossible for tech companies much larger than us to ignore disaster response.

If we could do it from Africa, they could do it from Mountain View.

This wasn't as simple as putting the news in front of everyone on the platform. Much like these companies did with digital advertising, crisis messages had to be targeted. They had to be put in front of the most relevant individuals and communities at the right moments. On a global scale, there's too much happening all the time to notify every person of everything happening. That would result in notification fatigue.

People in Fresno probably didn't need to know about a landslide in Indonesia. They might if they had friends or relatives in Indonesia. This meant messages had to be prioritized and filtered. Other times, those boundaries had to be blurred. Mass shootings in America might be relevant to people around the world because the place where the event happened was connected to family, friends, and colleagues.

Facebook also recognized these alerts served more than people's curiosity. What's more important to the users of social media users than the safety of the people most important to them? These were dynamics my colleagues and I knew very well. In 2011, we launched our first platform allowing people and first responders to check in to events and locations. Around the same time, apps like Foursquare and SCVNGR were on the rise and we recognized the things they were doing to simplify and speed up documenting the location of people and things. You can now check in as safe during critical events on Facebook. What's more important to your friends than knowing that you've been marked safe?

On these apps people could leave digital notes that essentially said, *I was here and these are my thoughts about this place.*

Waypoints.

Memories.

Invisible connections made visible.

Those notes would be digitally tied to physical locations in the real-world: restaurants, bars, clubs, hotels, etc. This creates what you might describe as a digital cloud around specific places that allows future visitors to read through the messages of past users. I was a longtime fan of GPS technology and an avid user of these location apps. Internally, at Ushahidi, I pushed my colleagues to build on these concepts. How could we let people check in to emergency situations? How could we help them share information with others who needed that information either during the event or after? The products we developed in this space built upon each other, beginning with my team's work on a product we released called Crowdmap. This led to an ever-evolving roster of solutions that iterated on this basic premise following my departure from the company. Projects like Crisis.net, TenFour, RollCall, and Ping.

We were cautious. When the big companies came knocking, people in the open-source world were naturally skeptical of their intent. They had billions of dollars in funding, highly paid software engineers and a seemingly infinite ability to scale their products at a moment's notice. We on the other hand had a core team of fifteen or so, and a few hundred volunteers who only worked with us when they were available.

Our products were mostly useful for other technical people. Those who were highly proactive, capable of fixing software bugs, and who could do their own troubleshooting. We lacked the stability and reliability these bigger companies could offer. Our products were also open source. Big companies could contribute their teams and resources to helping us improve our open-source solutions, but when it came to shipping products of their own, they needed to own everything. They wrote proprietary code that often couldn't be shared. Out of necessity, Google and Facebook began to create their own solutions for humanitarian problems.

When an Egyptian Google engineer was kidnapped during a youth movement protesting the country's government, a lot more people at the company became aware of the need for innovations in safety technology. Suddenly, open-source tech orgs like ours were a little less interesting. We couldn't really help them at scale. We didn't have the resources they did. Google responded swiftly, deploying solutions like Google PersonFinder (which helped families reunite during times of crisis) and Google 2FA (two-factor authentication, which helped activists and corporate users better protect access to their Google accounts). Other open-source tech companies found that they were being steered to pursue for-profit models as well. The movement had been co-opted by capitalists. For a while, everything was free and open. Guys at LAN parties willing to work for pizza. That all ended when there was money to be made.

When I first began working on tech projects like this, the internet was a very different place. Then, it was a thriving environment for experimentation that built upon ideas born and shared by others. That was the spirit of open source. Freely building on each other's work. From open source came open protocols for sharing data between different software applications. When Twitter first launched, large amounts of raw data could be pulled from its platform freely and cheaply.

Ushahidi had been heavy users of Twitter's real-time data feeds, which allowed my team to pull messages from all over the world that we could sift through to discover information related to crisis events. This allowed us to operate faster and more accurately than many journalists who hadn't yet figured out how to manage real-time feeds of information. Twitter was a commercial company that had to make money. Their corporate messaging up to that point had been about remaining the world's premier source for open, free-flowing information.

In many ways, they were like us, except they were focused on commercial uses for real-time data versus philanthropic ones. At its first annual developer conference in 2010, Twitter announced new pricing tiers for its firehose of tweets. Unlike us, they were now aggressively pursuing growth in revenue to appease their new venture capital backers. What we used to be able to get for free, we would now have to pay them for. On the cheap end, it was going to cost hundreds of thousands of dollars per project.

My head dropped.

The world's best source for open, real-time, global messages had just slammed the door on us.

#TheNairobiReport

"But her emails..."
—American meme circa 2016

The morning of August 29, 2007, a PDF file, 3.909093 megabytes in size, with cryptographic identity SHA256 eb7d9f08f73c4d-88c6e84002f7b22f56c36171cc7318d6b307d6a 01a749cb177 was leaked to journalists around the world. The email heading read *Findings of Graft in the Kenyan Government*. The document was also released online via a number of early whistleblower websites, among them a then-little-known site called Wikileaks.

Wikileaks was an organization that promoted itself as a platform for whistleblowers. It called for the to release sensitive information via its platform, securely and expediently without fear of retribution. Their methods were fairly straightforward: users emailed documents that revealed high-level corruption or scandal, and the Wikileaks team would publish them. First, they said, they researched the allegations to determine their veracity, then scrubbed them of any metadata that might reveal the identity of the leakers. Once sanitized, they released them to journalists to amplify whatever information the leaks contained. The documents would be uploaded to the organization's internal servers, distributed via torrent, or emailed directly to reporters within major news organizations. By then, the organization had made a controversial business from collecting and releasing highly sensitive information. Leaks of information exposed crimes and brought down governments.

To ensure the veracity of the files being distributed, the Wikileaks platform maintained a directory listing. It contained information about each document's file size and type, cryptographic hash values, and other information that could be used to ensure the files were identical to the originals and had not been altered materially. This meant that journalists who received the files from third-party sources had a way to ensure they were looking at original versions of the leaked docs and not manipulated copies.

John Githongo was the whistleblower at the center of this exposé of rampant corruption within the Kenyan President's administration. Githongo's official role was the President's personal advisor on Anti-Corruption and Governance. He had been brought in to expose any corruption that might implicate the former administration. His investigation resulted in numerous allegations compiled into a dossier that was delivered to the sitting President, Mwai Kibaki. In the report, Kibaki's predecessor Moi was said to have used a system of shell companies to embezzle more than three billion dollars from the Kenyan government. When Githongo exposed this alleged corruption in 2004 by bringing it to the attention of the administration, it was hailed by some as a breakthrough. He intended it to be the beginning of a major asset-tracing and recovery operation to bring back the billions looted by Moi's collaborators. However, that would never happen.

The report was not released as originally intended.

It was suppressed. Years later, the results of a second investigation alleged wrongdoing by President Kibaki himself, the same President who requested the first investigation. Githongo had implicated Kibaki, the man who had hired him, in what would become known as the Anglo Leasing Scandal. A second investigation suggested that companies controlled by friends of President Kibaki were bidding for government contracts deliberately inflated so money could be siphoned in ways that would seem legitimate. As President, Kibaki could manipulate which companies won the tenders. Once under the control of his cronies, they could direct money wherever they desired. In this way, State finances were allegedly laundered to buy real-estate holdings and privately held companies around the world. One of these companies was called Anglo Leasing. It alone had been awarded $770 million dollars in contracts. John's research found that the company didn't even exist in any operational form. It was a shell company.

The second dossier was perhaps even more scandalous than the first. It revealed just how widespread and deep-rooted corruption in the Kenyan government was. It wasn't just one President or a single party abusing power. The report became an indictment against the entire Kenyan political elite. When those indicted attempted to claim Githongo's allegations were baseless, he released audio recordings to substantiate his claims. Githongo's exposé led to threats to his safety. He was formally exiled from the country, and the asset recovery operation abruptly ended.

These threats were what motivated his sudden departure from his home in Kenya shortly after producing the report. His exit was recommended by his friends at Kroll & Associates, the auditing firm he worked with to expose the corruption. Kroll wasn't a stranger to offering financial services to the elite and at protecting high-value assets. Githongo was now one of those assets. While it was his work with Kroll that got him into the situation in the first place, their people now worked to get him safely to London. Once there, he was to rendezvous with a Reuters reporter to continue exposing the corruption.

Once in London, Githongo remotely resigned from his post in Kenya. He then watched as the reports he had helped prepare were leaked to the media. They found their way to media outlets 100 days before Kibaki was up for re-election in Kenya in late 2007. The leaks included the original investigation of Moi as well as the Kibaki dossier. As a result of the publicized allegations, the two former Presidents announced an unexpected alliance, lest the allegations of corruption bring them both down. The public reaction to these scandals, as well as accusations of election tampering on Kibaki's part, was explosive. During Kenya's 2007 elections, Kibaki's opponent Raila Odinga took to the radio waves and called on his supporters in Kenya to protest what they saw as an unfair election. *Burn it down!* The protests turned to violence. First with the police who tried to keep peace, then with fellow citizens as groups turned on each other along ethnic lines.

Thousands were injured, killed, or displaced as they rushed to escape the violence in Nairobi and surrounding regions. Looting and destruction of property were rampant across the country. Kenya hadn't seen violence like this in over a decade. To end the ongoing violence, a coalition government was established. The constitution was changed to create an official role in the Administration for Odinga. He would become Prime Minister while Kibaki remained President. Githongo remained in exile. His reports were damaging but in the end, they proved existential only to his own career in politics.

Even though the actual leaker remained anonymous, threats were targeted towards any individual alleged to have been involved. Not knowing who to blame for the leak just meant those implicated in Kenya directed their anger towards the one person who they knew for a fact was involved, Githongo. It was his report. Guilty or not, he was the high-profile name they could identify and target. His allegations were the root of their problems. Journalists referred to him as courageous and heroic for attempting to take on corruption at the expense of his own livelihood and safety. The Kenyan government pointed to his refuge in Britain as proof that he had been a spy.

If the internet itself is a Petri dish for experimentation and the exchange of ideas, John Githongo would soon find himself *patient zero* for an era of leaks that irrevocably changed the course of government in his country. These new types of targeted, well-timed information leaks were to have a swift, measurable impact on government, and the lives of millions.

* * *

I reflected on all of this the morning of November 29th, 2010, as I stood on an escalator carrying me to the first floor of The Guardian headquarters at Kings Place, London, U.K. The Guardian was one of the most prolific news organizations in the world, founded in 1821 as The Manchester Guardian. It would later become the home to Glen Greenwald, who would go on to found *The Intercept* with Pierre Omidyar, the billionaire founder of eBay. Pierre, ironically, was also the patron of the company I was representing on my visit. Specifically, my team's expertise processing unwieldy rivers of data was now becoming essential to every global news organization. We were experts at turning location data and people data into the types of insights that news organizations needed. We were the experts at a time where there were few others. Even more daunting, journalists had to verify the reports culled from millions of questionable sources. Then they had the task of parsing it all, attempting to turn it into comprehensible stories for readers.

The Guardian had been following our work, covering our company at many points during our evolution. For this meeting, they invited two of our staff to demo our platform for their editorial team. The goal was to brainstorm with them on how they might better process information from day to day. The day didn't go quite as planned, though. The staff at the Guardian was about to face an information crisis of a different type.

This happened to be the same day that Wikileaks released thousands of diplomatic cables consisting of the behind-the-scenes communication of world leaders. This massive leak was coordinated through journalists who partnered with them, housed at various news outlets around the world. A man named Daithi, a staff member at The Guardian, had been tasked with being our escort at their office for the day. He explained how Guardian journalists and others around the world worked with Wikileaks representatives well in advance to verify some of the more controversial leaks to come. A team of technologists at the Guardian had built a platform to codify it all, digitizing it line-by-line, in order to make it easier for reporters and the public alike to search. The various newsrooms also worked together to keep the leaks quiet. They needed to synchronize the release globally. It was an act of solidarity, so no one organization got credit for the scoop. Unbeknownst to me and my team, this was all planned to release Sunday night, just as we were touching down in London from Kenya. By morning UK time, the American news media was exploding with coverage. It was the largest release of confidential documents to the public in history—an event that would become known as *Cablegate*.

Though we weren't affiliated directly, the volunteer communities behind Ushahidi and Wikileaks overlapped quite a bit. Members of both were adamant about transparency and freedom of information. Like us, their origins were in Kenya, where one of their first reports originated. They were also champions of open-source software. Some advocated that the public's need for open-source information trumped any need for political privacy and state secrets. They, like us, aimed to give a voice to the voiceless, challenge corruption, and change the way information flowed in the world. In fact, it was a line Erik bellowed frequently: "We want to change the way information flows in the world!" I'd have to remind him we borrowed that mission from Wikileaks. It wasn't just mutual admiration. The Guardian itself made the comparison on November 29th, 2010, writing:

> *We are at a pivotal moment where the visionaries at the vanguard of a global digital age are clashing with those who are desperate to control what we know. WikiLeaks is the guerrilla front in a global movement for greater transparency and participation. There are projects like Ushahidi that use social networking to create maps where locals can report incidents of violence that challenge the official version of events. There are activists seeking to free official data so that citizens can see, for example, government spending in detail.*

Other publications followed suit, recognizing the similarities. Wikileaks was not yet viewed in the light they are now. In fact, the world didn't quite know what to make of it then. Were they hackers? Were they journalists? The tide of public opinion would eventually turn against them. At the time, they were still champions of transparency. That said, if we at Ushahidi were the media darlings, the goody-two-shoes of cyber hacktivism, Wikileaks were the bad boys who tested authority.

"We sat on this for months," Daithi told me. "This many global editorial teams working together, collaborating to scrub and verify every email and every document, all in order to mutually time the release for this morning. I've never seen anything like it."

"That's pretty amazing," I said. I was intrigued. I had heard so much about Wikileaks. This was a propitious moment. To be at the two companies worked together, orchestrating their own beautiful game. A two-hundred-year-old newspaper and the organization who claimed to steal secrets.

Daithi showed me how the various groups worked together to index and analyze the leaked data. They had created a massive database that other journalists, and later the public, could quickly sift through. This made it easier to understand all the information the database contained. It also made it easier to surface interesting stories from the archives. Essentially it was a search engine like Google, but contained only the leaked cables.

"It really highlights the need for more programmers to work with our editorial teams. People who can program, analyze data, and editorialize it. Your team seems to be doing that well; that's why we invited you," he said. The staff at The Guardian were among the first to recognize the need for data scientists like me in the newsroom. "Looking for a job?"

I smiled. It was an honor but the I felt that my colleagues and I had only scratched the surface of our own potential as an organization. It was too early to jump ship, "I don't think so but this is interesting."

"Yes, I'm afraid we're not going to have the audience I thought we would for you to present your group's software today. I was going to bring in the whole editorial staff to watch your presentation…" He looked towards a conference room where people in suits huddled over a phone and watched global headlines about the leak scroll by on a flat-screen TV.

"…but as you can see, their attention is elsewhere."

#OpenSources

"Agitation or excitement; flutter. Twitter."
—Nick Bilton, American journalist

"Can't say we've heard from many data companies from Africa," a gentleman in the room quipped. Everyone chuckled. He was the guy calling the shots. I watched the eyes of the people in the room. Theirs were fixated on his. No one stopped laughing until he did. "So, show us what you got!"

I stood at the center of a circular conference room at Lockheed Martin. Some thirty officials had convened, flanking me on all sides. Another member of the Ushahidi staff was in the corner, taking notes. She and I agreed that I'd kick things off to talk about our technical capabilities, then pass to her to handle logistics and next steps. I felt like an imposter who had somehow hacked my way into the room. The square jawed stoicism of blank-faced men in suits was a work environment I wasn't used to. For software developers, it wasn't uncommon to show up wearing shorts, flip-flops, and a rock band tee shirt. For this meeting, I bought a suit and tie and practiced my posture in the mirror. These were straight-backed career military men like my dad. To close a deal with them, I had to look the part.

"We're the leader in the market. In Africa, we represent virtually the whole market," I said. Everyone laughed again. In all fairness, I couldn't think of any other location data companies that had emerged from the continent. We were the market.

Innovation isn't about being the smartest guy in the room. It's not about being the most accomplished or best funded. When the whole world is looking at a problem one way, the person who looks from the other direction becomes the genius. The fresh perspective becomes the most valuable one.

I was a dropout film major who threw away a career in film and music to go on random adventures around the world. I hadn't done anything particularly special when it came to this technology. The team at Ushahidi hadn't either. In the community of *open-source* innovators, it wasn't even the custom to claim ownership if you had. Innovation happened as part of a greater collective. You didn't need to be individually brilliant; anyone could make rather mediocre contributions to a movement that was more powerful because it represented a collective. It didn't make individual contributions matter any less. Without the participation of many, there is no open-source movement. That was the point.

Radical collaboration.

The people at Lockheed were infinitely better staffed and re-sourced than we were. In theory, they didn't need us at all. We just happened to be looking from the other direction. We had to. Africa was the other direction.

"Here in the military, you call it open-source intelligence. We call it crowdsourcing but it's the same thing," I told them. "We organize and map the data. The hardest part for us is verifying it all."

In the military-industrial world, they used the term "open source" differently than we did. To them, an open source was an individual who was unknown, unverified, and while not neces-sarily a threat, not to be trusted. In our world at Ushahidi, open source meant software that was written to be shared freely with the masses. The crowdsourced data we worked with was the type of data the folks at Lockheed had been taught not to trust at all. I explained that what I had been working on in my role at Ushahi-di was a thesis for verifying real-time information collected from untrusted individuals.

"How do you do that? Verify the reports? Is that what the little dots on the maps are?" the man asked dismissively.

"Those are called nodes, sir. The size of each node represents the number of people affected by an event in that location. The color represents the category, in other words, what they have been af-fected by."

"How do you verify…"

"Our users send us information however they can. From Twitter, text message, Facebook, or web forms—whatever it takes. The goal is to get some information versus none."

"Doesn't that mean some of the information is going to be spam or fake?"

"Yes, it does. We anticipate that. We've got filters to separate the wheat from the chaff, if you will. The first layer is that we prioritize known phone numbers. If we recognize the number from a person we know we can trust, it's because they've provided quality information in the past. The second layer is contextual. It means the information came from someone physically close to the event itself. We can deduce their proximity using metadata we get from the mobile network providers. The third layer is relational. If we don't know this individual, who else does? The fourth and final layer of data we use, combines the previous three into new metadata that our systems use to make decisions. A contextual meta-layer.

"What does it all add up to?" I continued. "Every message we receive that doesn't pass the above criteria gets filtered out. For those messages, we have human volunteers comb through to be sure nothing of importance was missed. They then manually check each message. They use their own experience and knowledge of the situation to study photos and video. They individually determine if it was misclassified and retrieve it if it was. If there was a message of importance missed, they ascend it in our queue."

"How long does all this take?"

"Near real-time, sir. In a crisis, speed and trust are priorities. The focus on accuracy and incremental improvement is ongoing. By working in this manner, there are always trustworthy messages to display while the laborious task of dealing with unknowns can happen in as much time as is required."

The room was quiet.

Walking into a room full of career military men and rocket scientists requires a different type of code switching. I didn't have the academic background to impress them, but I knew I was able to work in areas they couldn't. I was able to look from the other direction, something their superiors often didn't allow. They seemed impressed with our methods.

"Any questions?"

Hands shot into the air. I pointed to a gentleman across the room, "Sir."

"Are you sure you're not looking for a job?"

It was after our work around Haiti that I was invited by both the Pentagon and Lockheed Martin (LHCO) to discuss Ushahidi's involvement in the 4636 Haiti response. As open and inclusive as our company was, we wouldn't take all meetings. Interaction with Federal agencies and contractors was tenuous. Some of our most active users were considered dissidents in their home countries around the world. An activist in one country might be considered an antagonist in another. Who the heroes and villains were depended entirely on perspective and goals. Incidents where the U.S. government decided to support one side might put us at odds with our own community if they supported the other. As a corporate mandate, we tried to remain as neutral as possible.

It's not uncommon for the U.S. to side with governments to squash resistance movements deemed a threat. Therefore, if we did choose sides, it would be impossible for us to be on the right side all the time. We chose to avoid most government-related work, especially military work. Plus, the products we made were free and open source. Our stance was anyone could download and use our products. We didn't need to be involved directly.

We needed to maintain neutrality. After some deliberation, the team and I initially decided to turn down the invitation from the Pentagon. Working with the U.S. military-industrial complex while trying to support activists in Libya, Egypt, Syria and other countries wasn't going to work. It undermined our open forum. Also, we didn't want to be accused of weaponizing our software against anyone.

I also recognized the importance of being at the table. "If you aren't at the table, you're on the menu," was an aphorism often repeated by my African friends. After all, they could relate.

Following World War II, the continent was carved up without regard to ethnic and linguistic differences. The dividing lines that now form the continent's many countries were arbitrarily decided by European leaders at The Berlin Conference in 1885. No African leader had a meaningful say in where those borders fell. No Africans were in the room in Berlin.

Africa was not at the table, it was on the menu, and the World leaders in attendance were starving.

I knew if we didn't at least participate with some of the stakeholders in government responsible for coordination and response to wide-scale human incident, we too would end up on the menu. Lockheed just wanted a presentation. They hadn't yet decided if they wanted to deploy our software. I convinced the team that they were worth at least talking to. That much we could agree to do, surely. It didn't commit us to continue working with them. If we were part of their conversations, we could better control outcomes that affected us and causes we were empathetic to.

The other reason for pushing for this meeting was the pressure to increase the earned revenue our company was bringing in. These were still the early years of the organization and we were trying to grow to meet increasing demand. Although Ushahidi was a non-profit first, we were a tech company second. Our funders wanted us to supplement grant funding with earned revenues from products and services. I'd learned from friends working at groups like Booz Allen and Deloitte that a single consulting agreement with a group like Lockheed could easily net between $50,000 and $500,000 dollars. Sometimes more. We'd have the opportunity to compete on bids for several contracts with them. So, in March 2011, I visited Lockheed headquarters in Bethesda, Maryland. They wanted to learn about the upstart powerful data platform from East Africa. I was eager to share our story.

The discussion was surprisingly interactive with lots of questions from the room. I came in with the perception that powerful people can't relate to the rest of us. This wasn't the case here. These guys certainly knew their stuff, but after years working at the ground floor of the emerging data industry, I was surprised at how much we knew that they didn't. We had been looking the other way, when they hadn't. It made us the experts in areas they'd yet to investigate. To them, our crowdsourcing methods might as well have been voodoo.

How do the dots get on the maps?

You mean you just ask people to send you their data and they do it? Why?

We get our surveillance data from our satellites. Do you have your own satellites?

It took about an hour to answer their questions.

The Ushahidi platform expanded. The general purpose of these products we made was not dissimilar to how people used mapping apps like Waze to avoid traffic. Think of it sort of like Twitter, but with every message displayed on a map instead of a time-line. Our maps had Waze like indicators of which messages were most important. Our team were the contributors to many of the open-source technologies that would find their way into mapping apps like Waze. In fact, many of our former employees and contributors went on to work at Google, Waze, and Uber. Some are still there. We didn't necessarily invent those technologies, but neither did the big tech companies. It was all one big radical collaboration around location, filtering, real-time data processing, and mapping.

The mapping tech that now powers many of these technologies still leverages the open-source components we helped create. Collaborative software development is people all over the world contributing lines of code. Line by line. It was a beautiful game. Using algorithms to map the best routes to people in distress is the same concept now used by any person who has ever heard Waze say, *"I've found a better route."* I called it adaptive dispatch, automating directions and updating a route in real time.

Crowdsourcing was hailed as a new way of organizing people and culture. My peers and I made the tools that helped people from all over the world self-organize and respond to disaster, election meddling, and oppression. We essentially helped our users do two things: organize people and the things people were concerned about.

Towards the end of 2010, I was flown to San Francisco to speak to engineers about data analysis at Twitter HQ. Twitter was already huge and spending money like crazy. This was before they were the publicly-traded company they are today, but long enough into the company's life that they were barely considered a startup anymore. Their offices were located on the top floor of a building on 795 Folsom Street, south of Market Street, an area they called SoMa. Twitter was subletting the office from AOL. As

I approached the door to their office, I stepped over half-a-dozen or so homeless people sleeping in the inlet that led to the lobby.

Welcome to San Francisco.

It took some getting used to being back. Abroad I was the American Black, a man with a different shade who was full of ideas and impact. In the U.S., I was back to being an African American. In any case, I was other-first. A woman in the lobby asked if I was in the right place. When I told her I was there to meet some people in the C-suite, she called up to verify. As I sat there, she eyed me suspiciously until I got on the elevator. In San Francisco, which was becoming overwhelmingly homogenous and affluent, I found code switching to be pointless. It reminded me of the suspicion NGOs had of African businessmen and women. Cautious and skeptical for no clear reason. I made no attempt to mold myself to the room. These were some of the wealthiest people in America. One out of every 11,600 people in San Fran was a billionaire. It was a sort of bubble of wealth, tech, and business. The least I could do was make them the tiniest bit uncomfortable, to remind them there was still a country around them. I borrowed a lesson from my old friend, Leila Chirayath. I wouldn't adapt to their rooms; their rooms would have to adapt to me.

My presentation at Twitter HQ was detailed and technical. I spoke about my methods as the architect behind the data analysis platform we were building at Ushahidi called SwiftRiver. Ushahidi mapped data, SwiftRiver analyzed it. Together they worked like a petri dish and a microscope: one collected and presented the data while the other observed and digested it. It was the analysis part that many companies were struggling with. Before you can organize information, you need to know what it's telling you. In crisis scenarios, there is no time to slow down; it has to be analyzed as quickly as possible. This was something Twitter's engineers were experts at. I gave a brief talk and went back and forth with their teams for an hour or so. Working sessions like this were called *teatime*. A guest speaker was invited to visit the company and speak to its staff over lunch or snacks. It gave their software developers the opportunity to exchange knowledge with outsiders, learn different topics, and helped break up the monotony of their day.

The problems Twitter was facing were problems the data world knows all too well now. First, how to organize the torrents of information, flowing through their platform. Literally every second there were hundreds of thousands of new tweets posted by people from all over the world. Every message might cover different topics. In the early days of Twitter, one user, a young technologist named Chris Messina, had proposed a solution rooted in an old programming format called *microformats*. By prefacing certain words in each message with the 'hash' sign (also known as the pound or number sign), users could have a means of assigning categories for their messages. This would allow the sender to distinguish certain words in the text as the active keywords. This might be used, for example, to help people identify groups they belonged to or events they were attending. These tags quickly evolved beyond just group distinction to identify the intended topic of the message or funny keywords the message sender wanted to add (ex. #lol #wtf). They would become known as hashtags.

> *How do you feel about using # (pound)*
> *for groups? As in #barcamp [msg]?*
> **—Chris Messina, ("@factoryjoe"), August 23, 2007**

The power of the hashtag was that it helped make the Sisyphean amount of information flowing through Twitter slightly easier to organize. When a person wanted to search for a specific message that mentioned a certain word like "bar" or "camp," they might surface millions of unrelated messages. Instead of 'I went to the barcamp last week in Nevada," it might return a message that said, "I camped out at the bar last week in Nevada." Even though both messages contain the right keywords, the second one has a completely different context. If the message used hashtags (like #barcamp), this unrelated content wouldn't surface at all. Only messages specifically containing the hashtag would be discovered. Hashtags were a way of embedding context into text messages without relying on metadata or other software.

The problem was that hashtags placed the burden on the user to type them. If they forgot to add a hashtag, their message would still be filtered out. It was a search and discovery problem, one we shared.

Hashtags would become essential to our team at Ushahidi. When an environmental disaster or conflict around the world happened, we were among the first to notice. When people deployed our software, they could do so at will. They didn't need to pay us or ask us any questions. They could use it, and we'd often never know. This did present a challenge where we wanted metrics on how many users we had or where they were around the world. David Kobia, one of the company's co-founders, set up a script that allowed the software to ping company servers whenever our software was downloaded and used.

This was like our Bat-Signal.

When word reached us about an earthquake, a flood, or a fire, the Ushahidi team would spring into action, calling volunteers to help strategize a response. We worked from what Erik dubbed our war room, an online chatroom we used to strategize and communicate with our staff and our global volunteers. Hashtags became essential to translating our strategies into directives everyone could act on.

If we needed to share information about a flood in Queensland, Australia, we didn't want to inadvertently pick up messages about a person *whose house had flooded over the weekend in Queensland* or someone who wanted *to flood the streets and party.* Hashtags like *#HaitiQuakes #QueenslandFlood #DeepwaterHorizon* were used to help collect the right messages instead. Other custom tags like *#Uchaguzi #Wonzomai* we used to brand activities related to things like election monitoring. Those were nicknames or phrases our team coined to tell one election monitoring set of data (say, elections in Kenya) from another (elections in Egypt).

The tags made it easier for computers and people to find the information they were looking for. Our volunteers adopted the tactic as well, sending tagged information from the scene of disasters in real time. The more information got tagged about what had unfolded, the more likely it would make its way to someone who could respond. The discoverability of information went way up. Our goal was to standardize a common syntax for disaster communications, something early Ushahidi employee Patrick Meier pushed for:

Untagged: "Fabiola needs medic at Sarthe 20, House no. 10"

Tagged: "Fabiola needs #medic at #Sarthe20, House 10"

Ushahidi and Twitter were around the same age as well, both founded in 2007. Ushahidi was born from the meeting of the founders in Arusha, Tanzania only a few months after Twitter, founded a few thousand miles away in San Francisco. As the architect of the methodology Ushahidi used to manage real-time streams of data, I was facing some of the same engineering challenges the team at Twitter were. Those challenges meant storing all the data we were collecting, combing through it, and handling the load of many different users. Instead of surfacing data around the random things people talk about on social networks, we were hyper-focused on messages during crisis scenarios and the news about those crisis scenarios. The stakes were that much higher for us to sift through and prioritize data without spending a lot of time doing so. For our users, it could mean life or death. Hence, the invitation to speak to the Twitter engineering team was mutually exciting. I wanted to learn from their team, and they, it seemed, wanted to learn from mine.

What Twitter had that we didn't was engineers. Lots of engineers. It didn't hurt that they had just raised $200 million dollars in new venture backing to hire those engineers. And more importantly, they had the commercial freedom to build a highly scalable plat-form. Ushahidi was not poorly funded, but we weren't anywhere close to being as well-financed as they were. For the type of hard data problems we were tasked with solving, I couldn't help but feel like we were grossly under-resourced. This constraint was something I was increasingly concerned about. I had also come up with a solution.

I wanted to form a new company around the SwiftRiver software, to get it out of the constraints of a non-profit. I was concerned about the name as well; it was rather generic. The whole product began as a series of collaborations between academic organiza-tions, but after I began working with them, I was intent on fo-cusing our efforts and shipping a product more like a traditional software company. We had several examples of startups like our own scaling and becoming successful; Twitter was among them.

I suggested this should be a for-profit company that spun out of the organization to stand on its own. That way, it could take on investors and customers without compromising Ushahidi's non-profit status and humanitarian mandate. At the time, compa-nies that profited from solving these types of data problems were springing up left and right. One of them was a company called Palantir which would later go on to dominate the human-scale data marketplace. These companies were unbearably white, lacking geographic and racial diversity, and often weren't attempting to solve the type of human problems we were and certainly not for the same reasons.

Why not launch our own company and compete? Why not put Africa at the front of the emerging data science movement? At least as it related to crisis matters, this was a discipline we practically invented. We were big data experts hailing from the land of dial-up.

I wrote a proposal that I sent to the founders. In it, I laid out a business plan and cost justifications. I clicked send and grinned. Were we about to change the world again? This time it would be through a new company that was about processing humanitarian data fast and efficiently.

This new company would be called *Swiftly*.

#Hush

> *"Your friends will believe in your potential, your enemies will make you live up to it."*
> **—Tim Fargo, American speaker**

Wifi connects your computer to a router; your router connects you to an internet service provider; your internet service provider connects to another service provider; that provider delivers content; which might be an email; a text message; a tweet; or article. This is how information moves across the internet. However, there's an inherent problem with communicating online: each semicolon in the opening sentence represents an opportunity for eavesdropping.

In the real world, if someone is listening in on your conversations, you can speak in hushed tones to stop them. If they are looking in your window, you can pull the blinds. If they follow you, you can run.

The physical world has boundaries. People can't hear what you don't make audible. They can't look where you put up barriers. If you flee, the other person needs to run faster. Or they need to find out where you're going in order to track you down. To get around those challenges, they'll need assistance, some tool or device that lets them overcome their physical limitations. The world is bound by rules humans can't easily change – biology and physics.

Unlike the physical world, in a digital system, your options for avoiding surveillance are surprisingly limited. Yes, you can use virtual private networks (VPNs) and encryption layers to protect yourself, but that is just more software. Software has few boundaries. It's all an illusion controlled by the kernel. It's limited only by the machine it runs on. The rules that govern the software are written by people. This means the rules can be bypassed, broken, or rewritten.

Improvised.

Remixed.

Hacked.

No software is unhackable. All systems can be compromised. The only people bound by the rules of software are people who lack the knowledge on how to change the rules. That's not a limitation of the software, it's a limitation of the mind. A good hack is a mental one.

Mind-fucked.

Either the root of the hack is the person's cognitive ability, a limitation of their biology, or they literally can't move fast enough to stop a brute force attacker, which is a limitation of physics. For anyone with the right knowledge, there are many ways to change the rules and compromise a system.

All you have to do is introduce the right slang.

The slang becomes normalized.

The syntax is redefined.

That's how radicals change rules.

* * *

In early 2011, tensions throughout North African countries reached a tipping point. In Algeria, Morocco, Egypt, Tunisia, and Sudan, young activists and dissidents sparked a different kind of trend, one driven by their disgust with the corruption and indifference of politicians in their countries. Discontent had been building, in some cases, for generations. What changed that year was twofold. One, the rise of social media, which allowed activist users in one country to inspire activists in another. And two, the ubiquity of mobile phones allowing communication to happen anywhere.

Mobile phones, Twitter, Facebook, and YouTube were all now ingredients in a recipe for revolution. Eventually, a groundswell of dissidence would wash over these countries, in some cases ousting government officials and presidents.

This movement became known as the Arab Spring.

It was a type of humanitarian crisis we had yet to face. I'd become accustomed to crisis events where there were no human aggressors – hurricanes, floods, earthquakes, even the threat of nuclear fallout. These scenarios were the result of circumstance or nature. An earthquake happens, the damage is done, and then cleanup begins. Scenarios that had a clear beginning, escalation, and conclusion.

Human conflict is different. It is messy and prolonged. It presented new challenges. A hurricane is not going to try to hack you. An earthquake isn't going to arrest you. A flood isn't going to hold a gun to your head until you denounce your political allegiances. Even when tensions quiet down, it isn't always clear if the crisis is over, or awaiting another opportunity to flare.

From late 2011 through early 2012, I saw a rise in demand for my work from organizations that needed our products for crises where the adversary was human-led, sustained, and dangerous.

There were essentially two types of requests from activists who assembled to protest or from the authorities who attempted to diffuse or detain them. One side coordinated to strike; the other side coordinated to strike back. These were high-stakes encounters with loss of life occurring on either side. The players on both teams were constantly moving in many directions but collectively had one goal—*win*. Activist movements formed and took to the streets. The governments they rallied against countered with plans to infiltrate and subvert those movements. They would use force if necessary. Politicians and humanitarian organizations lined up to take one side or the other. They all worked together and against each other, weaving in and out of each other's paths until they are stopped.

A twisted version of the beautiful game.

Digital activists were now facing an existential threat we'd never really considered, that someone might try to rewrite the rules of digital engagement. The playbook used to target activists was simple: *surveil, infiltrate, compromise, neutralize.*

It began with surveillance.

Activist groups were communicating on digital platforms like Twitter and Facebook, run by privately-held corporations in the United States. The platforms were stable and secure for posting memes and selfies but for anyone trying to gut a sitting government, these social networks were flawed. For starters, there were the domestic interests those companies had to consider as they related to their home country's national security. The U.S. government wasn't just going to sit by and let an American company undermine and remove an allied government. Then there was corporate interest. What did the shareholders of these companies stand to gain by supporting activist movements if those movements became unpopular with the public and investors? Nothing. Plus, these were social platforms designed to track everything possible about their users so it could be sold to advertisers. As a result, they were increasingly hard to use anonymously. Advertisers will pay a premium for data that identifies and qualifies millions of people online. This made these social networking applications easy for interested parties to watch, while waiting for opportunities to advance the next phase of attack.

Then came infiltration.

These platforms are only effective if you are in a network of other users and actively communicating with trust. If you aren't a part of the network, there's no point communicating because they don't trust you. You have no influence within the group. Any activist using these tools to organize will, by definition, be part of the network of trust and will remain active within it. Since these platforms and all communication on them are public, a potential attacker can first watch communication patterns to see who was following who, who communicates with who, and who is friends with who. This allows the attacker to learn who to target, the easiest to prey upon.

The attacker could come up with a plan to join, perhaps by posing as a new member, or a friend of a friend already in the group. Once in, they lurk, waiting to see what the activist group's plans are.

From there they advance to the next threat level...

Compromise.

The attacker has now slipped into the trusted network of activists undetected. They might record and archive communications of the group—names of friends, locations, or the dates of a planned protest. They might profile individuals in the network—where they like to go, what they like to do, the times of day they do it. Ultimately, this information could be used to compromise the whole network's integrity.

They may attempt to undermine the groups mission, dissuading members from protesting or talking its members down from any planned activities. Or they might do the opposite and encourage the group to protest in locations where they know forces in the real world will be waiting. Either to arrest them or confront them. Or, to truly compromise the network, they might descend on one of the individuals in this group of activists. Take them away. Put pressure on them, using torture or other methods, to convince them to work against their friends. If they can flip a member of the group, making them an informant, they gain an asset embedded in the groups network of trust.

Once an activist group is compromised, the crackdown can begin. It starts with the equivalent of a nuclear bomb in the digital domain, taking away the entire domain. Total communication blackout – a weapon that was increasingly used between 2011 and 2014 across North Africa.

No mobile communication.

No television broadcasts.

No Internet.

No radio.

An information blackout is how a government eliminates the members of a compromised network. They can do it in ways that won't ever reach the outside world, at least not until it's too late. When there is no possibility of sharing information within the country and no information coming out, the government controls the narrative. This is when the most horrific things happen, while the world is blind to them. No BBC, CNN, or Al-Jazeera coverage. No war correspondents from the Associated Press. No aid workers decrying violations of human rights.

If done correctly, when the blackout is lifted, activist networks will still seem intact online, except that everyone behind the individual accounts will have been silenced. Detained, jailed, killed, or disappeared. Other activists in the group who haven't yet been eliminated or captured may not even be aware of what happened. They'll have no clue who is behind their friend's digital accounts as they come back online. Members of the network would have no way of knowing if the person on the other end is friend or foe, or who might be coming for them next.

Mind fucked.

There are other ways an activist network might be compromised. The most obvious way is through mobile cellphone towers or internet service providers, which allow governments to employ technologies capable of compromising activist accounts from afar. With some tools, mobile phone signals can be intercepted right out of the air. In these situations, as soon as an activist picks up a mobile phone, they may be compromised. At every step, the tools we once used to help people were becoming weaponized, turned against them.

On February 3, 2011, I was on a group thread in an email. It came from an activist in a neighboring country:

"Things are getting worse in Egypt, and it seems they will get even more worse before they can get better. We are interested in seeing in what ways we can help with the situation there...but we want to... *need* to do more."

I continued to receive emails from activists, protestors, human rights organizations and the like. Radicals trying to change their systems of government. All aimed to be more active in countries participating in the North African protests. I made it known that they were all asking for something I felt they needed but we weren't prepared to provide. *Security.*

The official stance of people in our network of volunteer hackers was that security always fell on the user. After all, it was open source. There were no central platforms to run everything from. If you use Google or Facebook, in theory there is a single business responsible for security and protecting its own users. With decentralized software, it's not like that. By definition, there is no organization responsible, so users are on their own. If we promised we could protect people, it would be a feckless promise. If it took six months for my colleagues at Ushahidi to fix the smallest software bugs, how on earth were they going to protect activists from the resources of an entire country willing to go as far as possible to achieve their goals?

Reports of disappearances of activists continued to rise.

"We aren't equipped for this," I said at a meeting. "This isn't routing Red Cross workers around potholes. In these situations, our mistakes could lead to people being kidnapped or tortured. I don't think we're prepared to be the cause of or deal with the aftermath of anything like that."

This was the type of code switching I wouldn't do—pretending that we knew anything about protecting people in these kinds of scenarios. Bluffing when we knew we didn't hold the right cards.

Everyone agreed. Others around us continued to be involved in the activist communities behind the Arab Spring uprisings. I wanted to do more for the protesters too, but it would have to be done responsibly. Our being under-equipped was the constraint. It began to dawn on me that some of the technologies we created had evolved in the wrong direction. The tools our open-source community was advocating seemed to be far more effective when weaponized *against* our activist networks than it was *for* them. Organized governments or groups were more effective at using them than unorganized pockets of radicals. It took months and the coordination of lots of volunteers and institutions to turn our form of digital activism into real-world outcomes. The movement was non-linear and messy. But it only took one incorrectly encrypted message on a server to get someone silenced—neutralize.

I found myself agreeing with some of our critics. What came after the maps and data streams? Was our community giving people in dangerous situations a false sense of security? Were we vocal enough about our software's shortcomings? Were we inadvertently putting our community of activists at risk?

#Swiftly

> *"Ideology is the enemy of problem-solving."*
> **—Steven Soderbergh, American film director**

In December of 2010, I walked into a penthouse overlooking the Meatpacking District of Manhattan. It was a pristine, one-bedroom, one-bathroom loft. The oversized sun-filled windows almost reached the ceiling and led to an outdoor terrace. A Lutron smart lighting system gradually illuminated the room as I tapped the switch. Motorized blackout shades enclosed the premise on command. Soft music played from Bang & Olufsen speakers wired throughout the living room.

Ory Okolloh, Ushahidi's own muse, was on the phone asking me, "Are you in?"

"Yes. I didn't expect such a nice place!"

"It's a friend's place. A very successful one. The place is yours for the week, so take care of it. And don't tell anyone, yet. Bye!" She hung up the phone.

It wasn't yet public knowledge, but Ory had just resigned as the Executive Director of Ushahidi. She was leaving to join Google in a new role as their policy manager for Africa. It was a big move, one we were all proud of. Still, the departure rocked the company.

I was visiting New York as a guest of the New York City Economic Development Corporation, which had created a mentoring program for young entrepreneurs. The goal of the program was to attract foreign companies that would consider making New York home. They connected us with investors, recruitment firms, real estate agents, anything we might need to make a move. I met with venture capital groups like BetaWorks and Bloomberg Ventures who showed initial interest. In the tech industry, we call it a *roadshow*, where startups visit a series of investors looking for one or more who are going to participate. For most, funding Ushahidi directly was a non-starter. It was a non-profit and non-profits traditionally can't issue shares to investors. However, almost as predicted, my pitch for Swiftly as a for-profit seemed to be resonating.

In the tech industry, it was rare for Black startup founders to raise money. Less than 3% of venture capital went to Black founders in the U.S. The numbers for African startups, surprisingly were worse. Somehow funders found a way to fund predominantly non-Black entrepreneurs, even in Africa. It was a trend I was determined to break. As a member of Ushahidi's leadership team, we were already breaking the mold of traditional non-profits. I saw Swiftly as our opportunity to break the for-profit mold.

Swiftly was still operating under the Ushahidi umbrella as a sub-organization. We decided that was best until we could figure out own viability. We had somewhere between eight and ten full-time employees at the time and thousands of active volunteers around the world. Our team had become largely removed from the rest of the Ushahidi organization. We were already thinking about the new venture, Swiftly, and the autonomy of being able to solve different problems as a newly independent company.

We now worked on completely different projects and used different software than our colleagues. The core Ushahidi platform used a framework for pretty much everything. The hypertext processor (PHP) was a language known in software engineering circles as an accessible technology choice that made programming easier for novice programmers who wanted to build personal home pages, blogs, and web applications. However, where PHP excelled with accessibility, it failed in performance. It was the security weaknesses that were becoming most alarming. Also, the system's ability to perform the data analysis and computations we needed wasn't there either.

For the harder data analysis work, my team at Swiftly were using Python and newly emerging non-relational databases like Mongo DB. A white paper I wrote about this was circulating with statisticians and computer scientists at institutions like Carnegie Mellon. It was my attempt to find allies who knew far more than I did about machine learning and data processing. We were attempting to push the boundaries of computer science, implementing methods and computational solutions for managing the amount of data we needed to process. I felt my team had a real need for the same kind of funding contemporary tech companies received.

Without real funding, we would continue to be constrained by Ushahidi's non-profit limitations. We also needed the autonomy to put together a proper team of computer scientists and security experts. As a non-profit humanitarian organization, Ushahidi had other priorities that weren't tech or business related. That fact didn't need to change. To solve the big problems I was working on, my team would have to transform. The tech industry evolves rapidly and the window for disrupting and capitalizing on shifting trends was tight. If we wanted to remain at the forefront of this data revolution, we'd need to move quickly. Our own products wouldn't be limited to Africa or even humanitarian efforts. The opportunity around Swiftly had become way bigger than what I'd originally been aiming for. We were poised to do far more.

"The next big tech companies are going to be data companies. We spend all our days solving data problems that few else in the world have. We've become experts in solving problems that most don't even know about. Right now, we're well positioned to be the leaders," I said at a company retreat. I was making an impassioned pitch to sell my team's vision. "Location data. Real-time data. Verifying data. Analyzing data. Visualizing data. Each of these will eventually be a business vertical. We do them all."

"If we spin out one company, what happens when the next employee wants to spin out?" Ushahidi's CEO Erik asked.

"I don't know," I replied. "What I do know is that this unique moment is a market opportunity that only exists because of timing. We're working with some of the biggest companies on the planet and at least for right now they can't do what we do. We're ahead of the market."

"Who's going to pay for it?" someone else asked. The implication was that the company wasn't interested in financing what they saw as an experimental venture. That was a fair question, because if the company failed it would mean wasted resources.

"Look, I will find the money," I said.

"Who's going to own it?" Erik asked.

The organizational structure of the new company would, of course, matter. Would the old company own the new one? Would the new company become the parent of the old? Would there be some other partnership structure?

I shot back, "Who cares! Would we rather outright own a non-profit that has to hunt for grants constantly, or do we want to own a piece of a profitable, self-sustaining for-profit company? Heck, the for-profit may eventually fund the non-profit, and then we won't need grants at all. Or we could go public or get acquired. It could be good for the staff, too. We could offer perks like stock options that aren't possible in our current non-profit form…."

These were real problems that non-profit organizations often struggled with. Most non-profits were on a spinning hamster wheel of fundraising and grant applications. Their work was often hindered by how many rich donors became passionate about the causes they cared about. If a non-profit didn't know the right donors or wasn't able to appeal to their interests, they struggled to get any funding at all. At Ushahidi, we'd been quite successful raising money from wealthy benefactors, but it was still exhausting having to raise millions of dollars for our annual budget every year. Meanwhile, when successful for-profit tech companies went out to raise money from venture capitalists, they often raised tens of millions of dollars meant to last them years.

Then there was the issue of employee incentives. For-profit companies could offer staff healthy bonuses, stock options, and other perks that the strict mandates non-profits had to abide by didn't allow. For the average non-profit employee, they collected a modest salary and did the work, but there was no long-term upside other than the occasional award. Nothing wrong with that. It becomes a problem when their organizations are under-resourced, leading them to become over-worked and stressed. Burnout was real.

It was no surprise that many non-profit staff eventually found their way back into the private sector when they decided they wanted benefits, a 401K, health insurance, and increased earning potential over time. We had just lost one of our own, Ory, to one such company, Google.

The mood in the room became tense. There were two camps, people who were excited by the prospect of the new venture and those who were reticent. I didn't feel my passion for this spin-out company was driven by hubris. I simply recognized the opportunity for us to capitalize on the momentum we'd built as experts in emerging uses of data. We were well ahead of the curve, but the moment was fleeting. Perhaps those who were reticent just didn't appreciate the potential value of the opportunity. Or perhaps they didn't want to get left behind at the non-profit. Or the founders didn't like the idea of losing control of their baby. Whatever the reason, this call to action wasn't going over nearly as well as when I rehearsed it in my head.

"We're the same age as Twitter and they just raised $200 million dollars, I continued. "We reach millions of people around the globe, just like them, and we've hired some of the best computer science engineers in the industry, just like them. We have every major news organization in the world covering us. We have a great humanitarian mission and great software. We only lack resources."

Silence.

I looked at my colleague Matt. He shook his head. It wasn't an argument we were going to win. Matt was someone I met in Uganda, a software developer who I initially hired at my other company, Appfrica. Matt was such a good engineer that when Ushahidi approached me to moonlight with them, I encouraged him to join me. Eventually, they hired him at my recommendation. He was a more experienced programmer than almost everyone on their team and excelled at creating data-driven software. Swiftly became his vision as much as mine. He and I would go on to build multiple successful startups together over the years. But for the moment, we were confused about what to do next.

I proposed a compromise: "If I find the money to pay for this, will you at least consider it?"

The team was still quiet. They seemed reluctant to make any decision at all. "That's reasonable," Erik said.

It was frustrating. Nonetheless, I had my marching orders. *Find money.*

In fact, I had already started. Weeks earlier, I had successfully pitched the idea for Swiftly to a group called the Knight Foundation. Knight was a philanthropic group that had a billion-dollar endowment that they wouldn't be able to spend in several lifetimes. Instead, they engaged in various initiatives aimed at helping communities around the U.S. One of those programs awarded grants of between $10,000 and $500,000 to projects aimed at fostering informed and engaged communities. They had a particular interest in news and data-oriented projects. Knight had previously funded Ushahidi, so they knew us well. We were like a case study for them, a success story. I already knew they were keen to fund any new ideas that might emerge from our team.

I had received an email from the decision-makers at Knight approving funding for Swiftly a week prior to my conversation with the team. I was agreeing to find money that was effectively already in place.

Over the next few weeks, I made additional phone calls. With Knight's commitment, there was a good chance that we could also get money from the organization that had essentially bankrolled us for the first few years, Omidyar Networks. Omidyar remains a long-time funder and partner of the Ushahidi organization. It was among the company's first funders back in 2007. They agreed to $350,000 as a vote of confidence and would match and exceed whatever else we could raise. So, the first $250,000 from Knight, when combined with Omidyar's money, became $600,000.

The other funding would arrive via a meeting a few weeks after our retreat. It came from another organization passionate about the world's information, the Wikimedia Foundation. The Wikimedia Foundation maintained the open-source Wikipedia, the free web-based encyclopedia that was made up of information that could be edited or updated by almost anyone (with some restrictions). One of the problems they were having was how to improve how millions of people around the world were able to contribute, edit, and comment. They saw the potential in what the team at Swiftly was building and agreed to pay for a pilot. As a non-profit, they couldn't invest, but they would advance us money in the form of a grant, and we could deliver the services later. Boom, another $150,000.

In four weeks, I was up to $750,000.

In the world of venture capital, this amount of money was only a start. Still, it was enough to spin out the company, hire additional staff, and operate for about a year. That would be all the runway we needed. Within that year, we would continue to raise money, and hopefully begin generating revenue. There were likely additional millions waiting once we restructured and went back to investors. If we accomplished all that, it would mean the new company had proven its viability. All the pieces aligned and in record time.

This *had* to be the sign the Ushahidi founders were looking for.

I called Matt after the meeting with Wikimedia and said, "I think we did it. We've got the money."

We put together the budgets, the business plan, the pitch deck, and research necessary to satisfy our new investors and launch the company. It would be called Swiftly.org. The non-profit wouldn't have to pay a thing. We had even more interest from investors who expressed that they'd consider funding us once we'd launched. They wanted to wait until we were clear of any ownership issues that might arise while spinning out a new company from an existing one.

I was in California meeting with funders. As soon as we were done, I flew to Kenya to relay our success. I was now certain everyone would be elated.

* * *

"It's not happening," Erik said.

"What's not happening?" I was genuinely confused.

"We still don't think the timing is right to spin out a new company."

I couldn't believe what I was hearing. "But we have everything we need now. I raised nearly a million dollars in a few weeks."

"We just can't justify it," he said.

Was there more going on than he could share?

I was dumbfounded. The previous months had been a whirl wind. I'd put everything into scaling Swiftly: press releases, fundraising, partnerships, potential customers—everything the startup would need. A string of articles from the BBC, TechCrunch, ReadWrite, The Economist, BlackWeb 2.0, The New York Times, and Columbia Journalism Review had covered the company as if we'd already launched.

"If we don't do this now, someone else will. The need is too great. You know this. You're in the same meetings that I am. You have to see it!" I pleaded to his better judgement. No avail.

"This is a mistake," I said defiantly.

Technically everything Ushahidi did was open source. I didn't actually need anyone's permission to do what I was proposing. The software we built belonged to our community and the world. That's what our version of open source meant. The code could live on. The momentum, the partners, the brand and image were all ownerless. However, I had no desire to fight them for the thing that mattered most – the staff. The optics of a rift forming in the company that caused half of its staff to leave to form a new company would be a PR disaster for both entities. It would look especially bad that it was happening only a few weeks after our executive director Ory had left for Google. Also, since I began the process of raising money as an Ushahidi spin-out company, the funding was off limits. Sure, investors were betting on me and the team and our vision, but from a legal perspective, they had bet on us as a company spun from its relationship with the well-established Ushahidi. They had not bet on us as a completely new stand-alone company. If I did want to take Swiftly on as a solo project, the funding definitely wasn't going to come with us. This meant my entire team at Swiftly would have to quit their jobs if they were going to leave and follow me into a startup that was unproven. Investors and donors would be hard to appeal to. I knew they didn't want to choose sides.

We were at an impasse. A lose-lose situation. A series of small over-looked mistakes that had festered, culminating into one big cascading failure.

The founders of Ushahidi were unified in disagreeing with the idea of letting Swiftly spin out. There was a lot of agreement in principle that it was a solid idea, that the software we were building was progressing, and that it needed more resources. Yet they didn't want to let us go, and weren't going to allocate us more of the company's budget if we stayed.

"Investors bet on people not companies," one of our funders once told me.

I became more self-aware than I had been in a long time while in Africa. While I felt like living here had removed me from the legacy of America's own brand of racism and bias, I found a new kind. One where the American Black was perfectly fine to give his ideas to a company and work within it, but not one where the same company would take a bet on him as a leader. I'd assembled a team of machine learning experts and, with them, built a platform for analyzing and processing data that some of the world's most important institutions were begging for. I found the money needed to finance it. I had everything except for support of the people I needed. That was my mistake: I should have gone to them first. Instead of seeing the venture as an opportunity for growth, maybe they saw Swiftly as a threat.

Within a few weeks, the idea was shuttered – almost as swiftly as it had begun.

* * *

"Another one?" I sighed.

In addition to our organization's inner turmoil, it seemed the whole world was tearing itself apart in 2011. The Haiti quake relief efforts stretched on for months. Our volunteer network continued to offer ongoing support to the company, glowing reports in the press followed, and use of our products by first-responders, crisis response, and recovery teams continued well into the following year.

Then came the torrent: a conflict in Yemen; an Ethiopian Airlines plane crashed into the Mediterranean Sea, killing 90 people; heavy rain caused floods and mudslides on the Portuguese island of Madiera; 2.5 million liters of diesel oil was dumped into the river Lambro in Northern Italy; Central Chile was hit with an 8.8 magnitude earthquake; two suicide bombers detonated in the Moscow Metro killing forty; a train derailed in Italy; the eruption of volcanic ash from Eyjafjallajökull in Iceland led to the unprecedented closure of all airspace over most of Europe; the Deepwater Horizon oil rig exploded in the Gulf of Mexico spilling millions of gallons of oil into the ocean; there were contentious elections in Venezuela; Times Square was the target of a failed car bombing; Israeli soldiers raided the Gaza Flotilla ships leading to several casualties; Cote d'Ivoire had its presidential elections; an oil tanker exploded in the Democratic Republic of Congo killing 230 people; there was a hostage situation on a tour bus in Manila; a 7.1 magnitude quake hit Canterbury, New Zealand…the crises seemed endless.

Our software was designed to help respond to these tragedies. So we did.

For months, we were overwhelmed by the sheer demand. Talk about under-resourced.

My head hit the desk, exhausted. Our staff didn't have to respond to all these events directly, but we had to respond to the responders. They, after all, were using our software to address life-or-death scenarios. Bugs in our code might lead to casualties or failed rescues. Tech support was life support.

"This is unsustainable," David, one of our founders, said in a meeting.

"We don't have to respond to every single event. Let the volunteers handle most of the work," Erik, our CEO, said. He was a master of efficiency. I was still bitter about Swiftly, but I was committed to our mission of helping others. "We should only get involved in the big ones," he continued.

"You mean we can't be everywhere at once?" I asked sarcastically. How were we going to decide who needed our help more, the survivors of a plane crash or the victims of an earthquake? I knew we couldn't realistically be everywhere at once.

"We don't need to be," Erik said. "We just make the software. We aren't the damn Justice League."

He was right. In addition to our core staff, we had a network of community organizers who managed a larger network of volunteers consisting of students, academics, and humanitarians all over the globe. It's how our company always appeared to be on the scene all over the world.

Little did we know our network was about to show its strength once again by taking on our second largest disaster since Haiti. On March 11th, 2011, another major earthquake hit Japan off the Pacific coast of the Tōhoku region. It had a magnitude of 9.1. The tsunami that followed was even more devastating. The torrential waters disabled the power supply and cooling reactors at Fukushima Daiichi Nuclear Power Plant (福島第一原子力発電所). Cooling at the plant was no longer adequate, which initiated three near concurrent nuclear meltdowns.

For the people of Japan, this seemed like it wasn't possible. They'd been told since 1967 that Fukushima was built to withstand even the most powerful of earthquakes. Forty years passed, and the entire country was convinced it was quake-proof. Apparently, it was—but it wasn't tsunami-proof.

The damage caused by the tsunami, whose waves reached as high as 45 feet, was to blame for the reactor's meltdown. Japan spent nearly half a century preparing for an earthquake only to be left reeling from an ancillary event they'd never anticipated. The tsunami was an *unknown unknown,* an unforeseen event that converged with other unplanned phenomena in unexpected ways. A small oversight in the construction of Daiichi accounted for every contingency except the one decades later that broke everything, a cascading failure.

We now faced a triple-frontier crisis in Japan. An earthquake, a tsunami, and a nuclear meltdown. In a comic book, it's the type of scenario where the actual Justice League would have swooped in to save the day. By March 12th, 2011, thousands had been left stranded as transport systems came to a halt. Anxiety about the shortage of water, food, fuel, and electricity was high and exacerbated by the unfolding situation. In the hardest-hit areas, over 20,000 people were dead or missing, and hundreds of thousands had been evacuated to shelters.

One piece of Japan's infrastructure that did survive was its internet. We had been used to operating in countries where communication infrastructure was sparse, where we had needed makeshift cellphone towers and hastily configured servers. Here in Japan, there was no need to improvise communications using pirate towers or shortcodes. In fact, just hours after disaster struck, volunteers in Tokyo were able to jump online and begin mapping hazard zones and emergency services across the country.

With the internet completely functional, collecting reports from citizens was simple; they could fill out a web form. For those who had no smartphones, volunteers provided them. We coordinated a task force of responders to assess the damage to the city, dropping waypoints and taking photos. Our software was designed to help people react quickly to share as much information as possible in the aftermath of a crisis. Our goal was to put better data into the hands of the first responders and communities who mapped resources, shelters, safe and unsafe zones, etc. In Japan, volunteers repurposed the platform to collect information about the environment following the meltdown. Much as in Haiti, the Fukushima Ushahidi deployment became a case study cited for years to follow.

This was no Haiti. This was a resource-rich, wealthy, well-developed country. Emergency response was easily mobilized and prepared. There were a plethora of resources for getting information to citizens, even multiple deployments of our platform. The two with the highest-profile were Sensai.info and Safecast. The Safecast deployment was the most interesting. Their team flipped the idea of mapping crises on its head. Instead of using maps to report incidents of people needing help from first responders, their map measured radiation levels. In 2011, it was named as the largest radiation monitoring project in the world with 3.5 million data points. The other deployment in Japan, Sinsai.info, was a unique deployment relying on a heavily organized effort by Hal Seki and more than 200 volunteers who confirmed, geo-coded, transcribed, and uploaded more than 110,000 calls.

Erik was right. We didn't need to be everywhere at once, the software and volunteers could do that for us. The coordinated response to the quakes by Safecast and Sinsai in Japan proved that our community could thrive without us. Still, the world was enamored with our story. The misfit band of hackers from Africa had helped Japan through its own unprecedented catastrophe.

* * *

On June 5th, 2011, I was to speak at an event called the Personal Democracy Forum at Skirball Hall, New York University. The title of my talk was *SwiftRiver: Advanced Crowdsourcing*. Originally, it was meant to be an inflection point, an opportunity to publicly launch a project that had been languishing for years. Why shouldn't we build a sustainable company? I had joined Ushahidi and found we'd kick-started an open-source revolution around data, analytics, and access to information.

Our whole brand in Africa was about independence and resilience. The business of Ushahidi was the opposite. We had every opportunity to build a for-profit technology company 100% our way and yet here my peers were choosing to build another non-profit in Africa. Sure, a cool and better-run non-profit than most, deserving every award and accolade received over the years, but not the company it could have been.

"Everyone is expendable," Erik told me on a heated leadership call just before the event.

"Are you trying to force us to let you do this?" David said. "You've been doing all this press and these events. You're supposed to accept a big grant next week!" He was usually mild-mannered, but now here, he was quite angry.

"Calm down, mate. We just want what's best for everyone here," Matt chimed in. He was always more diplomatic than I. If I was the Steve Jobs, constantly selling the world on ideas, Matt had been Steve Wozniak, making the things I dreamt up happen.

Finally, I spoke: "Look, I've been to New York. I've been to San Francisco. I've been to London. I've met with the VCs and angel investors. People everywhere are hungry for what we're doing. We need to move on it!" The wave of data companies that launched between 2011 and 2013 would later prove I was on to something.

"We aren't going to be forced," David snapped back.

"That's not the right move," I muttered.

I was shouting into the wind. Whatever path we were on had already been decided by long-standing relationships and internal politics. The company was part of their brand. They didn't see it as part of mine. Plus, in the unlikely scenario where they followed this new company, they would be putting their own reputations on the line if it didn't work out. My team going rogue without their support was a kamikaze mission. The only way for any of it to work was if the founders agreed 100%. But they didn't.

I half-suspected to be cut from the speaker roster that day. One of our funders caught wind of the situation in advance. They knew things weren't good within the company and the person at the root of the trouble, me, was about to keynote on behalf of the company forcing him out. I had already decided I was going to remove myself from Ushahidi. I had nothing to lose.

Walking to the venue, I anticipated receiving a call where I'd be told someone else would be giving the keynote instead. I wound up speaking about the project's progress and our vision for what it could've been. Every word was painful. I was delivering a eulogy while making it sound like an optimistic product launch.

I imagined the company's future would be forever filled with questions: "What's your company's data strategy? What the hell happened with SwiftRiver? Whatever became of that Black-American guy?"

I walked onto the stage in front of a packed auditorium. I was wearing a t-shirt that read *Team Swift*. It was my silent protest. A defiant middle-finger about being shut down. I felt used and discarded. I had the shirt made custom by a screen printing company before the talk. The place that made it was also a tattoo company. I sat in the lobby and waited while men with ink guns drew on other people's bodies who grunted and contorted from pain. When the shirt was done, I held it up to look at it.

"Team Swift. What's that mean?" The guy at the register asked. "Some band?"

"No. It means screw the other guys," I said.

"Right on," he said, completely oblivious to anything I was talking about. "That'll be fifteen bucks."

"Trust me. It's going to cost a lot more than that."

* * *

After the keynote incident, I submitted my resignation to both Ushahidi and the board at Omidyar. I was scrubbed from the company Wikipedia page the next day. I knew where I stood. I was the American Black who had no supporters. I might as well actually be on my own. I didn't need anyone to bet on me. I bet on myself.

My experience with Swiftly was soul-crushing. I had successfully built a unique community, raised capital, and rebranded. Although I hadn't started the original open-source SwiftRiver project, I became its champion and its de facto leader. Now, I was walking away, leaving $1 million and carefully forged relationships in the process. I was starting over. Screw the other guys.

In the 2018 movie Black Panther, a brash, ideological American from Compton travels to Africa to challenge the kingdom of Wakanda who want to remain isolated and insulated from anything the outside world has to offer. I tried to do the same. Like him, I failed.

I was the Killmonger.

#Collateral

> *"You know who's going to inherit the Earth?*
> *Arms dealers...because everyone else is*
> *too busy killing each other."*
> **—Nic Cage, Lord of War (2005)**

The askari was bleeding from his temple.

The blood left a trail from the guard's house to the road beyond the compound's security wall. The guard had discovered the intruders as they were attempting to break-in to the house. As they scuffled, the guard yelled for help when a blow from something cold, hard, and metallic rocked him. The world blurred to black. As his senses came back, he could hear the skittering footsteps of his assaulters run towards the concrete wall then hurl themselves over.

The shuffle of feet continued into the darkness and the woods beyond the wall. He was too spent to pursue them. In too much pain to stand. He sat there on the ground, holding the back of his head and wincing until someone came.

* * *

An hour later, my attorney found him. His car pulled up to the gate. *Odd.* It wasn't open.

Usually, all he had to do is tap his horn lightly to signal that he was home. Then his guard would come to the gate to open it and let the car in. After a few minutes of tapping the horn, he became frustrated. Where was he? The attorney got out of the car and began fumbling with his keys to open the gate from the outside. As he did so, he noticed the silhouette of the guard crumpled to the ground in the beam of his headlights.

"My God!" he gasped. His compound was on a hill overlooking the city and was surrounded by a dense tree line and fortified walls. Realizing what had occurred, he squinted into the darkness, beyond the trees, to look for answers. He searched for signs of movement, traces of the people who had attacked his security guard.

Nothing.

Hours later, he stood in our compound sharing this story with Sarah and myself. His home had been burglarized. The guard was now in the hospital from the nasty head wound.

"They clubbed him from behind," he later told me. "They didn't get much. Luckily, he found them quickly after they entered."

"Thank god he's okay. What did they take?" Sarah asked.

"They just rummaged through things. They didn't get far before the guard found them."

"It's not the same Kampala," I said, thinking about the riots and the bombings. Peace seemed to be hanging by a thread. Security was more intense, yet crime was up.

My own paranoia rose as we spoke. This was my attorney in Uganda, sharing a story about a break-in attempt at his home. It was only a few weeks after I noticed strangers lurking around my own house. Break-ins in Kampala aren't exactly rare, but they aren't frequent either. Most homes are encircled by a seven-foot protective concrete wall meant to protect the residents from artillery fire and bombs. On top, barbed wire or shards of broken glass were set in cement. Each house was its own compound, with a large metal gate, bolt lock, and personal guard's quarters. For a break-in to occur, any intruder would need to account for a lot of variables. To get this far, it meant they had to have been watching the house for days before the attack. If they knew to watch my attorney, were they also watching my home? Were they watching us both? Why?

Being an activist in a country like Uganda is a dangerous affair. Being wealthy, having global influence, and being in the news constantly made it far worse. It wasn't unheard of for people to disappear without a trace, only to turn up again days or weeks later. Sometimes their opinions on subjects they were once so passionate about had changed. Other times they came back defiant and more antagonistic. Or they never came back at all.

I tried to keep my profile as low as possible. It wasn't easy. I had just appeared in CNN Money talking about the importance in investment in Africa. A reporter from the New York Times had left Uganda to meet me for a story. He wanted to work with me to expose the sources of illegal weapons trading across the continent and tie the sources of those weapons to their foreign financiers. BBC, The Economist, and TIME were all reaching out to schedule coverage on various open source community efforts I was involved in. Meanwhile, situations in other countries increasingly put my colleagues at Ushahidi on the side of prominent political dissidents. Radicals who were denounced as troublemakers and terrorists by the political elite they railed against.

Like I said, I kept a low profile as best I could.

After leaving Ushahidi, I remained part of a wider network of *liberation technologists* who, similarly, made technology that was used to support human rights, liberty, and transparency. Few technologists were prepared to actually be on the front lines. Instead, we made software for those who took to the street to protest. We provided them with the tools and technology they needed. Most people used this software altruistically, but others used it negatively. This is a struggle many technology companies have. Once you become aware of negative uses of the products you make, you're presented with an ethical dilemma. Do you remain neutral? Do you take a side? Which one?

If a company does nothing while hackers misuse their products, doesn't indifference benefit the attackers? Doing nothing enables them to do more damage. When lies and disinformation are spread on social networks who does inaction benefit most? The liars are still going to lie. Disinformation is still going to spread if nothing is done. In a conflict, there is no neutral. I once thought technology could be agnostic to human disorder. I was now learning first-hand why it isn't. We either encourage or discourage the abuser. Standing by and watching does nothing to limit abuse.

No choice *is* a choice, usually the most damning choice.

As I watched a wave of digital activism spread across developing countries, I became more self-aware about my own choices. I felt increasingly vulnerable. I was living in a country that didn't have the best track record with human rights. How exposed was I? Was I being a coward because I was focused on my own safety while the people who used the products I created bled in the streets? What did I owe them?

In Kampala, one year earlier, there was a bombing at a clubhouse called the Kyadondo Rugby Club. The club was in the Nakawa neighborhood and was very popular amongst locals and expats alike. It was a rowdy environment where bottles of *Guinness Special Export* beer were only a dollar and people blew high-pitched vuvuzelas to the tunes of hometown music stars like musician Bobbi Wine. A crowd had gathered to watch an exciting football match between Netherlands and Spain—the World Cup Finals 2010. Two loud explosions, timed so closely in succession that they probably sounded like a single blast, ripped through the shouting fans. Across town, there was another explosion. That one, at a restaurant named Ethiopian Village in the Kabalagala district. It was another venue popular mostly with expats and diplomats. It was often attended by friends of mine. The dual explosions killed a total of 74 people and left another 71 injured.

I was out of the country at the time, in Oxford, England where I was preparing to give a speech at a conference. As I rehearsed in front of my laptop, notifications began to pop up. Next to it, my cell phone suddenly buzzed as if panicked. Reports of the bombs flooded my timeline on Twitter. Friends were reaching out via text message. I called Sarah immediately. It wouldn't have been uncommon for either one of us to be at the restaurant watching the game that day. We weren't exactly soccer fans but most of our friends were. I reached her around midnight Uganda time.

When she answered I sighed with relief. "I just heard about the bombings."

"It's bad. But I'm okay and I'm thankful no one we know was there," she responded.

"What's it like there?"

"Eerie. Everything's shut down. I'll be glad when you're back. I'm scared, Jon."

As much as I wanted to rush to her side, if safety was the immediate concern, it would make far more sense for her to leave Kampala than for me to return. Also, the attacks weren't sustained. I was headed back in two days. I decided to stay to do my talk. What could happen in 48 hours?

"Only another day or two, babe. I'll be home soon. I love you." I hesitated before hanging up. Was this the right choice?

* * *

After the bombings, life in Kampala changed. There was no way back to the relaxed city that I had come to know. It had perished in the blasts.

Walking the streets in the weeks after the attacks was like visiting the city for the first time. Everyone in the city was getting use to this new reality and the heightened sense of vulnerability that came with it. Security was on everyone's minds and, soon enough, in everyone's faces.

At Garden City, a shopping mall, armed guards stood with guns drawn at the entrance. Every car was hand searched. Guards holding long rods with mirrors at the ends peered underneath vehicles, checking for bombs. Every person in the car would need to get out and be searched by hand and sniffed by bomb dogs as well. At the airport, a security perimeter was established about an eighth of a mile from the main building. Incoming cars were screened inside and out.

Kampala was now tense and anxious.

My own anxiety was fueled by this change in the city's atmosphere. I became more reclusive. I was alarmed by the unknown faces that turned to watch my car as it passed driving through the town. Before the bombings, I'd wondered about their faces with enchantment and curiosity. Now, I was fearful of everyone's intentions.

People became *unknown unknowns*. I made sure to never take the same route twice. Previously I frequented restaurants and events around town, now I mostly stayed at home. I stopped going to the Appfrica office. I stopped greeting people in the slums. I had no idea what they really thought of me and my mzungu wife. The long stretch of road now seemed desolate and sad. It was full of impoverished people who could be paid to say or do anything. I cursed myself for losing my optimism.

It's only paranoia when the anxiety comes from an unknown, unidentifiable threat. In this case, the threats were real and they were numerous. Paranoia was a gut reaction. I couldn't say for sure it was an over-reaction.

I felt dangerously exposed.

* * *

"So, you want me to smuggle guns out of Uganda for you?"

"You know that's not what we're doing."

"Yeah, I know that, but people like me don't just get the benefit of the doubt!"

He sighed. "Look, I was just asking..."

The man I was speaking with operated a charity that collected guns from war-torn countries and decommissioned them, to get them out of country. So, a gun smuggler...but for good.

He'd asked me if I could help him move guns out of the country. I didn't have a problem with any of that, in theory. It was a noble cause. Only, I felt I would be the one taking on all the risk. I was the one who lived in Uganda. I'd be the one with an armory stockpile in my office. Who were the drug dealers, guerrilla fighters, and more nefarious arms dealers going to target if they decided they wanted those weapons back? Who was going to protect me and my family in-country if security didn't come in time?

Also, what sort of watchlist would I end up on—the guy who popped out of the ether into Uganda for no clear reason? CIA? Interpol? And what sort of stance would the Ugandan government itself take if it decided moving guns like this was just a cover-up for some other scheme?

These were the types of projects I frequently came across in the philanthropic circles in Uganda. On paper they sounded crazy and half-baked, but in practice they were solutions to real problems in developing nations.

One such group trained rats to sniff out and detonate live land-mines in Liberia. Another project offered free legal services to people detained in Ugandan prisons. There was also a filmmaker who produced a documentary about going to Liberia to teach people to surf.

"Surfing will bring people together and help the country's people heal after a drawn-out civil war," he told the room at an event. I wondered if he believed his own words. Surfing was going to heal the wounds of two civil wars that took the lives of over a million people? Good luck with that, I thought cynically. It was a thoughtful film and the director meant well, but the wounds that lingered from war weren't going to be eradicated by surfing.

In the civic tech community, I noticed projects were most provocative when the creators were in one country working with activists in another. Usually because the people with the craziest (and riskiest) ideas were in the more developed, safer, country. They were shielded by protections the people in the developing countries they worked alongside often didn't share.

For example, a volunteer in a place like San Francisco might conceive of a digital platform that exposed the names of a country's most corrupt officials. Those names would then leak to journalists who would launch investigative stories. The volunteers were safe, tinkering away at digital systems far away. Meanwhile, the leakers living in-country could be targeted and chased down. The locals had no assurances of safety. They just had dreams sold to them by grad students in New Jersey and techies in San Francisco.

They were *collateral*.

Standing here, speaking to this do-gooder gun-runner, I realized I was now on the other side. I was the expendable one. If anything happened to me, I would be considered collateral damage and the project would continue on without me. I realized how naïve I'd been in my own digital activist pursuits.

Digital activism of that era was born out of the spirit of open source by people who wanted to use technology to benefit humanity. That meant the stakes were inherently high and there was less room for error. Digital security had a completely different meaning when it was needed to protect lives. I had a full team of Ugandans who didn't have the luxury of leaving this country if things got out of control. I had friends in Egypt and Syria who weren't using software because they thought it was cool. They used it because their way of life *depended* on it. They were facing an existential crisis. I was a willing volunteer in their struggle, whereas they didn't have a choice. For them, this was survival. My peers and I only faced these crises because we chose to. We had made their pain our luxury getaway.

Realizing this, I became a lot more selective about what sorts of activist projects I took on. Any project where I was at risk personally was debatable. Projects where my staff and friends were at risk I rejected without hesitation. I didn't want to be the person who lulled them into a false sense of security. The humanitarian sector was full of people around the world willing to experiment on the poor and powerless in countries like Uganda. For them, there was little risk if the projects failed and nothing but glory if the projects succeeded. I may have had all the benefits afforded to an American citizen abroad, but my staff and friends in Africa did not.

I had to be cautious on their behalf.

* * *

"When you follow the money, things get weirder," Ron said.

Ron was an investigative reporter for the New York Times. He was in Kampala and had asked to meet with me. He needed my help with a platform that he felt would put the world on notice.

"Do you ever ask yourself how all these warlords lurking in the jungle and poor countries keep getting access to high-grade military weaponry? How do they get the weapons? Where do they come from? What routes do they follow? Along the way, there are ports, customs, shipping routes – a whole illicit supply chain of this shit that no one is looking into!"

I could hear the excitement building in his voice.

"This supply chain is fed by corruption," he continued. "Connect the dots between how the organizations are operating here and what they report back home, and you get a richer picture of what's really happening."

His idea was simple enough. The platform he wanted to build was called *Ujima*. Its goal was to highlight discrepancies in budgets allocated for foreign aid, trade, and military projects. In countries like Rwanda and Nigeria, this type of information was hard to get. In fact, it was often suppressed and rarely ever made public. Trying to access it could cause very bad things to happen for you. However, on the other side, U.S. and E.U. financiers had to report any transactions because in their countries, they had a responsibility to report to the public because it was all taxpayer money they used.

"African governments don't disclose this information to the public. But since the other side is contained in U.S. records, we are able to work backwards to deduce where the money is coming from or disappearing to."

"Or where the illegal trail leads," I said.

"Exactly. Why not help people see what their governments are doing with their money?"

His plan was to train journalists across Africa to help him collect information. It was similar to what the data collectors in Japan had done. Instead of reporting damage to buildings and radiation levels, Ron would train these journalists to search for documents and expose political corruption. He found forty reporters, split between Rwanda and South Africa, and taught them how to use an app to find information on government programs, arms sales, and medical supplies. He showed them how to become experts at search engine queries on Google by typing things like *'keyword *.pdf'* or *'keyword *.docx'* to limit search queries document types that might contain official documentation. He pointed to external resources like AidData, WorldBank's data portals, and Form 990 public filings by humanitarian organizations who sometimes served as fronts for shady activity, intentionally or not.

Ron pointed to organizations that served as sources of legal info like the Dutch organization HiiL. HiiL operated out of Den Haag, Netherlands and worked in association with the International Criminal Court. Another group, the Conflict Awareness Project (CAP), was an organization that was dedicated to collecting and sharing investigative reports with journalists and prosecutors. Founded by former United Nations investigator Kathi Lynn Austin, CAP was dedicated to the investigation and litigation of major arms traffickers, war profiteers, and the criminal organizations fueling global conflict.

"In the world's bloodiest business, we're taking aim at business as usual," was their triumphant tagline.

"Approach this with *a document state of mind*," Ron told the room of junior reporters. "In any investigation, there is always a document, database, or website with the exact information you need for your story."

It was a tactic used by many investigative journalists, like the dogged reporters in the 2015 movie *Spotlight*, who won't stop until they've found what they're looking for. Ugandans were stereotypically relaxed and friendly people, docile even. Tactics like this were going against the grain of culture. These reporters stepped up to the task anyway.

"You have to adjust your thinking," Ron continued. "Don't ever assume you can't find what you need. Question who has what you need and how to get to them. Why haven't you found it yet, is what you must ask yourself," he continued. "What could be missing? Who might be deceiving you?" He gave an example. It was a case that was still playing out in the local news, "Have you heard of a man named Viktor Bout?"

In the early 2000s, a former Soviet military translator named Viktor Anatolyevich Bout allegedly used air transport companies he owned to smuggle weapons out of Eastern Europe and into parts of Africa and the Middle East. He was allegedly a close associate of Charles Taylor, the former President of Liberia. Bout's arms dealing is reported to have played a major part in fueling the decade-long Liberian Civil War, which began in 1989 and officially ended in 1997.

After the war, the arms from that conflict still flooded the country. The tragedies that stemmed from those remaining guns as stretched far beyond the war. As a result, Bout became infamous. He was known internationally as The Merchant of Death. In 2015 a documentary called *The Notorious Mr. Bout*, the filmmaker challenges the image of Viktor Bout as a cruel psychopath and death merchant. Instead, it portrays a man who is in love with life, travel, and who brushed with danger as a member of the entourage of

African warlords. In the movie, he rolls down a hill naked in the snow. He shakes his body wildly on the dance floor of a night-club. He delivers long poetic diatribes about entropy and chaos while cooking dumplings. Nicolas Cage was selected to play a character inspired by Mr. Bout in the 2005 film *Lords of War*.

It turns out the evidence pivotal to catching Bout was discovered in a long-buried United Nations report. The report made the connection between the trade of conflict diamonds from parts of Africa and arms dealers like Bout traveling through Uganda. The flight plan of a plane headed to Guinea hid destinations that weren't in other publicly available records. The plane was dropping off illicit payloads. Somewhere the truth was hiding. That was the point. The truth was always out there.

Dig deeper, Ron encouraged.

It turned out Viktor operated through a series of oddly named holding companies: AIR CESS, AIR ZORY, AIR BAS, and ATC, Ltd. (owner of Centrafrican Airlines). A single holding company cited multiple addresses in the United Arab Emirates, Pakistan, Equatorial Guinea, and Entebbe, Uganda. From that thread, an investigator could weave a narrative that explained the potential route run by Bout's planes. From Islamabad, Pakistan to Entebbe, Uganda to Malabo, Equatorial Guinea. The Uganda connection in the middle of the route indicated the country's airport itself might be a source to trace the corruption. Any plane arriving or departing has to declare its manifest to air controllers. If reporters went there and requested flight logs, their discoveries might reveal airport executives or staff who were there at the time of the flight. Then, they too could be interviewed.

Tugging at the smallest thread might cause the whole plot to unravel. Follow the documents. Suddenly, a story that seemed to be the concern of other countries had consequences right here in

Uganda. It was revealed later that there were executives at the airport who helped Bout's team cover their tracks.

"The stories aren't hiding from us! We just don't always know how to turn the pages to uncover them! Keep looking," Ron said, pacing like a professor.

While none of this seemed relevant to my work at Appfrica, I listened closely. In order to help Ron build this software, I needed to understand how he worked, his logic, why he wanted to build this system. It became the same logic I later used as a data scientist, and analyst working on intelligence projects.

Trace every connection, determine if sources can be trusted. My staff at Appfrica was able to help Ron build Ujima. He later won awards and funding, continuing the project without us. I wasn't upset by this. To the contrary, I was glad he wasn't putting my staff in danger, incurring risks that would make them collateral. Unlike the proposed gun smuggling project, Ron's work was the type of project that was safe for us to undertake. We were only a service provider, while journalists were prepared to take such risks.

Well, most of them…

#SwapperCellphoneHackerSpy

"Never underestimate the determination of a kid who is time-rich and cash-poor."

—Cory Doctorow, American author

You never know until it's too late.

The first blow hit him in his kidney. The second, the gut. Before he could scream, a bag was placed over his head. Unseen hands grabbed him. Unfamiliar voices spoke in harsh whispers. His arms were pulled behind his back and bound with zip ties. Heavy boots thrashed the grass as he was pulled by the neck. He heard the shouts of people in the vicinity. His feet kicked the air as he was dragged to a nearby car. He was thrown in the back seat. Panic turned to terror as the engine roared to life. The vehicle sped away.

* * *

"That actually works?"

"Yes."

"Right out of the air?"

"Yes, ssebo."

"That's crazy."

"Yes."

When you're a technologist in resource-starved environments like Uganda, you learn to do a lot for yourself. It becomes necessary to know how everything works, from the most superficial level to the most granular. This meant I learned everything there was to possibly know about servers and computers—motherboards and operating systems, kernels, graphical user interfaces, even the underlying networks, and how undersea cables connected the African continent (and all continents) via the Internet.

When something wasn't working, I couldn't complain to customer service with a latte in one hand and the threat of a class action suit in the other. This wasn't America. I had to figure it out. If the undersea cables were severed and the whole country was offline, I had to arrange for backup connectivity through satellite connection SatFi, internet from space. The same went for the primary interface for computing in Africa, the mobile phone.

I learned the differences between complex technologies like CDMA (Core Division Multiple Access) and GSM (Global System for Mobiles) in addition to the newer protocols GPRS (General Packet Radio Service), EDGE (Enhanced Data rates for GSM Evolution), 2G (second-generation wireless), 3G, 4G, and 5G standards. I had to be my own security expert, my own forensics expert when data was lost, and my own therapist when all of this drove me insane.

My office looked like it belonged to a mad scientist. We called it frontier tech. Engineering at the ends of the world.

When you have to be brilliant to survive, the solutions you engineer often surprise you. This biscuit-eating Georgia-boy shouldn't have known any of this stuff. I didn't go to MIT or get trained by the military. I don't have formal training. I improvised. I had to learn to survive. There were no other options.

The friend I was speaking to was another local Ugandan technologist. He was warning me about *SIM swappers*, cybercriminals who were cloning SIM cards and spoofing cell phone networks in order to steal data. They didn't need to touch your phone anymore; they could just collect data from the air. Everyone was a target, that included me and my staff. I wanted to try to get ahead of it by understanding how these new systems worked.

Using feature phones, laptops, and the occasional Pringles can, the hackers could decrypt 64-bit A5/1 encrypted GSM signals. When done successfully, text messages would show up on their computers as they were sent from people's phones in real-time. This essentially allowed them to eavesdrop on your private conversations.

The GSM networks prevalent in Uganda exchanged subscriber location data via towers which routed calls and text messages to the right place. By using these new eavesdropping devices, the hacker could determine subscriber locations through simple internet queries. The results provided accuracy down to the city or neighborhood.

Once they had a location, the swapper could get in their car and drive to the area. Then they roamed around the neighborhood with their window down, makeshift antenna hanging out the window connected to a device that looked like a Garmin.

The antenna could be made from anything directional. Even something as innocuous as a Pringles can, with its aluminum interior coating and narrow tube pointing in only two directions. The hacker points the antenna at the building where they think their target is near and they wait.

This is called *sniffing*.

It's called sniffing because they don't actually know they've identified the right target. They have to sniff out the right signal. Like in a game of Marco Polo, they keep sending a call and response query until they figure out where the response is strongest and most consistent. The hacker's system waits for the digital payload, usually a text message. When there's a match, they've got you. You've been *pwned*.

From the software running on their laptops, the hackers sift through reems of data. Once locked on your phone, they can spoof the signal and send you messages. Perhaps they pretend to be a spouse, or girlfriend, or drinking buddy. It doesn't matter. The goal is to get the recipient to volunteer personal details that can be used to further exploit them. It's a technique called *phishing*. If the connection is solid enough, they can even recreate the phone's audio signal. The target's voice plays from their computer as they listen in from yards away, the replicated conversation lagging only a few seconds behind the real conversation.

In 2018, a news report from the Daily Monitor alleged that it was methods like these that allowed a group of swappers to hack several sitting members of Uganda's Parliament at the same time. The whole government was briefly held for ransom as a result. The actual SIM cards were compromised. They were removed from their phones, cloned, and replaced with SIMs that served a dual purpose – operating as normal while also relaying information to the hackers.

"What else could these methods be used for?" I wondered.

Cellphone hacking was shady business all over Africa. There were millions of kids in Uganda, South Africa, and Nigeria who were getting pretty good at it. They put the vermilion phone phreakers in Europe to shame. And many were getting good at it for nefarious purposes.

I wondered if there was a way to repurpose their misspent energy. Could their SIM hacking, cell spoofing, swapping, sniffing, and jamming be used for something more productive? This was another role innovation hubs like the one I founded in Uganda played, offering an alternative path to highly technical youth. It gave them options.

Without the chance to be entrepreneurs, to gain work as productive citizens, or find work with tech companies, they were vulnerable to the offers of terrorists and criminals.

In 2013, I founded a company called Abayima which offered software tools for hacking SIM cards. My goal was to undermine attempts by governments (or criminals) to surveil activists and journalists. It was an idea that came to me while working with activists during the early days of the North African protests. The digital security of mobile phones was limited. By making tools that allowed the circuitry of the SIM card to be modified, they would be more secure. My other goal was to offer another outlet to leverage, and redirect, the talents of young people. I drafted some of the developers at Hive to help build the first version.

This too stemmed from a critical election. In 2010, the Ugandan Presidential elections were coming up. People were excited to make their voices heard, but fearful of what was becoming a heated debate between candidates. They were worried contention might turn to conflict. Regardless of which candidate incited their ire, citizens were talking.

In Africa, the most widely accessible form of long-distance communication is the text message. In fact, the World Bank has reported that mobile phone penetration has reached more than 80% across the continent. The specific numbers vary per country, but the trend remains. Africa is a mobile-first and, in some places, mobile-only continent. Citizens use mobile networks for everything—paying for groceries, researching sports scores, ordering food, checking medical records. But the primary use-case for mobile is, of course, communication.

In the days leading up to the 2011 Ugandan elections, if one were to send a text message critiquing the President, the messages strangely never reached their targets. Friends took to Facebook to complain about mobile networks being slow, only to see that others were complaining about the same thing. We discovered that it was only the ones with a political tone that were somehow lost.

We soon realized what we thought was a standard network problem might be something more deliberate. Journalists both local and from abroad began to investigate. Was this a systematic attempt by the government to silence citizen protest? Meanwhile, political messages from the sitting party were broadcasting just fine.

"Vote for the guy in the hat," the messages read. Out of context, that may not make sense, but if you walked the streets of Kampala on February 2011, they were littered with pamphlets branding the visage of Yoweri Museveni wearing what looked like a cowboy hat.

Meanwhile, a friend wanted to send this message: *"Chase Yoweri out of power!"* He called shortly after to make a joke about it.

"What message?" I asked him. I hadn't received it. It hadn't gone through.

As a test, he sent a different message instead: *"chs ywri ut ov pwr!"* He called back. This time it went through and I got it.

After trying several other messages, some written normally and others abbreviated, we realized what was happening. There appeared to be some sort of filtering in place. It was a system that targeted words critical of the President. If a text message contained words like "power," "dictator" or "bullet," the system intercepted the message. Normally, messages were delivered fine no matter what they were about. Was the Ugandan government deliberately trying to shape the national conversation by censoring critique?

It wasn't long before we had confirmation. From the Kampala Dispatch, February 18, 2011:

> *A quick test sending SMS messages with the banned words revealed that indeed some of the messages were blocked. Or they just did not go through as is sometimes the case in Uganda. According to an internal email, SMS messages with words like "dictator,"*

"Egypt," "Mubarak," "police," "bullet," "Ben Ali," and "people power" will be blocked. We sent an SMS from an Orange line to an Airtel number and an MTN number with this text: "Favourite movies: The Great Dictator, Police Academy and Bullet with Steve McQueen." The message did not go through.

My first impulse was to figure out if there was a technology solution to the problem. The incident made me realize just how vulnerable mobile networks were. They were the lifeline of communication for Africans. Tampering with them was a big deal. In future scenarios, perhaps the conversation shaping would be more aggressive, more malicious. It was understandable that the local government would aim to suppress messages that might be perceived as calls for violence or otherwise incited the public. But simply critiquing the current President was not a call for violence. I, along with members of the staff at Appfrica and Hive Co-lab, felt it was an egregious abuse of the power telecom networks had. What could we do?

In countries like Egypt, Libya, and Syria, the world witnessed the mass disruption of communication channels. Communication blackouts became a weapon in wars between citizen and state. This represented a disturbing trend of silencing citizens. There were few solutions that could truly circumvent mobile networks. A few in the liberation tech community had attempted Bluetooth mesh-networks, hyper-local wifi networks, and ad-hoc cell towers. I studied their solutions. Most were impractical, but they did give me some ideas on what to do differently. Feature phones like the ones dominant in Uganda didn't have wifi or Bluetooth capabilities, so solutions that required either would be useless. Though the cost of smartphones had plummeted, the cost of data had not. It was definitely not proportionate to the income of the majority of working individuals in developing countries.

I wondered if it was possible to leverage feature phones as a platform for resilient communication as we had tried with our friends at Frontline in Gulu. My experience working in crisis response had taught me that text messaging wasn't always the solution. Without a network to send the messages, you had nothing. When networks went down, the ability to send text messages went down with it. The ubiquity of mobile phones wasn't as much of a strength as we thought it was, at least not when limited to text messaging.

As the elections heated up, a journalist working for a local radio station reached out to the team at Appfrica. A colleague of his, another journalist, had been missing for several days. Apparently, he had been taken by the Ugandan police on "suspicion of treason" for taking pictures at a polling station. When his colleagues went to find him, they found evidence of foul play – a broken cell phone and his notepad, things essential to his job that he wouldn't just leave behind. They came to our offices to get technical assistance after they found his phone. They wanted our help to find him.

"We think they got him before he could alert us. You usually never know until it's too late," the journalist told us. "They grab you and hold you."

The Ugandan Police were notorious for bullying activists and anyone critical of the Ugandan government. The two mobile phones the journalist usually carried had been smashed. Luckily, the subscriber identity module (SIM) card, which allows the device to connect to cell networks, had not been removed. The kidnappers weren't savvy enough to think the SIM could be traced to locations where the phone had been used. There was a second reason. By pulling data from the phone itself or the SIM, someone could recover the last few messages sent from the phone. The phone was destroyed, smashed into bits. Since we only had the

SIM, I hoped to be able to recover messages the journalist stored to its memory.

Surprisingly, there were unsent messages stored to the SIM. These were notes for a story the journalist had been working on. In this case, this journalist who couldn't carry a conspicuous laptop around with him in the field resorted to turning his normal text-only phone into a digital notepad.

Smartphones have virtually unlimited storage and apps. On the more basic phone he had, he improvised, using a long-forgotten feature to store messages to the SIM card in the phone. Different SIM cards could then be used to discreetly carry information around undetected, almost like a thumb drive. Unable to carry an expensive iPhone or laptop, the journalist had engineered another way.

My friend Leila Chirayath Jannah had taught me the Hindi word *jugaad* years ago. It was used to describe frugal innovations born from a scarcity of resources. "Innovate your way around the constraints," she had said. This was one of the more impressive examples I'd come across. In hindsight, I couldn't believe it wasn't used more pervasively.

Helping these journalists track down their friend gave me the idea for my next project. This new spin-out organization we would be subbed *Abayima*, which meant *guardian* in Luganda. I began to investigate new ways to tinker with mobile phone circuitry and memory. With Frontline, we helped establish a pirate cellphone network for refugees. With Ushahidi, I helped turn mobile phones into tools for data collection and mapping. Now I was trying to change the nature of these low-end featureless phones at the circuit-level.

SIM hacking.

People often talk about how prevalent mobile devices are. Over five billion people on the planet have at least one mobile device. These same people often have more than one device. As of this writing, there are 9 billion mobile connections. SIM cards and micro-SIMs are just as plentiful, with one or more in each phone. There are more devices to put them in than individuals who own them. There could be as many as double.

SIM cards are used to couple the phone's unique device profile and the user's information. Those two data sets are then linked to a particular telecom network. If I place an AT&T SIM in my phone, my phone identifies itself as being ready to use on the AT&T network. If I change the SIM, it changes the network my phone uses to perhaps Verizon or Sprint.

It's quite common in African countries for users to swap SIMs frequently to take advantage of the cheaper rates offered between different networks. What if the SIM itself became the carrier of content? What if users could store messages deep within these simple phones that were hard to detect? Storing data this way would be slow and inefficient, but what the user gains is the ability to store and share information discreetly – security through obscurity. My staff at Appfrica began developing an open-source solution for reading and writing content to SIM cards.

There were many hurdles to overcome. The carrying capacity of a SIM is something like 164 kilobytes. For context, we usually talk about modern digital content in the megabytes, 1000 times more. The SIMs were also difficult to program, since the software needed to do so was usually exclusive to the maker of each SIM. It was essentially a microchip. Programming a microchip is lower-level programming. Low-level means programming for machines and transistors, not humans. It's a much harder discipline. For the two years, I went back and forth on the concept. I was torn between how I should move it all forward.

The answer came in the form of $150,000. It was a grant from the Knight Foundation, a humanitarian group that managed a billion-dollar philanthropic endowment. Each year, Knight donated a portion of their funds to information technology projects like Abayima. They had previously awarded $250,000 for the Swiftly project I led for Ushahidi. Now they were backing me again.

Journalists weren't my only users. This SIM hacking project was partially conceived to address the problems I'd observed in activist networks in Syria, Libya, Egypt, and Tunisia. Activists were disappearing for weeks, sometimes never to return. Their Facebook and Google accounts were often compromised, and the information they shared on those platforms often ended up creating the breadcrumb trail authorities used to track them down. This was meant to be an answer to the security concerns I raised while working with the activists in Egypt.

With the Abayima project, the goal was to create alternative ways for sharing information to help avoid surveillance. However, I was torn between building Abayima as a platform or not building it at all. Any technology has a dual nature. Proactive or destructive. Additive or subtractive. Our funders had similar concerns. I didn't have a convincing response for their questions about safety.

It was only a few years after the terrible bombings in Nakawa, an event that drastically changed my life in Kampala. I learned the detonation devices used to carry out the bombings were hacked Nokia phones. Nokia 3310s, to be specific. The world's most plentiful and popular mobile device. My fear was that we were unleashing a new product that had uses we wouldn't be able to predict or contain.

On the night of the Nakawa attack, three bombs had been planted. Two detonated as intended. The third one didn't. It was later found by the Ugandan police at a place called Makyinde House. Investigators were able to use the undetonated device to retrace who the phone had belonged to. It too was a basic phone with no smartphone capabilities. There were no sophisticated apps or gadgets. The phone had been hacked to connect to the bomb. It was rigged so that when it received the right message, the circuits in the phone would trigger the bomb.

The group who planted it got as far away as possible and then dialed the phone number. For whatever reason, the other two bombs exploded, the third didn't. Investigators were able to recover its components. This offered a huge break in the bombing investigations. Using the undetonated phone, investigators were able to trace the last phone that had called it, which was located in a latrine not far away. By tracking who frequently called the discarded phones, investigators were able to match the incoming numbers to phone records and track down the names of the bombers.

They put a tracer on of the phone lines of the suspects. This would alert them when the phone was used, and reveal the terrorist's location. They would immediately be able to locate and arrest the owner. Unfortunately, the suspect seemed to be aware of this. His phone had been turned off completely. This meant no signal. Concerns grew that the suspects knew authorities were on to them. They'd probably never answer this line again. One of the strongest leads in the case now looked like a dead end. Later, it was revealed that the suspects had already made their way home to neighboring Kenya.

On July 25, 2010, a phone worker at Kenya Power and Lighting Company received a call. It was from a man complaining about a mistake on his electricity bill. The call came from the same line that had long been dormant, a line everyone thought was going to remain unused forever.

The investigators had finally found their signal.

* * *

I thought about this investigation while wrestling with the future of Abayima. On one hand, the project had been created to avoid this kind of misuse of technology. On the other, an untraceable way to communicate between people with ill-intent was not something I wanted to be responsible for creating. It was the exact type of tool that would have made catching the people behind the bombings much harder to find had they used it.

Were good intentions enough to create technology I knew I couldn't contain? I decided it wasn't. It wasn't worth it. It was a luxury to me but essential to them. Just a year after launch, I shut down the Abayima SIM hacking project.

Sometimes the genie needs to stay in the bottle.

#Thespian

"Laisse tomber les filles, laisse tomber les filles!
Un jour c'est toi qui pleureras!"
—France Gall, French musician

"Je ne peux pas."

The woman leaned back against the terrace sipping her wine. Her dark, caramel skin drank in the moonlight, glistening, melting with beads of sweat from humidity. The horizon sky was purple. Black ocean waves licked at the ankles of an oil rig miles away.

"Are you sure?"

"Do you know what you're doing? I could have you...*taken out.*"

"Lots of important people can do lots of things," I said. I stepped closer and kissed her neck. She leaned in and wrapped her arms around me.

"We should go, someone will see." She looked around shyly.

"Who? The beach is empty. The terrace is empty. Everyone's at the party."

We were standing on the terrace at the Palm Royal Hotel in Libreville which overlooked the sanguine beach below. The discovery of oil off the coast of Gabon had made the country one of the richest in Africa. You wouldn't know it from the intense levels of poverty. Eighty percent of the country's population lived on less than $1 a day and 40% were unemployed. Only around 8% of the population had access to the internet. In recent years, the costs of connectivity have plummeted tenfold allowing for more widespread access. Meanwhile, the remaining 20% claimed the country's $14 billion dollar GDP for themselves. Much of it went to those in the governing administration, led by Ali Bongo Ondimba, President of Gabon.

"People will talk," she whispered.

"Are you going to tell them what they should be talking about?" I asked. She laughed. Her family was among the wealthy and powerful Gabonese who earned nearly 90% of the country's income, either from their government affiliations or from oil profits.

"*Non.* I suppose not." She looked around terrace and into the room one more time. It was quiet and dark. She set down her glass and shifted out of her Saint Laurent heels. "Well then," she said finishing her wine with one rushed sip. "*Aller!* We must hurry. Security will come looking if I'm not back downstairs by midnight."

She grabbed my shirt collar and pulled me closer as we collapsed to the floor.

Resonance.

* * *

We'd met before at other conferences, immediately losing all interest in everyone around us. This time it was in Libreville. The next time maybe Kinshasa or Cape Town or Casablanca, perhaps. It didn't matter. If the conferences weren't interesting, we made them interesting.

After the conference, the attendees broke for afterparties and private cocktail affairs. My relationship with Sarah had suffered a great deal at this point. My concerns around security and safety while we were living in Kampala caused me to become depressed and withdrawn. I didn't want to share my fears with her. If I couldn't protect the other people around me, how was I going to protect her? I knew that my life while in-country made us both vulnerable. I was worried it was only a matter of time before we weren't so lucky. Then she hit me with news that changed everything once again.

She needed to move back to the U.S. It was her career that had brought us Africa, now her career was taking us back. It should have been the news I wanted to hear. Going back to the U.S. would presumably make us safe again. Yet I felt like I was being yanked back and forth across the planet with no regard to my own work, needs, and my own successes in Africa.

Despite my fog of worry and mistrust, I loved our home here. I had learned so much and gained so much from working and traveling across half the continent. I had become one of the most visible entrepreneurs on the continent. I feared going back to the U.S. meant going back to being the guy whose former employer forgot to take him off payroll.

"You can't be serious. I've built a whole new life here," I said.

"I know, but you came because I asked you to," Sarah replied. "On the other hand, I don't have a choice. This is my career. I have to go where it takes me."

"How is that a reason? What am I going to do with the staff?"

She was also upset. "I know this is going to be tough. I don't know where I might need to go next. But we can think things over in the States."

"I can't believe this."

A rift began to form between us as wide as the Albertine. I now resented Sarah's career and she resented mine. Africa is where we had bonded. It turned out whatever was left of our bond would stay there. On Mutungo.

Although it was a relief to be heading someplace where we would both feel safer, it was tough to leave behind a place I had come to love over those years. I had built several companies, funded several more, and there were many friends and colleagues I was now leaving behind. It wasn't easy to leave it all but I tried again to make it work with Sarah. I followed her back to the States.

I spent the next year traveling back and forth between the U.S. and Africa quite a bit. This alone put a lot of stress on our relationship. We got married shortly after returning. After a year as a married couple, we divorced. They say if something can work in Africa, it can work anywhere. This wasn't true, at least not for us.

The event in Gabon was one of my many trips back to Africa. I now found it difficult to code switch back into being American. America was home, of course, but this was no longer the only place I felt at home. Home, now, always seemed to be elsewhere. I couldn't resist getting on a plane to go find where else that might be. Travel was its own trap house. I spent much of the time flying back to Africa or other parts of the globe to briefly get my fix, the high of living and working abroad. I was also chasing a different kind of thrill.

Meanwhile, during our year back in the U.S., I started my second company, MetaLayer. I received word Comcast was going to fund us as part of their startup accelerator program. That would take me to Philadelphia. If we were going to stay together, could the next move be for my career? Then came the other blow. Sarah was applying to work at the U.S. Department of State, a job that might require going as far away as Afghanistan.

"I'm not going to fucking Afghanistan with you," I said immediately.

"I don't know for sure where I'm going. But these kinds of jobs, you have to prove yourself by going where no one else wants to go."

"I just moved across the planet with you twice! I started a whole new company, and Matt is moving here from Uganda." I wanted to be supportive again, I really did. But I couldn't give someone everything when they were giving me nothing back.

"You're moving as much for your own work as you are for us," she said.

"Yeah, and you're always moving for *you*."

"That's not fair!"

"Is it fair to move again? To *Afghanistan* or some other random place? For me to have to keep putting my life on hold to be with you?"

She didn't answer. We withdrew from each other. After that it was pretty much done. I found it hard to code switch my way into being a husband. At least not the husband she needed me to be. Likewise, there was no room in her career for her to be the wife I needed her to be.

It felt like we were in roles that had been miscast from outset. We worked in one setting, Africa, but not anywhere else. I was pre-occupied with various projects. She was anxious about her future career path. We clung to each other while there but after leaving Africa everything seemed to be pulling us in different directions. We had more arguments. Accusations of infidelity were more frequent as I spent more time abroad. I wasn't faithful but I also wouldn't admit it. Instead, I was defensive. The arguments got worse. She felt betrayed. I felt abandoned.

The fancy Gabonese socialite and I talked the night away while meandering away from the gala. She was elegant and witty, neither a bobble-head nor an activist. She was wealthy, in one of the poorest nations on the planet. She was a contradiction, a distraction. A temptation I couldn't resist. As she and I walked the corridor of the hotel, we noticed the terrace was unattended. The room had been sectioned-off for an event being prepped for the next day's conference. For the moment, it became a secluded space—just the two of us.

The conference we were attending was for private equity investors interested in Africa. It was attended by kings from around the world, prominent journalists, and hedge fund managers. Like so many of these conferences, it was largely a convening of the wealthy and the powerful to discuss solutions to problems they had caused. Former Presidents spoke out against corruption. Billionaire oil executives spoke of how to save the oceans. Popular tech CEOs denounced wealth inequality. The powerful came here to absolve themselves. Their solutions were all the same: "Give us more money and we'll spend our way to redemption."

It was an echo chamber. Where the elite of industry dined with the elite of government.

People in the audience listened carefully for how they weren't responsible for the world's problems, while drinking $400 bottles of champagne. Outside, I envisioned the citizens of Gabon struggling to find their next meal. I was depressed about my collapsing marriage. The juxtaposition of poverty and wealth was a reflection of a love dying. Like this party, our relationship seemed beautiful from the outside, while up close, it was flawed. I buried my emotions as I flirted with this new woman.

"Why do they call it the New York Forum when it's about African investment?" I asked.

"Would you have flown so far to the Libreville Forum or the Gabon Forum?" The Gabonese woman said as she held up a silver compact, using the mirror to touch up her make-up and hair.

"Touché," I said buttoning my shirt.

"Had you even heard of Libreville before coming?"

"You got me."

"New York is the financial center of the world. This is why we call it New York Forum Africa – to bring you dumb Yanks. If they reference New York in the title of an event about finance in Africa at least some of you will end up here." She lifted her satin dress over her head, letting it fall into place, hugging her slim frame. She quickly slipped back into her shoes and bent down to buckle the clasps.

"I feel deceived," I joked. I sat down to slip on my loafers.

She took one last look in the mirror to make sure her hair wasn't out of place. She looked me up and down, smirking. "So do I..."

"Ouch! Maybe I should explain exactly what happened here to the audience when I'm on stage tomorrow?"

She rolled her eyes. "Don't you dare mention a word." We kissed one last time. "Remember, I could have you taken out." She giggled. "You're fun, but we've been gone long enough. I don't want you to be late for your presentation tomorrow."

She gave me one more deep embrace and a wet kiss on the mouth. When we left the room, she left first. I waited a few seconds, then headed in the opposite direction through the corridor and down the stairs.

For the rest of the conference, we ran into each other several times. Each time we were introduced by oblivious guests. We played along, acting as if we were meeting for the first time. It was our secret game. We exchanged secret looks at each other from across the room. We wanted to see if anyone around us noticed we weren't strangers at all. On the contrary, we'd been quite close.

Enchanté, Monsieur Gosier!

Pleasure's all mine. Do you know where the nearest bathroom is?

Welcome to Libreville, Mr. Gosier!

Are you a speaker? You look familiar.

You don't look like you're from Gabon, are you a Yank?

The next morning, I was hungover and exhausted from the night's fun. I woke up thirty minutes before I was supposed to be on stage. I scrambled to shower and iron my suit. I rushed over to the venue and quietly slipped into a working session just as they were calling panelists to the stage. On the panel, we spoke mostly about investment and venture capital and how to grow Africa's private sector through entrepreneurship. These were all topics I'd become comfortable with and, luckily, could rattle on convincingly without much preparation.

I looked around the room for my lady friend. She was nowhere to be found. I assumed she was still in bed sleeping it all off. When the moderator of the panel asked me a question, I smiled, turning on the charm and responding as best I could.

The transition was seamless.

#1UP

"When has the ordinary ever been news?"
—Rita Dove, American poet

"We're going to charter a 747 and fly it to Parliament," said the woman from IDEO.

"What are you going to do when you get there? *Steal the Magna Carta?*" I thought I was being funny.

She hesitated. "No, we're flying to the G8 Conference."

"You're serious."

"Very serious, sir. Your company Appfrica came recommended from a few different sources. You're on our shortlist. Can we
count on you to attend or would you rather nominate someone
else from your team? We need to know in the next 24 hours, or
we have to find someone else."

I paused.

Her organization, IDEO, helped big institutions rethink their
strategies around business operations, social impact, and product creation. It was a design company in every sense of the word.
They had hand-selected one hundred and thirty thought leaders, bloggers, entrepreneurs, and tech executives to fly to London to participate in the follow-up to 2013's 39th Annual G8 Summit called the G8 Innovation Conference. The guests consisted
of people like Prime Minister David Cameron, Richard Branson,
Boris Johnson, the Director of the Clinton Global Initiative and
executives from organizations like Google, Zappos, Andreessen
Horowitz, and Stanford. The goal was for British Airways to do
something to highlight their support for a wide array of social
impact causes, interesting new technologies, and global humanitarian concerns. Given Appfrica was an organization that often
dealt with all three, we were called.

It was only a week or two before the flight. At the last minute, one
of my colleagues, Bahiyah, had told me IDEO was interested in
our presence.

"You should go," she told me. "For what they're trying to do, we
should be on that plane."

"You don't want to go?" I asked her.

"I mean, I will but they'll only take one person. It's got to be you, you're the CEO. Plus, you're the one who's been investing in Africa for so long....but there's a catch."

"What's the catch?"

"They were going to invite one of the founders of one of our portfolio companies. I don't think they're going to take you both."

"Who is it?"

William Senyo was one of the young inventors I had invested in a few years prior. He was a natural star. Smart, likeable, and ambitious. He was running a startup called SliceBiz which we were eager to help grow. The success of our entrepreneurs was important. Without companies that win, it's hard to be an investor.

"Well that's obvious. William needs to go. He'll light up that room," I told her.

It was true. In every investor's portfolio, there are one or two founders you root for more than the rest. It's not that you don't believe in them all, it's just some founders stand out. William was one of them. Something he would do one day would be big, I was just glad to play a small part in his current company.

"This will be better for him than it will be for us," I said.

Bahiyah was also torn. She knew it was a big deal, that it would be good for our company, and she agreed with my logic, but I could tell she wasn't sold on my not being there.

"How about this," I said. "Ask them if we can both go and if they really can only take one. If so, it needs to be William. The companies are our priority."

What did we have to lose? You don't get what you don't ask for. Bahiyah was smart, confident, and demanding with an attention to detail that made her excellent in negotiating. In true form, she succeeded. Both William and I were on the chartered plane the next week.

For 10 hours and 5,351 miles, the UnGrounded plane flew non-stop to London. British Airways promoted it as their "innovation hub in the sky." One-hundred and thirty people meant that only around a third of the seats on plane were occupied. Once we took off, after the usual safety remarks, someone from the IDEO team stood in the middle of the aisle and recapped the purpose of the flight.

"This concept began as a partnership between the United Kingdom Trade and Investment Council, British Airways, the G8 Summit, and IDEO. Our goal is to spend the time we have together in the air brainstorming on how to encourage pursuit of science, technology, engineering, and math careers in developing countries. At the end of the flight, we'll choose two ideas to present at the Summit. A winner will be picked and funded by Richard Branson."

Absolutely insane, I thought.

"This whole plane is our workspace. We've got pens, paper, laptops. Whatever you need. Let's get to work."

I had been to a lot of think tanks like this. They always lead to a lot of great ideas. It was rare that anything useful was ever done afterward. What made events like this worthwhile was the people. I was sitting in the upper deck, the first-class section of the plane. The airline called it Club World. Twenty people from the group were separated and ushered up. Everyone else was in the main cabin. We had turned a whole damn plane into our playpen. Drinks flowed freely as people ran back and forth sharing ideas and writing them down on large sheets of paper. Eventually, all the ideas about how to save the world gave way to drinks, laughter, and conversation.

I was sitting next to an executive from British Airways. I was trying to do the math on what an event like this was costing. "This had to be a fortune," I said.

"Not that bad," he responded. "The cost of operating a 747 is roughly $25,000 per flight hour and around $15,000 of that is fuel. Do the math. Roughly 12 hours in the air from L.A. to London. Throw in the trip back, the lodging, the drinks, tours, and snacks and you get the point."

"Holy sh—! One million dollars for a two-day event."

"You're the data guy." He smiled.

He explained why this wasn't as big a deal as it seemed. "The planes have to fly back anyways. Sometimes empty, for maintenance and electrical work. So if they need to come regardless, it's part of the cost of doing business. Sunk costs and all that."

I couldn't help but laugh. I had struggled for four years trying to make a million dollars last investing in tech startups across Africa. Here we were burning through a million in *two days*. So a bunch of smart, well-meaning, attractive people could flirt with each other over the Atlantic while discussing poverty. I nodded as he spoke to show that I was still listening, but my mind was elsewhere. I thought back to that day at 795 Folsom Street to where I went speak to engineers at Twitter, a company owned by young billionaires Jack Dorsey, Ev Williams, and Biz Stone. I remembered stepping over the homeless guy to get through the door. Now we were doing the same thing, in an airplane.

We landed just in time for the Innovation Summit in London. It was another glitzy conference in another part of the world. The conference was held at the 4.4-acre Seimen's Crystal, a building lauded for its sustainable design. Later that evening, we received a private tour of the House of Lords by Her Excellency Baroness Patricia Scotland of Asthal followed by dinner at British Parliament. In the mix was American TV presenter Van Jones.

I left the party early.

After our innovation in the sky, I was tired. All these expensive, exclusive events where the attendees talked a lot about innovation and global good were tiring. Then we'd go back home and do it again at the next conference. And the next. Charter a flight. Or a yacht. Whatever one-upped the last event. The philanthropic world was one big opulent trap house. Apparently, the world could not be saved without extreme luxury. Yet, many of the activists I knew struggled to find funding at all. This was the kind of bloated aid my friend Stephen had railed against at the party in Nakasero years ago.

I had code switched my way into the epicenter of wealth, influence, and excess. I was now living the life of a *bon vivant*. I had become what Stephen warned me about all those years ago.

A bobble-head.

Act #4

Clearance

#Predestination

"Your assignment, should you choose to accept it..."
– Mission: Impossible

"Do I need a security clearance?" I asked.

"You shouldn't," the woman told me. "The data you're working with is unclassified."

"Okay. Well, we're ready."

After moving back to the U.S., I convinced Matt to join me. We started a new company called MetaLayer, leveraging my years in the emerging sector combining statistics, analytics, visualization, location data, programming, and research. This new industry was called *data science*.

Data science was a new name for an old discipline. Professionals—I'll call them data detectives—had long used a combination of math, statistics, and intuition to get to the root of human problems. In 1854, the physician John Snow used maps to deduce the origins of a cholera outbreak that left more than 600 people dead. My mother was a data detective as well. After working on the first flights of the Concorde, she graduated to a desk where she worked in labs to trace the origins of plant diseases threatening crops. Growing up, she told me stories about plant diseases that were so aggressive they could alter the American economy in catastrophic ways.

I got into data science initially while working with my team at Appfrica. We were often hired by multinational organizations to help conduct surveys in African countries. Then they would hire us again to work with the databases we created, to make sense of it. What did it mean to have millions of people living on a dollar a day in countries that still seemed to have growing economies? Where was the growth coming from? My mother was a plant pathologist. She investigated the condition of plants and their health. I investigated the condition of people and the health of economies. That put me in the position to work with the folks from Ushahidi. From there, I became immersed in a network of activists, liberation technologists, and investigative journalists who used data science to investigate corruption and human rights abuses. Eventually, around 2011 someone finally came up with a name for this combination of computer science and statistics. People who had been doing the work for years, like myself, overnight became *data scientists*.

My colleagues and I were recognized among the first people to call themselves data scientists for our work on high-profile humanitarian crises in Haiti and Fukushima. Other lesser-known projects, like the kidnapped journalist in Uganda, and my role in the response to the Kampala riots, had put me on the radar of people in the U.S. Intelligence agencies and the Department of Defense. Matt and I began freelancing with them, using data in ways that could benefit their efforts.

One of our first tasks was a research project for the Wounded Warriors and Veterans Association. The two groups spent millions of dollars conducting surveys every year that took forever and gave no quick results. First, paper surveys were mailed to vets receiving benefits. The surveys asked things like:

Which is more most important to you?

- ☐ *time with your pets*

- ☐ *freedom to travel*

- ☐ *time with family and friends*

- ☐ *time at home alone*

The results would come back then be sent to a processing center and tallied by a consulting firm. Then, the consulting firm would spend a few weeks, or months, compiling a report that drew conclusions. This would be followed by recommendations on how to better serve the veteran community. Those recommendations would then be mailed back out with another survey asking the veterans if they wanted different programs designed around the firm's findings. If a lot of them indicated they wanted more support for their pets, the VA would design initiatives that offered care to veterans and their pets. The whole process to determine that veterans liked to spend time with their dogs and cats could take anywhere from months to years.

After collecting messages from veterans on social media, we proposed a system that would extract keywords (and of course hashtags) from social media messages. These extracted words were used to create word clouds that showed the most popular terms in use by veterans. Word clouds were a way to rank words in a document by the number of times they appeared. The more frequently the word was used, the bigger they appeared next to other words. The idea was to pull the top ten keywords from the veteran's conversations online. We could then make recommendations by deducing what those keywords meant. We used the proximity of keywords appearing around them to guess some larger meaning.

The computers couldn't actually read and understand the text. Humans still had to make sense of it all. Yet, there were millions of messages. Way too many for us to read one by one. By identifying keywords and using word clouds, we were training the algorithms to reduce our workload. Normally, such studies would take years and cost millions, even tens of millions.

"We can do this in six weeks for one million dollars," I said.

"Do what? The surveys? They usually take a few months," the military researcher replied.

"Not just the surveys. All of it. We can buy historic data to form a baseline and capture new data going forward. The old data will allow us to make recommendations as soon as next week. The hardest part of this will be figuring out what fonts we want to use for the reports."

The researchers looked at each other in disbelief.

"Well, son. Can't beat that. Let's get you guys paid and get this project underway."

After a few weeks, Matt and I developed a deep understanding of everything in the veteran community. Yes, they liked their pets, and they also liked exercise and driving pick-up trucks. There was also the dark side. Suicide. Homelessness. Domestic violence. Racism. Our job was to find the most useful insights and summarize them, no matter what they said.

We worked with data sets pulled from social media where veterans used hate speech to vilify then President Obama or denounce Black and Hispanic service men and women. We had to sift through messages of white nationalist communities and others who became radicalized against the military or the local police. Others complained about the crushing weight of medical bills and contemplated suicide. Some left their final goodbyes on Twitter and Facebook and were never heard from again. It was like surfing through the psyche of millions of people. Somehow, we had to translate all of this into something proactive the VA could do to improve their support.

Eventually, our software was able to help us get ahead of the information. By analyzing recurring keywords, we learned we could predict with a high degree of confidence which ones were going to end up being the most useful. We could run the software and make educated guesses about what the results were going to be after only a few days. We had taken a process that normally took months, even years, and brought the time expectation down to a fraction of what it had been.

"No problem, son," the man at the desk said. "By the way, we're hiring. Let's talk if either of you ever think about a new line of work."

* * *

When I founded my company, MetaLayer, it was based on observations of the way large organizations work with data. I had spent
the better part of two years working with non-governmental organizations, governments, banks, telecoms, and other companies
trying to make better use of their data. Changes in technology
meant there were all sorts of new tools and technologies to make
use of new databases, new coding languages, and new ways for
different software programs to talk to each other. The amount of
data available to the world was growing at an exponential rate.
Working with these institutions in the early 2010s made it clear
that data-overload was a growing problem. There were too few
ways to collect, analyze and redistribute streams of data. At the
same time there were too many technologists offering too many
different solutions aimed at addressing these problems. Too
much of everything and not enough time to do anything.

Peak big data.

At MetaLayer, we asked the question: *How do we simplify managing these data tools?* Normally, data collection and analysis took
expert computer programmers and sophisticated algorithms. We
believed that MetaLayer could do the heavy-lifting and give our
users a simple platform that explained it all. If there were thousands of documents that needed to be analyzed, users could give
the system some minimal information and it would automatically
analyze, transform, or improve the datasets. We wanted to make
working with data as easy to learn as software like Photoshop.

The complex algorithms made it an exceptional platform. The
guessing we trained the computer to do was called *natural language processing*. We could point our code at hundreds of thousands of electronic documents and the code would tell us what
was in them. We used a different technique called *sentiment analy-*

sis which told us the emotional tone of the documents. Was there an urgent message or stern warning buried in a pile of emails? If so, we could surface those messages easily. We could also pull out relevant locations referenced in the documents and automatically display them on maps. This was useful if there was a need to take unclassified documents about incidents, people, or places, and get a quick visual reference of what was happening where. Our programs eliminated the need for humans to organize the information manually.

Perhaps the most powerful algorithm was our code for predictive analytics. In 2012, predictive analysis was rare and hard. It required using techniques to not only draw conclusions about the documents right now but using statistics to determine what would happen next. Companies like ours had turned predicting the future into a business. I'm joking, sort of. Predictive analytics was a method of computer science that made an educated guess about the future based on observations of the past.

What were the uses for this type of technology? One example might be analyzing torrents of financial documents in order to anticipate stock trades or business acquisitions. This was something hedge funds and Wall Street wonks paid companies millions for. Or perhaps we could sell it to investigative journalists who aimed to get ahead of a story. In other projects, we attempted to predict economic patterns of countries.

Before we could confidently sell software into those spaces, we needed use cases that gave us credibility. We found our most lucrative contracts in Washington, D.C. with the Department of Defense. For those working in counterterrorism, defense, and surveillance, our software's ability to anticipate outcomes had huge implications. They became eager early adopters willing to experiment to see if there was any advantage they could get for intelligence. Their goal was to look for any edge that would help them ahead of situations like planned bombings or terrorist movements.

"Reading the tea leaves of terror," the one of our first customers said in a dramatic voice. "This is some comic book-level shit!"

I laughed. "Well, I did read a lot of comics coming up."

"Does it work?"

"Only one way to find out," I said.

The offices of Thomson Reuters were at the corner of H Street and 14th Street Northwest in Washington, D.C. The man sitting across from me was the head of Thomson's Innovation department, a division named Special Services, or TRSS. Special Services offered custom solutions to select customers in the federal government. Their team focused on testing new tools and technologies that might be useful for the wider organization. The gentleman who had invited me had read about MetaLayer and invited us in to collaborate. The benefit of working with Thomson was that they could become a reseller. This meant that if the intelligence agencies didn't know or trust MetaLayer, they would recognize that it was a product that was co-signed by Thomson as our big brother. Additionally, we had access to some of Thompson's troves of unpublished research, billions of documents digitized, archived and indexed over decades.

"Let's give it a shot," the TRSS head said. "How much data can we throw at you?"

"We're ready for anything," I replied.

I was lying. The truth was I didn't know how much data our platform could take. Closing this deal would be a win. Whatever they gave us, we'd just have to figure out. TRSS went on to give us the largest data set we'd ever worked with at any company. Ask and you shall receive.

Now we had more than 50-gigabytes of data, containing 2.9 million documents from the prior fifteen years of Reuters reporting. We were to use our suite of data tools to comb through them and identify trends. If we were successful with our predictions, they would know we were on to something. Then their reporters could use our software to monitor events on an ongoing basis. Events that had not yet happened would be flagged and ranked. They would receive a risk score that displayed the likelihood that they would happen. It was like a weather forecast but for bombings, civil wars, and other human conflicts.

"If we're successful, the case-study that comes out of this will be worth bank with DOD," I told Matt after the meeting.

"I know, mate, but we're not ready for 50 gigabytes of data. Not a chance."

"Our job now is to get ready."

Matt chuckled. "Your job is to buy me a pint for all the new work you just dumped in my lap!"

It turns out we were ready. The project with Thomson Reuters was indeed a success. Tasking our computer systems to look through nearly three million records, we were able to analyze events across Tunisia, Egypt, Libya, Yemen, and Syria. We were then tasked with sifting through documents, both classified and recently declassified. The documents related to numerous wanted people and suspected terrorists. People like alleged Yemeni terrorist Anwar al-Awlaki, would-be Nigerian bomber Umar Farouk Abdulmutallab, Osama bin Laden, and disgraced former Egyptian President Hosni Mubarak.

We were in the big leagues.

The tea leaves of terror, indeed.

* * *

"Done."

"Seriously?"

"1.5 hours. Ingested and analyzed. All 3 million. Now what do you want us to look for?" Matt said.

"We're looking for *oh shit* moments," the guy said. "Places in the documents where these suspects line up with places that become important months or years later. Almost like looking back to see what we might have missed."

I laughed. "This is a startup. Aren't they all *oh shit* moments?"

#FailedState

"He has put a knife on the things that held us together and we have fallen apart."

– Chinua Achebe, Nigerian author

Blame Will Smith.

In 1998, the movie *Enemy of the State* portrayed the looming threat of a surveillance state as an action thriller. Smith's character Robert Dean is an aggressive lawyer in Washington, D.C. He's hot on the trail of a mob-affiliated teamster, Paulie Pintero. Meanwhile, an NSA executive has a sitting Congressman murdered, an act caught on video. An accidental witness to the crime is also murdered by the NSA. Before he dies, he passes off a copy of the recording to Dean. Unbeknownst to Dean, he is now an enemy of the state as federal agencies throw everything they have at him. They'll do anything in order to stop the leak of the video.

The film does a good job of making the audience question just how much of our lives were, in fact, being watched by the prying eyes of the government. They had satellites, hidden cameras, bugs, and the ability to hijack electronic communication systems without a warrant. The movie was a huge hit, grossing $250 million dollars on a $90 million dollar budget. The film also caused people to question how much power groups like the NSA had over their lives. Did they really need to do their jobs by invading our privacy?

The movie was prescient. It preceded the 2001 passing of the Patriot Act by three years. The Patriot Act granted the types of sweeping powers to the NSA the film had warned about. The launch of Wikileaks in 2007 manifested a different idea portrayed in the film: the threat of inconvenient leaks and the damage they could potentially do to governments. This too played out in the form of leaks by Edward Snowden in 2013.

I remember sitting in the theatre when *Enemy of State* came out thinking, *that's not how any of this works.* But I missed the point. The movie wasn't about what was a technical reality then. It was about the public's fear of what might become possible later. Fear of what technology in the hands of the wrong individuals would be used for. People fear what they don't understand and can't control – technology represents both.

In May of 2013, 29-year-old Edward Snowden was motivated by the same concerns. He wanted to expose just how much of the public's fears were vindicated. While working for the NSA,

Snowden snuck away to Hong Kong with tens of thousands of documents he allegedly stole from the US government. He felt the documents demonstrated that the NSA had gone off the rails in the name of protecting the public. Using the screen handle *Cincinnatus*, Snowden made contact with journalists, letting them know that he was in possession of sensitive information. A disgruntled NSA employee steals away in the middle of the night with terabytes of data and gives them to a journalist who uses them to challenge a broken system? It sounds like it could have been a draft for the plot of *Enemy of the State 2*. It was far more consequential. Vanity Fair later described the event as "the defining espionage story of our age."

If Wikileaks was a wake-up call for those concerned with the secrets that governments kept, the Snowden incident was a blaring alarm for those concerned with how those secrets were obtained in the first place. The timing of the scandal was personally disastrous.

In May of 2012, I was sent an RFI from a city in the United States that described the need for a system that sounded remarkably similar to what I'd been building at Swiftly. Matt and I were invited to work with them on their disaster preparedness strategy. The project would start with a few hundred thousand dollars in funding but would scale up to the millions if deemed a success. FEMA, the Department of Defense, and the Department of Homeland Security were each allocating billions of dollars to help American cities like Houston become "smarter." In short, they were underwriting the cost of new digital systems to automate or replace old emergency response processes.

We were well-positioned to win the bid. A substantial portion of these budgets was allocated to projects that leveraged data science for humanitarian response. The group responsible for the RFP, the Regional Emergency Public Information System Administrator of Fortbend County, reached out after I spoke at a conference about some of my work in East Africa.

"You might just have something we need," their representative told me.

The request for proposals was entitled *Software to Monitor Social Media Intelligence for Emergency Management*. It requested a system that could notify 4.5 million people of any public threat (terrorism, hurricanes, mass shootings) by leveraging real-time data feeds from social media. For weeks Matt and I worked with administrators in Houston to map out a strategy. to deploy and scale a version of our open-source Swiftly code. They were aware of my departure from Ushahidi, who were trying to build a different version. After my departure, Ushahidi still recognized the need for a robust data platform. Unfortunately, their new version was severely limited in scope.

The people behind the RFP were aware of both projects. "We need it to be able to do much more than that." I assumed he was referencing the other project, otherwise, he wouldn't have reached out us.

After we submitted our proposal, we received another email: "Great news, your bid was selected for negotiations by Commissioner's court last week."

We were excited. It had been weeks of back and forth with them. With a paying customer, and an exciting first project, we set out to revive our Swiftly platform. Even though we were now operating as MetaLayer, the Swiftly software was purpose-built for disaster preparedness and had different features. We didn't mind that they wanted us to return to the old code, we had built it. Our plan was to revive and release this new code as a branch of Ushahidi's SwiftRiver project. There was no reason to fight for ownership. It was all open source. We didn't mind gifting our code

317

back to their community of volunteers. This was something that happens all the time in open source. Other open-source projects like Linux have many competing versions, branches of the same underlying core kernel customized by different companies. Our work with Fort Bend had the potential to scale to any city in the world. It was a huge opportunity.

Our work on this continued for over a year. We slowly navigated the bureaucracy of government procurement. When the Snowden leak happened on June 5th, 2013 with an explosive story in The Guardian, I became worried. The public's growing anxiety around data and privacy was going to be a problem. I could feel it. People woke up on the wrong side of the bed to face big questions around data governance and digital privacy. I thought back to the types of questions I got after the release of the diplomatic cables, watching everything play out from inside The Guardian's HQ in London. This was worse.

This time it wasn't diplomats who were vulnerable, it was everyone. Senators, civilians, federal employees, corporations – everyone was now hyper-concerned with privacy.

"We need to be prepared that this isn't going to move forward, at least not in the way we thought it would," I told my team in an email. "The spotlight is going to be on companies like ours for a while."

I completely understood why the temperature had changed on privacy. Data was powerful, and people were intimidated by this power. They were already wary of people who knew how to wield that power for seemingly any purpose; now they suspected it was being misused. Every person in America now felt like Will Smith's character in Enemy of the State. The smartphones in their pockets, their laptops, their systems at work had all become weapons that could be pointed at them. It didn't matter if

MetaLayer was trying to use data to protect them; that was the same argument the National Security Agency used. It turned out the digital fence they were building around the country to protect it was also a prison to contain it. This was the dual nature of surveillance.

Up to that point, communication with our client was daily. Emails ping-ponged back and forth with municipal officials who were eager to get the MetaLayer system in place. "Negotiations Final," one email read. We were almost in the home stretch. So close.

The day Snowden's leaks broke, their tone changed.

June 5th. No contact.

June 6th. No contact.

June 7th. No contact.

June 8th. No contact.

June 9th. No contact.

June 10th. No contact.

June 11th. No contact.

I found out what happened from a press release in the Houston Chronicle released June 12th. No one ever called to tell me. Instead, I used a web crawler. It notified me whenever our company name was mentioned online.

The article said that the type of data systems we proposed was toxic because there were "too many unanswered questions about invasion of privacy." Those were words cited from a ruling where the funding for our project was placed under review. A judge pointed out his staff had received numerous phone calls from citizens concerned with data and its use. He agreed. With no easy way to reassure them, it was probably better to steer clear of anything that might put them at risk. It may have been out of an abundance of caution, but it was necessary.

"The question I got from constituents was, 'Isn't this similar to what the federal government is doing with [collecting data from] Verizon, AT&T, and Google?'" he said. "I asked staff to explain how this system is supposed to work [differently] so I can confidently explain it to our residents…that the safeguards being put in place can't be changed for malicious use later."

Lawyers representing the city and our team attempted to explain our products didn't have the ability to be invasive. We weren't violating any one individual's privacy. I also pointed out that unlike the corporations mentioned, our product was open source. That meant that authorities could always see what was happening in the system at any time. The code was auditable, and the data collected belonged to them, not us. My argument was too little too late.

"This is not something that can access people's emails or private posts on social networking sites. It can't collect non-public information about a citizen," a lawyer said on our behalf.

By then, news about the NSA collecting information from private personal phone conversations and emails was at a fervor. Paranoia was palpable and cast too many doubts on any program that sounded like theirs.

"There's just too much uncertainty and the timing is horrible, if you will," the Judge responded.

He ruled against us.

There would be no more negotiations or emails beyond a few courtesies thanking us for our work. There were expressions of disappointment on all sides. Once again, I felt I'd been positioned well ahead of the curve. We had everything in place to help the city, perhaps even the country, rethink how data could be used during times of wide-scale emergency. That vision was now shattered.

What if we'd got the sign-off on June 4th? I wondered. Everything would have been different. Startups are like that; every single day has the potential to lead to unfathomable success and wealth or cascading failure of epic proportions. This was the later.

After all the false starts, three different software development teams, 40 different code repositories, and losing funding on three separate occasions; this proved to be the fatal blow to the Swift-ly/SwiftRiver initiative. Later that year, Ushahidi would shutter its own branch of the open-source Swift project. It was ill-fated from the start. Matt and I moved on to work on other data science products. We shut down the Swift project for good.

It had failed for the last time.

#ThreatLevels

"Hold my hand, close your eyes, and pretend to be dead."
– Westgate shooting survivor

Our black hoodies were everywhere.

They skipped between attendees like Microsoft Founder Bill Gates, comedian Reggie Watts, lawyer Bryan Stevenson, and scientist Bill Nye. People wearing our hoodies ran through the halls, they laughed by the stage, they were at exclusive dinner parties, morning yoga sessions, late-night runs on the beach, skateboarding sessions, and strolls on the boardwalk. Hoodies were tossed on the floor of hotel rooms as people made out.

To celebrate the launch of MetaLayer and new financing from investors like Comcast, I decided to hack the annual TED confer ence in Long Beach, California. It was common in the tech world for rising startups to host big launch parties celebrating new rounds of funding. It was a signal to potential investors and customers that things were going well. We used new funding we'd received from Comcast to stage a guerilla takeover of the event. I brought 60-odd black hoodies, super comfortable for the brisk February weather. I gave them all away for free to peers in the TED Fellows program, part of that year's highly coveted TED gift bag. On the back of the hoodies in bright white letters, I printed the name of the company: MetaLayer.

In the exclusive, highly curated TED community, two thousand of the most influential people on the planet flew to listen to powerful talks and network. By giving 60 attendees my hoodies, I all but ensured I could photo bomb many of the photos taken at the conference that year. I estimated that as many as three percent of all photos taken that year featured some attendee lurking in the background with one of our hoodies on. It was even more obvious if you happened to be there. People took notice.

Who the hell is MetaLayer?

Did this startup send their entire staff? They're everywhere!

Can you tell me more about this company MetaLayer I keep hearing about?

You founded MetaLayer? I've heard a lot about them. Here's my card.

How much did you guys spend on this activation?

With MetaLayer, Matt and I got to operate the startup we had always envisioned Swiftly would be. Potential customers and VCs responded with enthusiasm. Some were aware of our work and others were curious how we'd been able to generate so much hype. The doors were open. I took meetings with venture capitalists including Bloomberg Ventures, Kleiner Perkins, NEA Ventures, and Kapor Capital. Doing the "Sandhill shuffle" meant traveling up and down Sandhill Road where billion-dollar venture capital firms are densely populated to raise capital. Despite our momentum and a memorable launch, MetaLayer never succeeded at raising much capital at all.

Instead, we survived off a lucrative niche we'd discovered working with the intelligence community. The same things that made MetaLayer attractive to Reuters made it interesting to others in the defense community. They had come across a white paper I had written for InQTel, an organization whose primary mandate was investing in the tools and technologies the CIA might be interested in.

One of those Defense projects was a counter-terrorism project focused on Kenya. It was my history in Africa and reputation in disaster response that led to these projects. It was rare to have an American who had carried out technical work in Africa. It meant I had context that would be lost to people who'd never lived in East Africa.

The project was compelling. The *youth bulge* in African countries was of growing concern to threat analysts in the intelligence community. Over 80% of the African continent was under the age of thirty. Unemployment and poverty were high. Large populations of desperate young people with idle time were potential recruits for extremist organizations. One such organization was a group known as *al-Shabaab*, which translated to "the youth" or "the youngsters." They were a fundamentalist group with origins in Somalia quickly spreading throughout Africa.

An analyst contacted me about a proposal U.S. Special Operations Command (SOCOM) was reviewing. The project aimed to combat the digital recruitment efforts of al-Shabaab extremist cells operating in Kenya. His group had successfully won the opportunity to test the concept. His company needed our team to help handle the construction and deployment of software that could track and analyze the digital evidence they were collecting. Doing this, we were to undermine al-Shabaab's recruitment efforts in Kenya.

It wasn't long before the system built using our technology was tracking tens of thousands of messages per day. We scraped data from around the world, tagging, sorting, indexing, and organizing the content. Our system surfaced content that seemed to indicate heightened risk as it related to specific locations or individuals. We were trying to find the hidden connections between people and places that might reveal some hidden plot, increased threat, or communication about an imminent attack. Once successful, the software could be sold to other agencies within the Department of Defense and Homeland Security who were also concerned with the rising threats out of East Africa.

In this case, the threat was Al-Shabaab. The group emerged with its own doctrine and ambitions, but soon pledged an alliance with another fundamentalist group known for terrorism—al-Qaeda. Al-Shabaab focused much of its efforts on recruiting and indoctrinating youth. In the increasingly connected world of Kenya, their recruitment efforts had evolved. The explosion of the Internet in Kenya meant there was a surge of youth in chatrooms, on web forums, on Skype, and other platforms. Al-Shabaab, well aware of this trend, had launched a digital recruitment campaign. It was aimed at targeting Kenya's disenfranchised youth. From early 2010 to late 2011, the ranks of al-Shabaab were increasing. This indicated they were an imminent and increasingly formidable threat.

Homeland security began to issue notices like the following:

Warden Message: Nairobi (Kenya),
Continued Threats to American Citizens

Anti-American sentiment; Terrorism; Threats

Africa > Kenya > Nairobi

5/20/2011

U.S. Embassy Nairobi released the following Warden Message on May 20, 2011:

This Warden Message is to notify American citizens that the U.S. Embassy in Kenya continues to receive information regarding threats against American citizens and interests in Kenya. In addition, Al Qaeda and Al Shabaab have made repeated public announcements threatening to avenge Usama bin Laden's death. The U.S. Embassy in Nairobi reiterates its advice to all Americans in Kenya to take measures for their safety and security at all times. These measures include maintaining good situational awareness, avoiding crowds and demonstrations, and keeping a low profile. U.S. citizens should avoid setting patterns by varying times and routes for all required travel. U.S. citizens should ensure that their travel documents and visas are valid at all times. In addition, over the next several days and weeks, we advise U.S. citizens to avoid areas where foreigners are known to congregate, such as nightclubs, shopping centers, and other crowded public spaces.

– American Citizen Services Unit

Matt and I were helping their team of analysts make sense of the data. We were trying to predict the statistical likelihood of real-world outcomes based on data collected online. Our software was able to do this by sifting through information from hundreds of online communities. It operated like a big search engine, only the contents were in Arabic and limited to conversations of suspected terrorists.

It was like a digital wiretap.

MetaLayer's job, as the software vendor on contract, was to supply this agency with the algorithmic means of collecting and sorting the data. Then we could expand the project. Instead of running in short cycles, we could run nonstop. It would quickly become the world's largest and most expansive repository of digital chit-chat by extremist groups throughout East Africa.

When we handed over the servers in late 2011, the group's team of analysts were ecstatic. The dashboards were lighting up with dots on maps indicating regions of the world that demanded more attention than others. A ticker counted off the number of messages collected in real time. It jumped from 343,343 to 347, 245 in three seconds.

They were floored by how much data we could process and how quickly.

Our software allowed analysts to sort through the messages. They were trying to understand who was targeted and where. The system could also translate the content from Arabic, so they could understand what was being said. It was like the localization work I had done for Google, only in reverse. Everything worked perfectly. Or so we thought.

Our celebration was short-lived. A few weeks after launch, we heard back from the executives. For reasons unknown, they were not open to expansion.

We'd been unfunded. Again.

Without additional funding, we had to deprioritize the whole project. The costs of running servers that collected this amount of data 24/7 easily ran in the tens of thousands of dollars per month.

"How can they shut us down? Has anyone looked at these dashboards? Something's clearly up in Kenya," I said.

"I know," the analyst replied. "But we're a private company just like you are. There isn't much we can do about it. We can't afford to burn this kind of money indefinitely."

Matt and I looked at each other. "So what happens now?"

"Well, hopefully, someone higher up the ladder reads the report we all produced. Best case scenario is they realize we were on to something and bring us back online later. Worst case scenario is they don't even read it."

"What's your gut tell you?"

"Maybe they've already got something like this. Something better. Maybe they don't need us."

I sighed, "That could be the case. Even if it is, are they looking for threats in the same parts of the world? Kenya, Somalia, Sudan, Libya, Tunisia, Algeria, Mauritania, Nigeria, Niger, Mali, Uganda, Sudan, Central African Republic? What about languages? Are they doing it in Somali? Farsi? Swahili? Oromo? Sangho?"

"Maybe Africa isn't a priority either. They only care about threats to U.S. interests. Whatever the case, what are we going to do about it? We're civilian contractors," Matt said logically. He sounded as defeated as I felt.

Everything came to a halt. A few days later, I sent an email, "Just letting you know that I shot one of your analysts an email to ensure that shutting down our old servers was okay. I think he has everything backed up and running elsewhere at this point, but we wanted to double-check."

"Yup. Nuke it." *Nuking* was a phrase we used to refer to zeroing out servers so that there was no trace of whatever happened on them. It was a way of resetting things, almost as if they had never been used at all.

That evening I opened my laptop to take one last look at the dashboard of raining text. As the streams of data flowed, I sat back and sighed. I watched digital lines representing different threat levels in East Africa zig-zag off the charts.

* * *

On September 21st, 2013, heavy footsteps echoed throughout the corridors of the mall as four assailants, wielding assault rifles and explosives stalked down men, women, and children with horrific efficiency. Some people who were trapped in the mall during the attack covered themselves in blood and played dead. They were shot and killed anyway. The gunmen who circled back needed to be sure. The mission of the assailants was to end all life within those walls. They carried AK-47s, reams of backup ammo, and grenades. The official death toll topped seventy, mostly tourists and native Kenyans who had been out for a day of shopping. They were caught completely off guard as the men raided Westgate Mall located in the affluent Westlands neighborhood of Nairobi.

When the attacks began, I must have been in the air. I had been hired to give a guest lecture at Rollins University in Winter Park, Florida, en route from another event in Montreal. Exhausted, I forgot to take my phone off of airplane mode. Instead, I went to baggage claim, collected my things and got in a cab. I headed from the Orlando Airport to Winter Park towards my destination. Once I arrived, I collected a key from a lockbox at a townhouse the University reserved for its guest lecturers and made my way upstairs to the bedroom. For the duration of my flight and the cab right there I was oblivious to any breaking news. That was about to change.

I turned on the TV. Shaky low-res footage captured by someone trapped in the mall showed the gunmen stalking victims, firing purposefully until they were certain there were no survivors before moving on to their next victims. There wasn't yet an official declaration of responsibility but the analysts on the news show were already tossing around the name al-Shabaab.

My stomach sank. I thought back to the work we had done months before. This was very much the type of worst-case scenario we'd worked so diligently to anticipate and prevent. I watched in horror as report after report emerged from Westgate. I called friends in Nairobi to make sure they were okay.

I can't know for sure if our work was capable of issuing any warning that would have been useful at preventing the assault on Westgate that day. Hindsight is 20/20 and historic data offers even higher fidelity. What I do know is I'd sat in front of enough screens in enough crisis scenarios to know what I was doing. I'd looked at enough dots on maps representing threats known and unknown to appreciate that we had offered a credible opportunity to intervene. Our mandate had been to look for, identify, and disrupt this exact scenario in this very location, targeting the group that eventually carried out the attack. If we weren't on to something, it was one hell of a coincidence.

I'm sure every person who's ever worked to defend the lives of others feels the same as I did. They feel the one thread they missed was their fault. If they had been better, or smarter, or more prepared, more people would still be alive. There's nothing any of us could have done, but it sure felt like a failure of epic proportions. We'd been looking at the right data, in the right place, shut down at the wrong time.

This was too much to process.

#AmericanBlack

> *"When marimba rhythms start to play,*
> *dance with me, make me sway"*
>
> **– "Sway (Quien Sera)," a song by**
> **Luis Demetrio and Norman Gimbel**

"Baltschug Kempinski."

The black limo pulled away from the curb and dredged through the melting ice. It was early evening in April and the city was warmer than I'd imagined. The drive from Sheremetyevo Airport was going to take an hour the driver said. His grey eyes glanced back at me from the rear-view mirror. He didn't speak much English and I spoke no Russian. We were silent most of the drive. He had the radio at such a low volume I could barely hear it. I looked out the passenger window and watched the horizon. I thought back to my time in Estonia, drinking with Miite, and being stalked by the Russian gang. Russia always seemed like it was a near-miss for me. I had finally made my way here.

In April 2013, I was living between Philadelphia and The Netherlands where I was attending an executive leadership course. I'd been invited to Moscow by executives at Google who asked me to speak at an event about data, privacy, and security alongside prominent tech entrepreneurs and politicians. It was from Amsterdam that I flew to Moscow.

Traveling on Google's dime as a distinguished speaker to one of the most expensive cities on the planet was the height of luxury. I'm not ashamed to say it was a lifestyle I'd become accustomed to at that point. I was always being flown somewhere, by someone, to speak about some world-changing project I was involved in. This Georgia boy from the farmlands of the rural South was in a limo on his way to visit stakeholders at the Kremlin, sponsored by the world's biggest search engine.

When I disembarked the plane, I was to look for a driver who'd be holding a sign up with my name on it. He had been told to take me to a black car and drive me to the hotel where I'd be introduced to my handler, the person whose job was to basically not leave my side. Also, the handler would ensure I was able to navigate Moscow freely and safely. In between conference events I was ushered into a green room where Google executives drank vodka and held court with politicians and diplomats.

We eventually arrived along the humming Moskva River to the palatial Baltschug Kempinski Hotel. Darkness had fallen, but it was still early evening Moscow-time. I checked in and rushed to my room, tired from the flight.

I sighed as I tossed my bags on to the bed. I opened them one by one. Strange. Things were in disarray, something not normal for me. I'm a little OCD when it comes to packing. Everything has to be in its place. I'd never just throw stuff in a bag like this. I assumed this meant my bags had been searched.

Usually, an airline will leave a card that explains that they'd done so, though. I didn't see any card. *Don't be paranoid, airlines search passenger bags all the time,* I told myself. I wasn't traveling with anything important, just suits and dress shoes. The important stuff was in my laptop bag, which I always kept as a carry-on. I rarely ever let it leave my side.

I thought back. Before boarding in Amsterdam, the security agent had made me turn on both my phone and my laptop to show that they worked. I placed them on the churning belt that ran them through their scanners separately.

Was there a moment when they were susceptible to tampering? When I was standing in line for the body scanner? How long had that taken? How about when I was patted down, or when I was putting on my shoes and belt?

There was a good ten to fifteen minutes that I'd been separated from my laptop. Enough time for anything to happen.

I turned my laptop on and carefully searched for any tampering. Nothing.

Perhaps lack of sleep was getting to me.

* * *

"We will be happy to organize for you excursion with English speaking guide. Only clarify, please, which half of the day will be more convenient—morning, afternoon, or evening," the Moscow booking agent told me.

Now that I had checked in and rested, the handler had arrived. She came to meet me in the lobby of the Kempinski. The woman was older, in her sixties or seventies, but she moved as quickly as a woman half her age. I was standing at Kilometer Zero, the meeting point she had given me in front of the Iberian Chapel, near the Red Square.

"Ah, yes. Mr. Gosier is it?"

"Hi. That's me," I said, shaking her hand.

"Your first time to Moscow?" She smiled.

"Yes, it's lovely."

"Well, you've come at the right time of year. You missed all the snow!"

Each speaker at this event was assigned a handler whose job it was to follow you around, translate for you, answer any questions you might have, and take you sight-seeing. They also told you where not to go and translated for you. Mine was a professional tour guide as well. She was eager to take me around.

"You are one of only four Negroes I've ever given this tour to." She paused, "Excuse me, they don't use that term anymore in America, do they?"

I feigned a smile. "No, we don't."

Her use of the word *negro* was fascinating to me. Although so much seemed to have happened in America since the 1940s and '50s related to civil rights, race relations, and tolerance, to the rest of the world, fifty years was a blip. It was nothing. Here, they had survived the collapse of an entire government, then they replaced it. In the scheme of geopolitics, American race relations were defined by much bigger events than the retirement of pronouns. Desegregation. The assassination of Martin Luther King, Jr. The election of President Barrack Obama. These were the racial milestones that had resonated throughout the world. All of American history could fit into the timespan of Russia's history four or five times over. American anxiety around race was invisible in Russia. That isn't to say Russia didn't have its own problems.

"Sorry!" she said, "Blacks. One of four *blacks* I have met!" She grinned and began our tour, beaconing me to follow.

She had been a tour guide for decades. Her personal highlight was the time she was part of the delegation that accompanied music superstar Michael Jackson at the peak of his fame. This would have been 1981 or '82. She told me that meeting him was her first interaction with a black person at all. It was hard to fathom; I was only her fourth *black*. The others being two American government officials and one Nigerian man.

It was a lonely list.

"You can't imagine how things were here when I was youth," she told me. "We were so very poor. But mostly it was insanely boring! My friends and I, we wanted nothing more than a pair of blue Levi's jeans. Of course, American products were banned – music and movies."

American musicians, our actors and actresses, our poets and writers, had unknowingly fought and won a different type of war for the hearts and minds of people around the world. Celebrities like actor Carey Grant, runner Jesse Owens, and singer Josephine Baker were not just entertainers. They were subverting authoritarian control by disarming the people and diffusing mistrust of America. Culture had become a weapon. I never fully appreciated the significance until I stood before this old woman whose eyes lit up and blushed as she fawned over jeans she never got to wear as a teen. It was that feeling and desire to be a part of pop culture that helped fray the social fabric of the Soviet Union.

The woman told me her stories of just how much sway American pop-culture had over Soviet youth in those years. They had embraced music and fashion, much of it American or British, to subvert censorship. A black market emerged for smuggling in music recordings. The youth gathered in the basements of friends to dance and listen to the latest jazz, rock, and crooners from the West. The *stilyagi* they were called. They had been members of a secret society of code-switchers, trading ideas and music that were forbidden by the State.

"Wow. Did you ever get a pair of Levi's?" I asked.

She laughed. "Oh, yes. Eventually. By then I was no longer a girl. An American tourist around my age and size, she gave me a pair of her Levi. Finally, Levi! I was so happy." She sighed, lost in fond memories. "Now you can buy Levi everywhere in Moscow, no problem!"

* * *

After the tour, she took me back to the Kempinski to get ready for my panel. The conference focused on cyber security, surveillance, and subterfuge. It was hosted by Google, the company holding more of the world's data than any other. We were near the beacon of Russian Cold War intelligence, The Kremlin, which was either horribly ironic or perfect. As I took my seat on the stage, I couldn't help but wonder if this had just been an elaborate ruse to lure all the most prominent security professionals and political dissidents to be rounded up. Here, anything was possible.

Many of the conference speakers, even a few on my panel, were Russian. Others were Israeli, Syrian, Egyptian, or from dozens of other countries. The speakers were each given a radio headset. The headsets could be tuned to channels where different languages were translated in real time by a person off-stage. As people spoke on stage, the translators in the headsets relayed what was being said in English or whatever language was native to each listener. The translators had to be fluent in multiple languages because not everyone on the panel spoke English. This enabled the presenters to speak, laugh, and argue with each other even if they had no common language.

The heavy use of digital tools during these events meant suddenly digital activism was a huge concern for tech companies. Executives from Twitter, Facebook, Amazon, and Google were there to offer their perspectives. Geopolitical conflicts were now talking points in their marketing campaigns.

I cited my many examples of high-stakes data science to conduct intelligence. I referenced projects at Appfrica, Ushahidi, Ujima, Abayima, MetaLayer, and Swiftly—where digital tools were built and used to save the day. I cautioned that the increasing needs of activists were changing the needs for tools that protected them as much as serving them in their efforts. I told them about the playbook used to take down activist networks: *surveil, infiltrate, compromise, neutralize.* How the very digital tools they were using to have a voice might also be the tools that compromised them.

As I spoke, I made a mental note to replace my own laptop when I got home.

#Freetown

"Please go easy with me."
- S.E. Rogie, Sierra Leonian musician

The sickness had come again.

It settled over the community like a storm front. For many, the disease took their loved ones quickly and unexpectedly like floods during the summer monsoons. Then came shame. They buried their people at night offering no explanation to the village as to where they had gone, fearful that if people knew the truth they too would become pariahs.

"Away," is all they would say, sadness swelling in their guts. They kept emotion as far from their faces as possible. *Away*. They did not want to be chased from their homes by anxious neighbors or shunned when they walked the town. If no one knew how their people succumbed to the illness, they could at least have a proper burial. At least their bodies would not be taken away on government trucks, never to be seen again.

At least, they could not be burned.

Hospitals were feared more than the sickness itself. People with the sickness could be prayed for. But hospitals were *godless*. Morose sunken faces lined the walls of the clinics, shrouded by the stench of feces, blood, and bile. The rooms overflowed with waves of death.

The government too had its shame, burning bodies at night in incinerators so the rising plumes of black smoke would not be seen for miles by grieving mothers. Soon, foreigners would come with their protective suits and mysterious medicines. They would wave their cameras and trample crops with their Range Rovers. The foreigners would feign smiles to mask their own foreboding. Everyone was humbled before this cruel fate.

The sickness, like Africa itself, was ancient, primordial, and feared by all.

Ebola!

* * *

Overwhelmed was an understatement. There were 45,000 Sierra Leonians for every doctor. In neighboring Liberia, it was even worse: 70,000 for every doctor. At the peak of the outbreak in early 2015 there were nearly 600 newly reported cases of Ebola.

Per week. The mortality rate was especially bleak at first, as high as 90%. As medical resources made to the countries and doctors became less stressed, mortality rates dropped significantly. On November 7th, 2014, I sat behind a table at the U.S. Department of State in New York discussing the outbreak with government officials and health workers. As a data scientist, I was being called upon to work with epidemiologists, medical teams, and journalists concerned with the outbreak in West Africa.

I was there to share my work as a member of a group that came together to address the situation. By its end, the pandemic would infect nearly 30,000 people and claim the lives of over 11,000. I wasn't one of the clinicians flying in to treat people. I had taken up with well-meaning humanitarians who worked from afar to support the work of first-responders and clinicians. From our homes in New York, Philadelphia, Hong Kong, and Atlanta we routed information collected from survivors in Liberia, Sierra Leone, and Guinea to journalists in multiple countries. This was now a familiar practice.

It had been years since I'd done it during Kampala's riots, phone in one hand, typing on my laptop with the other. Again, I sat behind a desk from thousands of miles away doing what I could, where I could. Again, I felt like we weren't doing enough, fast enough. Again, we were under-resourced and sinking in our own ambitions.

The feeling of trying to stay ahead of a virus is an urgency unlike any other. Viruses don't care about borders, ethnicity, or trade agreements. They are the nexus of math and biology. They spread exponentially and aggressively unless neutralized. In America, though people were afraid of Ebola, it was a misplaced fear. Most people didn't care that the pandemic was happening in Africa; they just didn't want it in America. They didn't understand the entire point of preparedness for an epidemic like this wasn't about how the virus started or where it came from. When a virus emerges in the world, by the time it becomes a pandemic, spreading internationally, it doesn't matter where they started. It will be everywhere, affecting everything.

Whether it's Ebola from Sierra Leone or the Spanish Flu (which actually emerged in France), by the time it becomes your problem, wherever you are, it's the world's problem. Americans wouldn't learn this until the Novel Coronavirus spread tore through the world in March 2020. In late 2019, when the spread of the virus could have been prevented through aggressive measures, Americans ignored that too. Eventually, *over there* was in the U.S. and 175 other countries. Viruses aren't xenophobic. Prevention and preparedness are the only ways to curb their impact. At the time of the Ebola outbreak, these weren't lessons that had been taught. American reactions to this disease were as racially charged as American's reactions to Africa itself.

It's over there, so keep it over there.

It was a particularly lonely feeling to face a global threat the people around me didn't yet understand. They minimized it and vilified the people they blamed. While most people were ignorant to the magnitude of the threat, I had to try to inform them without inducing panic. When this is done well, it will seem like the informer completely overreacted. The pandemic is contained, and they only get a glimpse of what could have been. Only people who faced the threat directly—epidemiologists, pathologists, and clinicians—will ever truly understand what disaster was averted. I spent my nights following closely along with news of the spread and death toll of Ebola. I found the normalcy of each day maddening. It was like fighting an invisible war with millions of oblivious civilians on the frontline going about their daily lives.

It occurred to me in that moment that I was following the path of my mother. While I had been drafted into the ranks of epidemiologists who traced the origins of diseases in humans and animals, her work was to trace the origins of disease in plants. I wondered if the strange, silent urgency I felt while trying to protect people from an enemy they would never fully appreciate was how she felt. If she and her colleagues did the job well no one would ever know or care. If they didn't, the agricultural supply chain in the country would fail and millions of people would face a food shortage and famine.

I was at the State Department to request help. I was working to build a computer system that sought to automate processes others had been doing manually. Across West Africa, health organizations received messages from people in countries affected by the Ebola outbreak. They then relayed them one by one to other health organizations, journalists, and government officials. Collecting and disseminating this information was painstaking and time-consuming. It couldn't stop, though. The various groups needed the data, since it offered clues that might reveal where the outbreak had originated and how it was spreading. Understanding the path of transfer was the first step at stopping the outbreak.

Without the right information, this wouldn't be possible. So, the workers found themselves overwhelmed by an avalanche of text messages, videos, and medical reports that grew day by day. The service our team proposed would make all of this cheaper and faster. By automating the collection of information and where it was sent, we could greatly improve their process. I proposed we replicate platforms used by big web publishers. Publish once, push once. One publication could be pushed across the cacophony of news services available to global audiences. This was how advertising and digital journalism had worked for decades. Could we apply the same logic to a global health crisis?

My colleagues were from an organization called *Ebola Deeply*. We were working to attack the multitude of challenges related to the outbreak. One of our goals was to better inform American audiences and the media. America has always held an irrational fear of Africa, but the trepidation was even higher where it came to Ebola. Likewise, in countries like Sierra Leone, Guinea, and Libera, misinformation was spreading wildly. They feared Ebola was a biological weapon being spread by foreigners who sought to wipe them out. As a result, many refused care for fear of being given the disease by medical workers. It was an irrational fear, but people often behave irrationally when they don't know who they can trust. By collecting and sharing quality information, we hoped to improve the situation on both sides.

The effort was spearheaded by a company called News Deeply. The company specialized in creating news portals that offered a vertical deep dive into different subjects. News Deeply built on the old concepts of journalism in digital form. They aimed to pioneer a model for single-topic investigative news sites. At the time, most news organizations covered many topics broadly. News Deeply argued that broad was the enemy of deep coverage. Imagine a CNN-like website that only covered stories related to water, climate change, or in this case, Ebola. Their goal was to help their editorial teams to do what has become increasingly uncommon in the digital era: focus.

Lara called them, "vertical impact and relief stories."

The Ebola project had been pulled together through meetings by my colleague, Bahiyah Robinson, and marketing executive James Andrews. Our other collaborators were Lara Setrakian, previously a correspondent for ABC, and acclaimed international journalist Isha Sesay of CNN. Isha was a woman I had watched many times from Uganda as she calmly relayed news of crises and casualties that the rest of the world seemed eager to ignore.

At the peak of the outbreak, Isha would fly to Sierra Leone herself to diligently work from the ground. There she hoped she could get her American CNN audience to pay more attention to the affected countries. American journalists often had to fight to get Africa coverage at all, she explained, a fact that was making misinformation even worse. She wanted to humanize the situation for her audience. She saw herself as the bridge to empathy and reason. She was Sierra Leonian and had more at stake than almost anyone. On our blog, she explained why she was involved:

"My family – mother, brother, grandmother and countless loved ones – are in Sierra Leone right now. My immediate family is in the capital, Freetown, while many others are scattered about the countryside. No matter where they live, their day-to-day lives, their routines, their normalcy, has been ripped to shreds by Ebola."

Sitting next to me on the panel was an executive from the International Rescue Committee (IRC). She had previously been embedded in Liberia, the country hardest hit by the outbreak. Her perspective was critical. She'd witnessed Liberia, a post-civil-war country with poor infrastructure and low-education, go from bad to worse. The presence of Ebola had several ancillary effects including disrupting the flow of medical resources needed to fight diseases like HIV and malaria. Doctors were so overwhelmed by the need for Ebola-related medicines that they couldn't keep these other medicines stocked. They couldn't rely on the normal supply chains, which had been co-opted to deliver treatments to fight Ebola. The doctors also had to contend with a growing shortage of hospital beds and other medical equipment. The supply situations in Guinea and Sierra Leone faced similar shortages.

The News Deeply team viewed the Ebola platform as an exercise in agile journalism. *Agile* was a project management methodology usually practiced by software developers. It's an approach to software development where requirements and solutions emerge from small self-organizing and cross-functional teams that work within larger groups. Those smaller groups take on portions of the project until all the tasks required to complete the project are accounted for, all were receiving feedback from stakeholders. The methodology encourages rapid and flexible to challenges called time boxes. A time box is a short increment of time where small tasks were tackled.

Each agile project has a representative who acts on the stakeholder's behalf. In the case of our Ebola project, one group represented journalists. Their job was to find out what the primary concerns of journalists were and what would help. A different group focused on clinicians, another, the people who were most at risk to Ebola. And so on.

By limiting the number of people involved with each cohort of stakeholders, it became easier to communicate as cohorts communicated information instead of individuals. These short feedback sessions allowed us to understand the issues of the smaller groups and address them properly. The smaller groups came up with solutions and brought their ideas and findings back to the larger group. We, as the managers, could allocate our collective time and attention towards executing their plans.

The process reminded me of my week at The Guardian, where the editorial division tackled millions of leaked documents in smaller teams who dissected them, organized them, and fed them back to leadership summarized and annotated. I wondered what kind of stories would come out of a task force like this when coupled with the document-state-of-mind set forth by Ron Nixon and his network of investigative reporters. What kind of stories would be produced by a team of agile investigative journalists?

When our potlatch team came together to form Ebola Deeply, we were like a group of paratroopers deployed from an airship. We convened, quickly raised around $200,000, used the money to report through the end of the crisis, flew our editors to conferences and in some cases to the affected countries to report from the ground. Then, post-crisis, we disbanded. All of this was done in the span of seven or eight months. There was no room for bloat.

Assemble, research, problem-solve, move on.

#RaceStreet

*"You were under full surveillance. We knew everything.
We even knew that you weren't man enough
to satisfy our little Christa."*
– The Lives of Others, German film, 2006

"If you view it from above, it looks like a pair of handcuffs," the officer told me in his thick Jersey accent.

We were speeding down Broad Street in a police squad car. A Lenovo ThinkPad was bolted to a black beam that stuck out of the dash. It hovered just above the car's armrest and gear shift.

On the screen, different data feeds streamed from bottom to top. A map dynamically adjusted itself as we drove, showing an animated canvas of streets and intersections mirroring the ones we saw as we passed by. From the outside the vehicle looked like it would be cramped. Now that I was inside, it was actually okay, comfortable even. As the car weaved in and out of traffic, I locked eyes with pedestrians, their heads turning as we passed. Their eyes were heavy and their faces stern. That was the look of resentment, I told myself. Or fear.

I met the officer at Race Street between North 7th and 8th Street, where the Philadelphia Police headquarters sits. The building had two spherical wings connected by a smaller boxy building with a straight edge. I was told they were deliberately designed by the building's architect to look like handcuffs. I was on a ride-along as the officer gave me a tour of the city's police facilities.

A day in the life of a data cop.

It was a year after the incident at Westgate Mall in Kenya. I wasn't eager to get back into counter-terrorism or anything like it. I had already seen the worst-case scenario, what happens due to failures of communication and bureaucracy. I was looking for new industries to apply my data skills as a consultant. One use case was in response to a police officer who asked if I could help improve their ways of working with data.

He explained that police were well aware they needed to collect and sift through streams of digital evidence left behind by criminals online, but they were starved for the resources to do so. Whether it was connecting the dots between individuals affiliated with gangs or collecting evidence on some elaborate scam, modern detective work had at least partially moved online. Could a data platform like the ones I had built for intelligence agencies be useful? Police needed methods and new experts. I, apparently, was considered one of the world's experts in the subject.

"Ever thinking of enlisting in the force?" he asked as he pulled up to the building. I had never been on the inside of a police car before, or even interacted with a police officer other than for the occasional speeding ticket.

"As a cop? I'm pretty sure there's a thousand skeletons in my closet that would prevent me from even getting past the background check."

He laughed. "Well you're in luck. The city needs people so we've lowered our standards. We'll take anyone. Even you."

"Not really my thing."

"You mean you don't want to help protect the fine citizens of Philadelphia with your data *voodoo*?"

"Voodoo? Listen, I don't often practice the dark arts but when I do, it's Python and SQL, not goat blood and candles. Also, that's kind of racist."

"Hey! Our HQ is located on *Race Street*. I like to think I get a pass on racism."

"Alright, Detective Fuhrman," I said getting out of the car. "Just don't shoot me. The object I'm reaching for is a laptop, not a gun."

Our friendly banter continued through the afternoon. It was another type of code switching. Humor could be disarming. Given a different context or situation, this might be tense relationship – a black male in his early thirties and a white cop in his mid-forties, together in a police car. Only this time the power dynamic was different.

I was there to them solve his data problems. It was part of an experimental predictive policing program happening outside the police department itself. It was a way of trying new things before they could be officially introduced into daily operations. In the movies, these systems were referred to as *pre-crime*. In short, it meant identifying crimes or suspects before they made themselves known through their activities.

The man who had invited me was a detective who worked closely with a police intelligence unit. The unit was called the Delaware Valley Intelligence Center (DVIC), located just outside of Philadelphia's city center. DVIC was part of a larger nation-wide program called the Real-Time Crime Center (RTCC). The purpose of the Real-Time Crime program was to provide specific Police departments in New York, Miami-Dade, Seattle, Fort Worth, St. Louis, Albuquerque, and Austin with access to advanced software like this. These systems made it easier to identify patterns in evidence by sharing data in real-time between the locations. The RTCC was powered by a data lake that contained billions of records and tens of billions of data points. The data lake, essentially a big database, was where data was stored so it could all be cross-referenced when necessary. Satellites mapped different regions from above, allowing officers to digitally navigate neighborhoods. Profiles of known suspects were used to link an individual to the locations they were most likely to flee to, like their homes or the homes of relatives. Crime centers are the central point of storage for data coming out of criminal records. It contained parole violations, complaints, arrests, 911 and 311 calls, and national crime reports. It had an index of billions of files considered public record. With the Department of Defense, I had helped build search engines that were limited to terrorist activity and communications. Now I was doing the same thing, only for police investigations.

"We've gotten pretty good at sharing information between departments," the detective began. "But making sense of it? That's a whole 'nother can of worms."

"That's why I'm here, I guess," I said as we walked into the handcuff-shaped building.

After a short tour, he took me to meet a team of crime analysts. There were only a handful of them. They huddled in a room that was probably once a closet. There was no window and only a single light that hung from an exposed cable. A card table had been jammed into a corner as a makeshift conference table. The computers weren't embarrassingly old, but they were old enough that I could tell they weren't useful for the type of computation necessary.

"I think I've identified the problem," I said. "It's hard to focus on data when you're cooped up in a room that strips away your will to live." Everyone laughed.

"When we're not working with data, this also doubles as an interrogation room," one of the men said. We laughed again. I wasn't sure if it was because that was clearly false or because it was clearly true. We made our introductions and sat down. I took my place at the table, glad not to be on today's menu.

"Okay guys. What have we got to work with?"

* * *

My ride-along and the handful of days spent working with the Philadelphia Police Department taught me two things. One was the sheer amount of criminal activity police officers have to respond to. Each incident is supposed to be carefully documented.

Even a cop on the street does his or her fair share of paperwork. The other thing I learned was how dangerous bad data could be.

Nationally, there was talk of using heat maps to highlight areas of a city where crime was occurring. These were normal maps with an overlay of colors indicating hot zones of activity. The brighter the red, the more dangerous the area. It was a baseline that predictive analytics could be applied to, allowing police to anticipate where crime might occur. It was the same concept as the Thomson and SOCOM experiments applied to police work.

To train the system, we would need to prep it with historical data. All the historical data they had was skewed by the level of crime that exists in communities that are already over-policed. These areas are heavily populated by African Americans, Latinos, and other immigrant populations. The danger, I thought, was that the baseline wasn't a true baseline. All sorts of failed policies had led to the policing of these neighborhoods. I wasn't being asked to come up with new ways to help them find crime. I was being asked to make what they were already doing more efficient. In short, targeting these communities faster. It had already been determined who the criminals were and where they lived.

Was this right? Do these communities actually commit more crimes?

From a data perspective, no. Police look for more crimes in those neighborhoods because that's where they are already looking. There's nothing that would suggest the same level of crime isn't happening outside of those communities. To get a true baseline, we'd need to first decide what type of crime we're looking for. Violent crime? White-collar crime? Sex crimes? Recreational drug use?

Change the type of crime, and you might find that there are entire neighborhoods not represented in police databases at all. In a biased dataset, potential criminals in those overlooked communities may as well not even exist.

Predictive analytics is not magic; it's algorithmic guesswork based on historical observation. If the underlying evidence isn't fully representative of the real world, then the output of a predictive program won't be either. This type of logic isn't exactly what police want to hear. From their perspective, their jobs are to use what they have, not redesign the system.

"What you have is bad data," I told them. That went over about as well as you might expect.

The data this team relied upon used circular logic. *Crime happens in this location; therefore, we need to increase our presence in this location.* It was all reactive. I suggested that in order to truly be effective, they would need to avoid looking at their data with any sort of pre-determined conclusions, "Let the data show you the story. Right now, you're only looking for what you already expect to find. We need to introduce some serendipity, some randomness to your discovery efforts."

"We don't have time to pull data from the whole world to make our cases. Here are the cases. Here's the data. Can you help us?" one of the men said sternly.

"That's not how it works. Pedagogically and ethically, this whole system is flawed," I told him.

It was the most inconvenient answer I could have given them. The room went silent.

After all the crime data and locations were mapped, there was another system in place that kept track of connections between key locations and people and their associates. Known suspects, especially those who were in gangs or other criminal organizations, were placed in databases that linked them to friends and family members. Those individuals were indexed, profiled, and surveilled very similar to how my company MetaLayer had previously helped track terrorists in Kenya. Their social media and mobile tech messages were archived. Communication with their friends, and friends of friends was indexed as well. Casually knowing the wrong person or being related to them seemed to make a person a target for surveillance.

"You're building profiles of people who haven't committed crimes. I don't know how to feel about that."

They were getting frustrated. They hadn't invited me here for my opinions. "Isn't this the same shit you did for the Feds?"

"We drew the line at surveilling people who weren't targets. It's not like we just started crawling the accounts of civilians because they happen to know someone who was suspected."

"Maybe that's why they can't ever catch them sumabitches!" another officer joked.

"Also, there are certain legal conventions we had to follow. At a state-level, don't you need warrants? At the very least a no-knock warrant?" I asked. I didn't have any legal training. For this type of surveillance data work in other circles, lawyers were needed just as much as programmers.

"It's called lawful interception," an officer said. "We cast the net and whatever we catch is what we catch."

He explained that they only scanned websites that were public. They were only conducting searches related to specific investigations. Information available on Facebook, Twitter, Snapchat and

YouTube was considered fair use. They were essentially in plain view of anyone using those platforms and therefore fell outside of the requirement for a search warrant.

"These are public accounts. If these idiots want to go online and talk about their crimes, it's all game. There is no search of the suspect's private accounts. No need for warrants."

"Right, but how are you getting some of these guys who do have private profiles? Do you have fake accounts friending them? If so, what are the legal grounds for tricking them to get past what is clearly a privacy boundary? That's a search. You don't need a warrant to do that either?"

He didn't answer.

"And what about profiling their friends? I'm now considered a bad guy because I've got a relative or an old college friend who ended up in jail?"

"Listen. You're not here to analyze our methods. Let legal do that. You're here to analyze our data and compute shit. Let us worry about how to do the job." He crossed his arms.

"I can appreciate that," I said. "I'm not your man, then. Maybe I'm making too much of it but it doesn't sit well." I closed my laptop.

For me, it wasn't just a question of what was legal. I understood that rapidly changing technology meant grey areas of the law were expanding. I had experienced as much working with activists and in response to other crises. Their bravery and desire to keep the public safe was admirable. But what they were asking for was laying the groundwork for a system that would continue to cross ethical lines.

Just because something could be done, didn't mean it should be. I'd learned that with Abayima. Without strict guidelines, computer systems would just replicate all the worst behaviors of people—only more efficiently.

We already had a flawed police system. My opinion was that the system needed to be reformed before it could be scaled. A different programmer might not care about these implications at all, but I did. I exited the doors of the police headquarters on Race Street and abandoned the project.

That night I scrolled through my list of friends on Facebook and wondered whose lists I might be on.

#BurnNotice

> *"Congratulations, you played yourself."*
> **- DJ Khaled**

In the intelligence community, a burn notice is an alert that someone has been *had*.

When a source or informant previously considered to be reliable
is revealed to be untrustworthy or deceptive, the federal the agency working with them issues a document that notifies other agencies the individual or group should no longer be trusted. In other
words, to disregard or *burn* all information derived from the now

questionable source. In some cases, this is the result of the source being compromised, flipped by the enemy. In other cases, it's because they'd been deceptive the whole time, making up stories, telling investigators what they wanted to hear. Either way, a burn notice serves as an alert to disavow the source. Nothing collected from them can or should be trusted going forward. Anything collected from them historically should be reconsidered.

In 2004, a man named Rafid Ahmen Alwan al-Janabi was serving as a federal informant. It had been alleged that he served as a chemical engineer making biological weapons for Iraq. Despite warnings from British and German intelligence agencies to the contrary, the US government used Rafid's case to advocate for military intervention in Iraq. This, in part, lead to the 2003 US invasion of the country. The prolonged armed conflict there would last nearly a decade. Rafid later admitted in an interview that his claims were lies. He was apparently just trying to get his green card. Informants often incur special favor with the government. They are offered things they want in exchange for information. With no real information to offer, Rafid made up an elaborate story. Subsequent to his admission, the CIA issued an official burn notice retracting hundreds of intelligence reports based on his first-hand accounts.

Agents gave him the nickname *Curveball*.

* * *

By 2014, the tools and technologies that gave me such optimism early in my career had evolved into something darker and more damaging than I had ever anticipated. More than once I watched as the tools and technologies of big data were weaponized faster than they could be used to solve human problems. In 2008, when I left for Africa, I was optimistic that technology was going to change the world for good. By 2014, I'd become cynical about the use of data. Not enough people were thinking ahead about where this could all lead.

In the months leading up the 2016 U.S. Presidential elections, allegations about former U.S. Secretary of State Hillary Clinton in Africa resurfaced. In 2012, Libyan leader Muammar al-Gaddafi had been ousted from office and subsequently dragged through the streets, killed by his own people. Across Africa, I noticed a concerning charge was being repeated. In the minds of many Africans, the reason the U.S. State Department got behind the effort to oust Gaddafi was because he wanted to unify Sub-Saharan Africa under one common currency that would empower Sub-Saharan Africa. Black Africa. It was a conspiracy theory that I believed had no kernel of truth. Still, it was popular.

The Libyan politician had been very outspoken on behalf of majority black countries, advocating for their independence post colonialism. He had also served as the former chair of the African Union. For an Arab leader, Gaddafi championed radical ideas of Pan-Africanism, a united Africa, and African Union. It made sense in late 2010 this was a rumor that I'd hear from Africans disgruntled with US policy. The ominous clouds of a revolution were forming over Libya, something many Africans viewed as the direct result of political engineering by America's elite.

They don't want to see Africa rise!

The US is afraid of Africa's true might!

It did not make any sense that these allegations resurfaced in the barbershops of Philadelphia in 2016. When I asked one gentleman where he had heard about this, he pointed to what had become a common refrain during the election: "I saw it on Facebook."

In his testimony before Congress in 2018, whistleblower Christopher Wylie reported a number of things that seemed to point out why. According to his testimony, Steve Bannon, media mogul and founder of Brietbart.com, worked with a company called Cambridge Analytica to target online audiences with negative coverage of Clinton. Wylie testified that the company amplified an enormous amount of negative messages about the candidate, including conspiracy theories. They only cared that people repeated the message.

In digital advertising, audiences are bought and sold almost like stock on Wall Street. Audiences are a currency that fluctuates in value. Speculators called media-buyers place bids on what they think the audiences are worth. The systems that collect the data offer profiles of uncanny specificity. Someone placing a bid could ask that their message be targeted to reach a specific type of person. How specific?

Mother of two in Kearney, Nebraska whose household income is $350,000 per year, who shops for romance novels on Amazon.com and who has $100,000 in credit card debt. Republican-leaning. Christian. Husband is having an affair. Visits Pornhub.com on her iPad and types the keyword 'lesbians' a lot.

Indian American male in Palo Alto, California. Earns $500,000 per year as the CTO of a tech startup. Sends $5,000 every few months to a Western Union pickup location outside Pune, India where he has family. Registered Democrat. Likes gangsta rap. Most frequently visited website after StackOverflow.com is Kink.com.

Latin American male in Miami, Florida. Earns $50,000 per year. Doorman at a luxury building in South Beach where the average condo sells for $1 million plus. Top streaming artists on Spotify

are Daddy Yankee, Romeo Santos, Marc Anthony, and Selena. In-
dependent. Spends three hours a day on Facebook, Instagram, and
Snapchat.

The information was detailed. Individuals were tracked by their
device identity numbers. Your device ID was like your computer's name and address. It was usually only used to talk to other
computers. You could have multiple IDs—for your laptop, iPad,
computer at work, smartphone, smartwatch, TV—anything you
connected to the internet. Those device IDs could be bundled together to create was called a graph identity. The graph ID essentially says all these device IDs belong to the same person.

Those IDs are then bought and sold on ad exchanges in the form
of units called impressions. Impressions are like the banknote in
this currency of audience data. Because there are two billion people on the internet and even more devices, the buyers of this data
usually can't be bothered with individuals. Instead, they bought
in larger swaths called segments. For example, they might tell a
data supplier:

> *I want to bid on only white males, who live on the east coast, who*
> *lean Republican and frequently visit Breitbart.com or RedState.com*

> *I want to bid on African American females who are college educat-*
> *ed, lean Democratic, and earn more than $100,000 per year.*

> *I want to bid on college students in the southwest who are liber-*
> *al-leaning and identify as Lesbian, Bisexual, Transgender or Queer.*

Once an order was placed, trading began. In the early days of the
internet, trading might consist of a martini lunch where impres-
sion prices were discussed for thirty minutes followed by hours
of drinking at strip clubs paid for on the company card. By the
early 2000s, the martini lunch was considered a waste of money.

Computer algorithms were capable of doing the bidding based on rules set by the media buyer. They didn't need to be wined and dined. Algorithms didn't have expense accounts.

Now sales executives would simply write the rules for algorithms. These rules are called bids. The salesperson would specify which groups, which audience segments, needed to be bought or sold. The algorithms would then talk to other algorithms, buying and selling all without human interaction. These bids are called insertion orders. They define the parameters in which you want to spend your agency's money, capped at a certain amount.

On the other side of the sales process, the supply side, publishers and aggregators of ad inventory scrambled to get the audiences they had access to in front of buyers. When the buyers started using algorithms to place bids, the sellers used algorithms to respond. Both sides let their computers do the talking for them, and after a set period, they audited to the transactions retroactively. At that point, it would be clear which audiences were bought and sold and at what prices. Accounts would be settled based on the people actually reached by an ad. Money was exchanged based on performance. It was like paying for a meal at a restaurant where you eat first, pay later. This day-to-day trading by computers resulted in a multi-billion-dollar economy called programmatic advertising.

In Wylie's testimony, he revealed that a segment of the population of particular interest to Cambridge Analytica was Black Americans. Blacks had been part of President Barack Obama's reliable base of supporters in both 2008 and 2012. If the opinion of Blacks could be swayed, it would have an outsized impact on the election. Perhaps they could be encouraged not to show up for Clinton in November. Cambridge Analytica designed campaign strategies for several Presidential hopefuls that year. One of them was the brash reality-TV star Donald J. Trump.

When you're trying to light a fire, it helps to blow on the coals. The team at Cambridge Analytica directed various media-buyers to audience segments they had profiled based on data collected from Facebook. Their thesis was some groups were more susceptible to believe certain information than others. Rather than target everyone, they could just target these groups. This type of psychographic profiling wasn't new. It's been done since the dawn of politics. Groups of people have interests that affect them collectively. It's how they self-identify. It's where the term *identity politics* comes from, the common experiences of individuals who tend to vote the same.

What was new was the ability of technologists to create psychographic profiles of millions of people at once. It became possible to place orders to target specific audiences with ads. It didn't matter if these ads were true or not, as long as they were believable enough to sway public opinion. Their campaigns could be aimed at identity groups with laser-like accuracy:

> *$50,000 order on websites like Pornhub next to lesbian content. Republican housewives seem to over-index there.*
>
> *$25,000 order for each frequent visitor to websites like TheRoot. com and Blavity.com, we want to hit affluent African-American females.*
>
> *$100,000 order on Spotify, we want to reach independent Latino voters who listen to Pitbull.*

Ad buyers could buy and sell any demographic segment they wanted. No platform made the buying and selling of people data easier than Facebook. The FBI later revealed that this disinformation campaign was pervasive. Cambridge Analytica apparently used questionable means to acquire targeting data from Facebook in the first place.

An FBI report later revealed Russian operatives launched bot networks (botnets) that were designed to spread and amplify disinformation. Whatever inflammatory messages needed to be sent out could be sent through programmatic channels where they had 90% accuracy of reaching the right person, in the right moment. The messages could be personalized to affect the voter based on the profiled audience segment they belonged to. The botnets posed as human users and mimicked humans who clicked ads. This helped give the appearance that it was truly viral content. By mimicking the attention of human viewers, botnets influenced ad networks, causing them to surface ads that were deliberately deceptive as if it were truly viral content.

There was also a coordinated cloning campaign. Russian hackers used their systems to clone Facebook accounts. They identified influential people and copied the text and photos from their profiles to create exact copies of their profiles. If your friend was *Brenda Applegate* on Facebook, another account named *Brenda Appplegate* might pop up. To anyone not paying attention, they probably never noticed the difference. They interacted with both accounts as if both were their friend. One account was not.

Then they would friend the unsuspecting user and share other disinformation as messages or posts. The messages looked like they were coming from friends. They looked real, so people shared them as if they were real. It was a way of hacking credibility. You might not believe a lie about political from just anyone. If it came from your friend, though, you might think twice. And if your friends got it from you, they might not think at all. They trust you.

All of this was done to give these messages the appearance of legitimacy. If your uncle shared content with your friends, that was one thing. If you shared it with your friends, that was something else. Ninety percent of hacking is social engineering, deceiving people into behaving differently. This was a massive hack of the American population through reverse engineering, using almost every single data technology that had emerged in the era: location data, programmatic advertising, graph theory, all weaponized and sold to the highest bidder.

Political media-buyers used Cambridge Analytica's research to target the audience segments most inclined to click on conspiracy theories based on their unique interests or concerns:

Don't trust her, she's molesting kids in pizza shops.

Don't trust her, she's part of a demonic sex cult.

Don't trust her, and definitely don't trust her emails!

In Africa, the rumors about Hillary Clinton's alleged disdain for Gaddafi first spread by word of mouth in circles of Gaddafi supporters. In the U.S. the rumor became an insertion order that followed people around the internet in the form of an ad. If it seemed like this type of ad was everywhere, it's because it was bought just for you. You'd been targeted. A different person had a different digital mix of ads (and rumors) targeted at them. The people in the barbershop in Philadelphia had a set target at them. The next person had theirs, and so on. Big data and ad-targeting became a potent political weapon.

Algorithms only know to amplify what you click, like and share. Algorithms don't care about the accuracy, the consequences, or the sources of information. If your uncle posts some salacious story, and his friends like it, and their friends like it, the algorithms amplify what appears to be an engaging message. The message spreads through your friend groups. When the message is popular enough, gets shared to groups outside of your own. Now total strangers see this message for the first time. To them, it appears as if it's legitimate news. They don't think to question it. If they are asked for the source, their source is Facebook.

In 2016, a burn notice could have easily been issued against digital platforms fueled by algorithmic activity. These sources were compromised. They were not to be trusted.

The spread of information through social groups is as old as religion and settlers on the plains of the African savannah. Storytelling is the kernel of culture. Culture can be weaponized. In Russia, my tour guide had told me tales of saving up her money to buy parcels of American culture: blue jeans, a Miles Davis record, a Snickers candy bar. That thirst for culture trumped her own national identity. It trumped self-preservation, too. She could have been carted away by the Kremlin for sneaking in American vinyl, yet she and the stilyagi did it despite the risks.

Forget the Cold War, a *culture war* is what finally pulled the rug from under the Soviet Union. A culture war and the youth revolution are what toppled regimes across North Africa during the Arab Spring. A culture war was also what subverted the Kingdom of Buganda allowing foreign occupation by the British for over one hundred years. Perhaps the outcome of the 2016 U.S. Presidential election was the culmination of a new kind of culture war.

If so, I hoped it wouldn't end the same way.

Options

#EchoChamber

"Fishing where there are none left to catch."
– Jon Gosier, Author and Entrepreneur

I approached the podium of the United Nations General Assembly at U.N. Headquarters on East 42nd Street in New York, NY. It was June 26th, 2013. The building was still undergoing a $2.1 billion renovation. The overhaul left some areas off-limits as scaffolding and materials were removed. Workers in paint-covered overalls darted back and forth between diplomats in ten thousand-dollar Italian suits and women in pearls bought with money earned four generations back. The interior of the assembly chamber stretched wide with high domed ceiling. A new acoustic system had recently been installed; the speakers were tucked away in nooks around the room's inner chamber. Any word uttered from the podium reverberated with gravitas. When I stepped forward to give my remarks, it was at a podium that presided over a vast audience of men and women still shuffling past each other to their designated seats.

I waited for them all to settle.

The grandness of the assembly hall made me feel both insignificant and larger-than-life at once. It was humbling. The command one holds at the podium is also intoxicating. I looked out at the audience. A spectrum of colored faces from countries around the globe dotted the room. Their expressions were stern and inquisitive, relaxed or disinterested.

I cleared my throat and began.

Executives at the United Nations had invited me to speak about the role technology played in the development of poor countries and how tech entrepreneurship creates wealth. I shared my story of moving to Uganda where I started Appfrica and, later, my association with Ushahidi. I spoke of my work in disaster response with my company MetaLayer. The U.N. representatives were there to learn how we operated, how these twenty-somethings from Kenya, Uganda, and the U.S. had started companies that garnered so much attention and achieved so much.

They were curious about our technologies, methods, and ideas. In short, how it all worked for us, under unique conditions unlikely to ever be repeated. They were interested in how they might replicate the successes of our companies in their respective countries. Successful companies created jobs that could lift people out of poverty. The jobs my companies created have kept people all over Africa employed and their families fed for over eleven years. These companies are still operational and scaling across Africa. It was the elusive outcome every entrepreneur hopes for: founding companies that live on for years beyond your own involvement. Most startups, ninety-nine percent to be exact, end in failure. The default of startups is failure. The odds of failure increase significantly in a developing country. There is no ecosystem for growth. No private equity. No banking institutions. Very few investors. Yet, here I stood with successes to point to in nearly thirty African countries. Most were technology companies.

"This is how economies grow. This is how the poor become more resilient and motivated," I told the audience. "Africa doesn't need more philanthropists or aid money from the countries represented in this room. Africa needs more investors."

The audience also wanted to know about digital activism. How Ushahidi, and my other project Abayima, helped activists subvert oppressive regimes and respond to human disaster. I was asked about our role saving lives following the Haiti Quake. I was asked about my efforts to equip Egyptian dissidents with mobile technology that could evade surveillance. I was asked about investigative journalism projects I had been involved in like Ujima. Why were they all so tech-oriented – why not focus on traditional jobs?

"Focus too much on the *what* and you lose sight of the *how* and *why*," I responded.

A light went on, indicating that there was a question from someone in the audience. I looked out into the sea of diplomats, civil society workers, heads of state, and humanitarian workers attending the session. Each row had its own table and array of chairs. Each chair was positioned in front of a microphone.

"To what end?" a woman said in a Sierra Leonean accent.

People in the room turned to look at her. "What is your goal?" she said. "What will any of this do for me? Or for my people? They are poor. They are *farmers* and *fisherman*. They are African. They do not know technology. What does any of this mean to them?"

The room murmured. She continued more confidently, "You want to put computers in our schools. What good are computers with no power? You want to put mobile phones in our pockets. We have mobile phones. Who's going to top them with credit? You are creating jobs with technology, but how many of these jobs will take farmers and fishermen? Who is this all for?"

She reminded me that these were all retrograde innovations—regression in the guise of advancement. I took a moment to think.

"Well, ma'am, I understand what you mean. Frankly, you're right. Technology jobs won't feed everyone in Africa, but this is a tale of two economies. The agrarian economy that our parents and our parent's parents knew, and the knowledge economy that the world knows now. I'm not going to argue that one is better than the other. The point is the world is changing. Global job growth is no longer agrarian or even industrial. Most new jobs exist in the knowledge economy.

"Tech jobs won't employ everyone, but for each technology job created, we've found that five traditional jobs and twenty unskilled jobs are created. What does that mean? This means every software developer who we employ creates a job for a teacher, a doctor, a lawyer, a mechanic, or an accountant.

"How? When they make money, they spend it. That spending is what creates opportunity and growth elsewhere in the economy. Those five newly earning people have their own expendable income and do the same, spending with cleaners, or at restaurants, or at butcheries, or at the mall. The collective spending of the secondary group creates twenty more jobs—for farmers, cashiers, and fishermen. Every dollar invested has a butterfly effect.

"By our calculations, the lifetime value of a single tech job for the local economy is over half-a-million dollars. *Per job.*

"For every one dollar my company has invested across this continent, we estimate that $220 dollars of value was created overall. Over the past five years, we project our little company from Uganda has created an estimated $110 million dollars of impact in the new economy. Not by investing in Africa's *past*, but by investing in its *future*."

I wanted to emphasize that while low-tech jobs like farming and fishing were easily scaled, high-tech jobs gave individuals the advanced skills needed to make them relevant in an increasingly global business community.

"When I started the company, there were one or two companies like ours. Now, there are hundreds like us across all of Africa. If they are all having the same impact, that's tens of billions of dollars in new wealth, jobs, and growth across the continent.

"Yes, fishermen may feel they need more fishing jobs, but if all their sons and daughters can hope for is to fish too, by the time they have their own children, there will be no fishing jobs at all. My work focuses on creating opportunities, choice, and options. It's one thing to choose to fish, it's another to fish to survive.

"Especially where there are no fish left to catch."

* * *

I was exhausted by the time I left the event. I hailed a cab and sat quietly with my head against the window. I didn't stay for the cocktail party. I was over talking to wealthy people in cathedrals about poor people in slums. I wanted time alone. I thought back to my first days in Kampala. Overcoming my fear of flying. Trap houses. Bombings. Shootings. Startup betrayals. My mother's journey. The phone hackers of Madrid. Sim-swappers in Uganda. Kenya. Haiti. The digital activists I'd been inspired by all over the world.

Every step was jotted down in my note pad; their coordinates saved to my Garmin. If need be, I could go back to rediscover the waypoints where those memories were made. I was an American Black, a data analyst, a music producer, an investor, a crisis mapper, an entrepreneur—a code switcher.

Most importantly – I was comfortable.

#End

CPSIA information can be obtained
at www.ICGtesting.com
Printed in the USA
BVHW010058080323
659912BV00011B/62